SATANIC ALCHEMY

ATROCITIES OF GILLES DE RAIS

SATANIC ALCHEMY

J-K Huysmans & others
Edited by Candice Black
ISBN 978-0-9838842-7-9
Published 2012 by Sun Vision Press

www.solarbooks.org

Acknowledgements:
Sorcery In Poitou translated by R.J. Dent, copyright R.J. Dent 2011
The Bloody Countess by Valentine Penrose translated by Alexander Trocchi, copyright © Creation Books 1996
"Sexual Life – War" and "Sexual Life – the Child Murders" by Georges Bataille from *Le Procès de Gilles de Rais* copyright © J-J Pauvert 1972; English translation by Richard Robinson first appeared in *The Trial Of Gilles de Rais* (Amok Books, 1991)
"Gilles de Rais" lecture notes by Georges Bataille translated by John Phillips, copyright © John Phillips 2004
All texts in Part Two translated by John Phillips, copyright © John Phillips 2004
The confessions of Gilles de Rais translated by Richard Robinson. First appeared in *The Trial Of Gilles de Rais* (Amok Books, 1991).
All other texts in Part Three translated by John Phillips, copyright © John Phillips 2004

INTRODUCTION

The figure of Gilles de Rais a.k.a. Gilles de Retz a.k.a. Barbe-Bleue, satanist and child-killer, eclipses French history like a dark star. A fallen general, once the champion of Jeanne d'Arc, de Rais' riches and experimentations led him to the very gates of Hell.

Not only does the juxtaposition of de Rais' obscene crimes and insidious aristocratic glamour contrive to lodge him in our minds as a medieaval Hannibal Lecter, but he is also believed to be the inspiration behind Perrault's classic fairytale *Bluebeard* – the transmutation of Gilles' actual atrocities (paedophilia, paedocide) into those of his fictional counterpart (serial wife-murder) being attributable to the author's desire to "tone down" the horrors for mass consumption.

Satanic Alchemy is a testament to the enduring myth of Gilles de Rais and his fantastic, if actually less frightening *alter ego*, Barbe-Bleue, and the way in which the two have fused in the popular imagination of centuries. The spectre of de Rais/Bluebeard has permeated French (and to a lesser degree pan-European) consciousness to almost as great an extent as that of the Marquis de Sade, to the point where Jules Michelet, in his *History Of The French Revolution*, could declare: "Societies perish under atrocity, the Middles Ages by a Gilles de Retz; the old order by de Sade, high priest of assassins". This fascination applies equally to literature; of the surrealists, Georges Bataille in particular engaged with de Rais, closely examining his case in *The Trial Of Gilles de Rais* (1965), while Antonin Artaud in the first manifesto of his Theatre Of Cruelty (1932) saw in a putative reconstruction of the Bluebeard story the chance for a "new notion of eroticism and cruelty". While Bataille's interests remain historical and anthropological, the story of Gilles de Rais has attracted as many novelists as historians, drawn to the mythopoeic aura of this most enigmatic of mass-murderers.

The first notable literary advocate of Gilles de Rais remains J-K Huysmans, famous for his novel *A Rebours* and its quintessential decadent, Des Esseintes. Huysmans' later novel *La-Bas* (1891), a virtual apology for Satanism, is threaded by a version of the de Rais story as narrated by the book's protagonist, Durtal. Punctuated by the author's own poetic interventions, this account depicts de Rais as an arch-decadent beset by demonic visions and ravening sexual manias – "the 15th century Des Esseintes". The most intriguing entry in **Satanic Alchemy** must be the first ever English translation of Huysmans' pamphlet *La Sorcellerie En Poitou* (also known as *La Magie En Poitou*), published in 1897 in a limited edition for private circulation only. Described by Huysmans as a reductionist, non-fiction version of *La-Bas*, it demonstrates the ongoing fascination exerted by de Rais over the author.

Satanic Alchemy continues with three more views of de Rais by notable, but very differing, authors: Valentine Penrose, Sabine Baring-Gould, and Georges Bataille.

Beautifully translated from the original French by Alexander Trocchi, Valentine Penrose's evocation of the de Rais legend is taken from *The Bloody Countess* (1952), her classic account of Elizabeth Bathory. Pitched as a black satanic fairytale steeped in blood, Penrose's version equates Bathory, murderer of hundreds of virgins, with the child-killer de Rais and conjures a dark-age Europe where superstition and witchcraft are a way of life, and peasants are little more than human cattle to be butchered at the whim of their depraved aristocratic masters.

Baring-Gould (1834-1924) was a vicar in the Church of England in Devon, an archaeologist, folklorist, historian and a prolific author; he was also an eccentric, and reputedly taught classes with a pet bat on his shoulder. His essay "The Maréchal de Retz" is taken from his classic study of lycanthropy, *The Book Of Werewolves* (1861).

The section entitled *Gilles de Rais*, by Georges Bataille, includes two extracts from his seminal *The Trial Of Gilles de Rais*

("Sexual Life – War" and "Sexual Life – The Murders") as well as previously unpublished notes from a lecture on de Rais given in 1955.

These diverse views are followed by a pair of comparative studies: taken from his *Perverse Crimes In History* (1963), R.L. Masters' "Two Extraordinary Monsters" again looks at the crimes of Elizabeth Bathory and de Rais, this time from a forensic angle of sexual perversion and deviant criminality; while Margaret Murray's "Joan Of Arc And Gilles De Rais", from her classic anthropological study *The Witch-Cult In Western Europe* (1921), examines the persecution of these intertwined figures in the context of secret covens and sorcerous hierarchies which may have permeated every strata of society during that period.

Satanic Alchemy continues with a section of six essays which look at other aspects of Gilles de Rais and his times, commencing with a detailed examination of the Bluebeard myth. Other subjects covered in this section range from an account of the alchemical arts to which Rais aspired, to details of the decadent banquets enjoyed by Rais and his peers, helping to evoke a complete picture of both the man and his historical milieu.

Satanic Alchemy concludes with an appendix of hard historical documentation; first, the actual court confessions of Gilles de Rais, as heard at his trial and first translated from Latin transcripts by Pierre Klossowski. These are followed by a biographical chronology of de Rais, and a resumé of the key players and places in his short but cataclysmic life.

PART I

SORCERY IN POITOU

JORIS-KARL HUYSMANS

Gilles de Rais, about whose childhood little is known, was born about 1404, on the border of Brittany and Anjou, in the château de Machecoul in Bas-Poitou. His father died at the end of October, 1415. His mother remarried almost immediately to Siegneur d'Estouville and abandoned him and his brother, Rene de Rais. He came under the tutelage of his grandfather, Jean de Craon, Lord of Champtocé-sur-Loire, 'a man old, ancient and of immense great age,' according to some texts. Gilles was neither properly watched over nor guided by that wry and distracted old man, who attempted to get rid of Gilles by marrying him to Catherine de Thouars, on 30 November, 1420.

Five years later, he is a significant presence at the court of the Dauphin. His contemporaries describe him as a rugged and robust man, one who was very handsome and in possession of a refined elegance. Information is lacking regarding the role he plays at court, but one can easily imagine how the destitude king greeted the arrival of Gilles, who was one the richest barons of France.

At that time, indeed, Charles VII was in extremis. He was penniless, devoid of prestige and without any real authority. The situation in France, exhausted by the massacres, and ravaged some years before by the plague, was deplorable. The country's resources were gone; it was drained to the marrow by England, which France was terrified of, for the English, like that fabulous sea monster, the Kraken, emerged from the sea and terrorized the strait of Brittany, Normandy, part of Picardy, the Ile-de-france, the entire Northern coast and the interior, as far as Orleans, razing towns and devastating cities, and in the aftermath of many battles, leaving many dead.

All of Charles's tactics: claiming subsidies, inventing excuses for exacting funds, and raising taxes, were useless. Ransacked cities and abandoned fields were ravaged by wolves. He was a king whose legitimacy was questionable. He was like a blind beggar, shuffling around, rattling a tin cup, begging for coins. His court in Chinon was a web of intrigue and sporadic murders.

Tired of being hunted, Charles and his supporters eventually hid out of the way in lodgings behind the Loire, where they took comfort in exuberant debaucheries, opulent dining and the wild drunkenness. The drink, food and prostitutes were paid for by constant raiding, borrowing and stealing, and they immersed themselves in hedonistic distractions, forgetting momentarily that disaster dogged the kingdom daily.

However, when the English armies united, quickly inundated the country, and then, after a concerted push forward, invaded the interior. The King considered retreating to the South coast, and then relinquishing France: it was at this time that Jeanne d'Arc appeared. Gilles de Rais, who was then at court, was entrusted by Charles to provide 'guard and defence' of the Maid. He followed her everywhere, fought at her side, assisted in the battle under the walls of Paris, and was with her in Rheims on the day of the coronation, where, as a reward for his valour, so Monstrelet tells us, the King appointed him – at the tender age of twenty-five – Marshal of France.

What was Gilles de Rais's attitude towards Jeanne d'Arc? Again information is scarce. M. Vallet Viriville (without any evidence) accuses him of treachery. The Abbé Bossard, on the contrary, says he was loyally devoted and watched over her, and he supports his opinion with plausible reasons. Anyway, after the capture and death of Jeanne, we lose track of Gilles, who we find cloistered, aged twenty-six, in the château de Tiffauges.

The iron warrior, the roughneck soldier who was an integral part of him, had disappeared. At the same time – just as the misdeeds were about to begin – the artist and the scholar develop in Gilles and completely possess him, inciting him, under the impulse of a perverse mysticism, to the most sophisticated of cruelties, the most delicate of crimes.

He was almost alone in his time, this Baron de Rais! In an era when his peers were merely simple brutes, but he wanted the delicate delerium of art and he dreamed of literature that was profound and contemplative; he even composed a treatise on the art of invoking demons. He adored sacred music, and surrounded himself not with everyday objects, but only rare things.

He was a Latin scholar, a brilliant conversationalist, a generous and reliable friend. He had a library that was exemplary for such an era, one in which all that was read was theology and the lives of saints. We have the description of some of his manuscripts: Suetonius, Valerius Maximus, and an Ovid on parchment, bound in red leather, with a gilt clasp and key.

All of these possessions were very expensive; though far less so than the luxurious court which made Tiffauges a totally unique place.

He had a guard of more than two hundred men, knights, captains, squires, pages, and all these people had their own attendants, all of whom were beautifully equipped at Gilles' expense. The luxury of the chapel and its collegial church was madly extravagant. All of the metropolitan clergy resided at Tiffauges: deans, vicars, treasurers, canons, priests and deacons, scholasters and choir boys. There were surplices, stoles, and amices, and grey chorus hats lined with miniver fur.

There was an abundance of sacerdotal vestments. Here one encountered gilt alter siding cloths, emerald silk curtains, an arras of crimson, purple and violet velvet with cloth-of-gold orpheys, another cloth of rose damask, satin dalmatics for deacons, canopies figured with gold birds from Cyprus; there were plates, chalices, beaten ciborium and cabochon, encrusted with gems. There were reliquaries, including a silver head of Saint Honoré. There was a mass of incandescent jewellery, which goldsmiths and artists, installed in the château, shaped and engraved to order.

And everyone was welcome. Gilles château was open to any guest. From all corners of France, caravans travelled to the château, where artists, poets, scholars found princely hospitality, warm fellowship, gifts of welcome and generosity at departure.

Already depleted by the demands that the war had made on it, his fortune wavered beneath these expenses. He began to follow the terrible path of usury. He borrowed from the most unscrupulous bourgeois; he mortgaged his châteaus, sold off parcels of his land, and was reduced at times to asking for advances on his religious ornaments, on his jewels, and on his books.

Frightened by his folly, the Marshal's family begged the King to intervene and, in fact, in 1436, Charles VII, 'certain' as he said, 'of the bad government of the Sire de Rais,' prohibited Gilles, in his great council, and in letters dated 'Amboise, 1436', from selling or disposing of any fortress, any château, or any land.

This ordinance simply hastened the ruin of the inderdicted. The largest skinflint, the master usurer of the time, Jean V, Duke of Britanny, refused to publish the edict in his states; however he did notify, underhandedly, all those of his subjects who dealt with Gilles. No one now dared to buy the Marshal's domains for fear of incurring the hatred of the Duke and the fury of King, so Jean V remained the sole purchaser, and fixed the prices of any property bought from Gilles de Rais.

It seems Gilles was completely dominated by the passion for alchemy, for which he ready to abandon everything else. But it is worth noting that this science – which threw him into demonomania when he hoped to make gold and thus save himself from impending misery – he had loved purely for its own sake when he was rich.

It was in fact about the year 1426, when his vaults bulged with money that he attempted for the first time, 'the great work'. We find him then, stooped over his retorts, in the château de Tiffauges, where he began on the series of crimes of magic.

Considering his time, it is easy to imagine that he had knowledge of how to transmute metals.

Alchemy was already highly developed a century before he was born. The writings of Albertus Magnus, Arnaud de Villeneuve, and Raymond Lully were in the hands of the Hermetics. Nicolas

Flamel's manuscripts circulated; there is no doubt that Gilles acquired them, for he was an avid collector of rare books. Let us add that during that time, the edict of Charles V prohibiting spagyric works under pain of imprisonment and death, and the papal bull known as *Spondent pariter quas not exhibent*, in which Pope John XXII fulminated against the alchemists, were still in force. These works were forbidden and therefore eminently desirable. It is certain that Gilles had studied them extensively, but from studying them to understanding them is a far distance.

These books contained, in fact, the most amazing nonsense, the most unintelligible scrawls. Everything was written in allegorical jargon and used obscure metaphors and incoherent symbols, twisted parables, riddles, ciphers, enigmas.

It is quite obvious that alone at Tiffauges, and without the help of initiates, Gilles was unable to attempt meaningful research. At that time, Paris was the centre of Hermetic science in France. Alchemists gathered under the arches of Notre Dame and studied the hieroglyphics which Nicolas Flamel had written on the charnel Des Innocents and on the portal of Saint-Jacques de la Boucherie, describing in kabbalistic symbols the rituals for the preparation of the famous stone.

The Marshal could not go to Paris without falling into the hands of the English troops who were blocking the roads, so he chose the easiest solution, he wrote to the most famous of the southern transmutors and brought them, at great expense, to Tiffauges.

Referring to the documents we have, we see him supervise the construction of the athanor, that is, the alchemist's furnace; buy pelicans, crucibles and retorts. He established laboratories in one wing of his castle, and he shut himself up in it with Anthonio di Palermo, François Lombard, and 'Jean Petit, goldsmith of Paris', all of whom worked day and night on the concoction of the 'great work'.

They failed dismally. Once the resources were gone, the hermetics disappeared, and there was from then on at Tiffauges an incredible coming and going of adepts and their assistants. They came from all parts of Brittany, Poitou and Maine, either alone or accompanied by sorcerers or acolytes. Gilles de Sillé and Roger de Bricqueville, cousins and friends of the Marshal, roamed the countryside, driving the game to Gilles de Rais, while a priest of his chapel, Eustache Blanchet, went to Italy, where metal smiths were plentiful.

Meanwhile, Gilles de Rais, undeterred, continued his experiments, all of which misfired, and he finally came to believe that the magicians were right; no discovery was possible without the help of Satan.

And one night, after John de la Rivière, a sorcerer from Poitiers, arrived, he and Gilles went into a forest that bordered the château de Tiffauges. Gilles remained with his servants Henriet and Poitou on the edge of the woods, while magician entered. The night was heavy and there was no moon; Gilles grew nervous as he scrutinized the darkness and listened to the muted sounds of the nocturnal silence, his terrified companions huddled close together, as they whispered and trembled at the slightest sound made by the breeze. Suddenly, a cry of anguish was heard. They hesitated and then moved forward, groping in the dark. Eventually they spotted, in a sudden flare of light, an exhausted-looking Rivière, trembling, haggard, manically gripping the lantern handle. In a shaky voice he recounted how the Devil had appeared before him in the form of a leopard, but had then rushed past him, the invoker, without so much as looking at him or speaking to him.

The next day, the sorcerer had gone, but another arrived. This was an incompetent named du Mesnil. He required Gilles to sign in blood a contract binding him to give the devil all the devil asked of him, 'except his life and soul'. To help the invocation, Gilles consented to have the Office of the Damned sung in his chapel at the feast of All Saints. Satan did not appear.

The Marshal was beginning to doubt the powers of his magicians, when the result of a new endeavour convinced him that sometimes the devil does appear. An invoker, whose name is lost, held a séance with Gilles and de Sillé in a room at Tiffauges.

On the floor, he drew a large circle and ordered his

companions to enter it. Sillé refused; gripped by a terror he could not explain, he began to tremble all over. He stood next to an open window, murmuring exorcisms under his breath.

Gilles, bolder than the others, stood in the middle of the circle, but at the first invocations, he shuddered and tried to make the sign of the cross. The sorcerer ordered him not to move. At one point, he was seized by the neck by something unknown, and was terrified. Full of panic, he wavered and begged Our Lady, the Virgin, to save him. The invoker, furious at that, threw him out the circle, and Gilles rushed out of the room. Sillé jumped out the window and they met below, both panting in fear.

Howls could be heard coming from the room where the magician was operating. 'A noise of falling blows, like large swords striking a wooden bed' is heard, followed by moans, cries of distress, and calls for help from a man being murdered.

Terrified, they stood and listened, and then when the noise ceased, they ventured back and pushed the door open, only to find the sorcerer lying on the floor in pools of blood, his barely-alive body mangled, his head caved in.

They carried the groaning man out. Gilles, full of remorse, put him in his own bed, bandaged him, and had his priest hear the man's confession, just in case he passed away. For several days the sorcerer lay there, hovering between life and death. Eventually he recovered, and fled the château.

Gilles was desperate to obtain from the devil the recipe for the sovereign magisterium. Then Eustache Blanchet's return from Italy was announced. He had brought with him the master of Florentine magic, the irresistible invoker of demons and larvae, François Prelati.

Gilles was in awe of this man. He was barely twenty-three years, yet was one of the most knowledgeable, most erudite, most polished men of the times. What had he done before coming to Tiffauges, where he would begin with the Marshal the most appalling series of crimes against the Holy family that has ever been known? His testimony in the criminal trial of Gilles does not provide much detailed information about him. He was born in the diocese of Lucca, at

Pistoia, and had been ordained a priest by the Bishop of Arezzo. Shortly after entering the priesthood, he became a pupil of a miracle worker in Florence, Jean de Fontenelle, and had signed a pact with a demon. From that moment on, he had delivered himself into the most abominable sacrilege and the murderous practice of ritual black magic.

Inevitably, Gilles fell completely under the influence of this man. The furnaces were relit, and together they searched frantically for the Stone of the Sages, which Prelati had seen and which he described as flexible, brittle, red, smelling of roasted sea salt.

They invoked hell, but their incantations were futile. Gilles, unwilling to discontinue, redoubled his efforts, but their invocations eventually went dreadfully wrong and Prelati barely escaped alive.

One afternoon, Eustache Blanchet was in one of the château's galleries and he saw the Marshal in tears; words of supplication could be heard through the door of the room in which Prelati had been trying to invoke the devil.

"The devil is in there and is beating poor François. I beg you, go in!" cried Gilles, but Blanchet, frightened, refused. Gilles then decided, and despite his fear, moved forward to force the door open. Before he could reach it, it opened and Prelati stumbled out and fell bleeding into his arms. Supported by his two friends, Prelati was taken to the Marshal's room and put into bed, but the beatings he had received were so severe he grew delirious and his fever worsened. Gilles, in despair, sat with him, nursed him, made him confess, and then wept with happiness when Prelati recovered and was no longer in danger of dying.

The fate of the unknown sorcerer and of Prelati, both having been dangerously wounded in an empty room, under identical circumstances, is a remarkable coincidence, but is also authentic, according to documents used at the trial of Gilles.

One can imagine how a mystic like Gilles de Rais would have believed in the reality of the devil, after witnessing such scenes.

Despite his failures, he could have no doubt – and Prelati, half-killed, must have doubted even less – that if Satan pleased, they would finally find this powder that would provide them with wealth and make them almost immortal – because at that time the philosopher's stone was not only able to transmute base metals such as tin, lead, and copper into noble metals like silver and gold, but also to cure all diseases and prolong life, without any infirmities, far beyond the limits previously assigned to the patriarchs.

Finally, Prelati, Blanchet, and all the sorcerers and the sorcerers' assistants that the Marshal had around him, declared that to invoke Satan, Gilles would either have to bargain his soul and his life to the devil, or else he would have to commit crimes.

Gilles refused to jeopardise his existence and bargain with his soul, but he was able to contemplate murder without any feelings of horror. This man, so brave on the battlefield, so courageous when he accompanied and defended Jeanne d'Arc, trembled before the devil and grew deeply afraid whenever he thought of eternity or Christ. And it was the same for his accomplices; he made them swear on the Holy Gospels not to reveal the confounding turpitude that the château conceals, sure that none of them would violate their oath, for since the Middle Ages, the most fearless of bandits would not dare to assume the unpardonable sin of deceiving God.

Gilles's first victim was a little boy whose name is unknown. He disembowelled him, cut off his hands, tore out his heart, gouged out his eyes and carried them into Prelati's chamber. The two men offered them, with passionate entreaties, to the devil, who remained absent. Gilles, exasperated, fled. Prelati rolled up the pitiful remains in a linen cloth and, trembling, went out at night and buried them in consecrated ground, next to a chapel dedicated to St. Vincent.

Gilles kept the child's blood for the writing of formulas for invocations and rituals. From it there flowered a horrible crop, and soon after, Gilles de Rais reaped the harvest of the most atrocious crimes ever known.

From 1432 to 1440, that is to say during the eight years between the Marshal's retreat and his death, the residents of Anjou, Poitou, and Brittany, wander along the roads sobbing. All the children disappear. Shepherd boys are abducted from the fields. Girls coming out of school and boys playing ball in the streets or at the edge of the woods, vanish and do not return.

At first, the frightened people told themselves that it was evil spirits that had dispersed their offspring, but little by little, horrible suspicions were aroused. When the Marshal moved, as he went to from his château de Tiffauges to the château de Champtocé, and from there to the castle of La Susa, or to Nantes, he left behind him grieving parents.

Whenever he passed through a region, the next day, children were missing. Trembling, one particular peasant realised that whenever Prelati, Roger Bricqueville, or Gilles de Sillé, or any of the Marshal's intimate friends had been in the vicinity, boys had disappeared. Finally, with horror, he noticed an old woman, Perrine Martin, who wandered around dressed in gray, her face covered – as was the face of Gilles de Sillé – with a black veil. When she accosted children, her speech was so seductive and her face, when she lifted her veil, was so friendly, that all of them were happy to the follow her up to the edge of the woods, where men would gag them and carry them off in bags. And the frightened people called this purveyor of flesh, this ogress, 'La Meffraye,' named after a bird of prey.

How many children did the Marshal slaughter? He himself did not know. The texts of the time enumerate seven to eight hundred victims, but this number is insufficient, and seems inaccurate. Entire regions were devastated, and the hamlet of Tiffauges had no more young people. In La Suze, there were no young males. In Champtocé, the entire foundation room of one tower was filled with corpses. Guillaume Hylairet, a witness quoted at the inquest, stated that "a man named Du Jardin heard that there was found in that castle a wine pipe full of dead children."

Even today, traces of these murders remain. In 1889, at Tiffauges, a doctor discovered an oubliette, and in it he unearthed piles of skulls and bones.

Gilles confessed to terrible atrocities and his friends confirmed the atrocious details.

The inhabitants of the regions where the Marshal's châteaux

were located now knew the identity of the inconceivable monster that stole and slaughtered children. But nobody dared speak of it. When, at a turn in a road, the tall figure of the predator was seen approaching, everyone ran away and either cowered behind hedges, or locked themselves in their cottages.

And Gilles passed, proud and sombre, through the deserted villages where no one ventured out while he was in the vicinity. Impunity seemed assured him, for what peasant would be crazy enough to tackle a master who could have him gibbeted at a word?

On the other hand, if the humble peasants had abandoned the idea of bringing Gilles de Rais to justice, his peers had no intention of pitting themselves against him for the benefit of peasants they despised, and his liege, the Duke of Brittany, Jean V, bestowed favours upon him in order to extort his lands from him at a low price.

Only one power could rise above feudal complicities, above human interests, and avenge the oppressed and the weak: the Church. And it was the Church, in fact, in the person of Jean de Malestroit, which rose up before the monster and felled him.

Jean de Malestroit, Bishop of Nantes, belonged to an illustrious lineage. He was a close relative of Jean V, and his incomparable piety, his assiduous wisdom, his Christian love, and his infallible faith, were venerated, even by the Duke himself.

The complaints of the flocks that had been decimated by Gilles finally reached the Bishop's ears. In silence, he began an investigation. His spies scrutinized the Marshal as he, the Bishop, waited for an ideal moment to begin the battle. And then Gilles committed an inexplicable crime that allowed the bishop to approach him and strike the first devastating blow.

To replenish some of his depleted fortune, Gilles sold one of his estates – that of Le Comte de Saint-Etienne de Mer Morte – to one of Jean V's subjects, one Guillaume le Ferron, who delegated his brother Jean le Ferron to take ownership of this domain.

A few days later, the Marshal gathered two hundred men from his military household and led them to Saint-Etienne. There, on the day of Pentecost, while the assembled people heard Mass, he rushed into the church with a sword in hand, swept through the ranks of the faithful, nearly causing a stampede, then stood before the stunned priest and threatened to kill Jean le Ferron, who was praying. Having deemed the Holy ceremony irrevocably interrupted, the congregation fled. Gilles dragged le Ferron, who was pleading for mercy, to the chateau. He ordered that the drawbridge be lowered, then took over and occupied the place by sheer force of will. Meanwhile he had his prisoner taken away and thrown in an underground cell at Tiffauges.

Gilles had violated the unwritten law of Brittany which forbade any baron to raise troops without the consent of the Duke, and he had committed double sacrilege by desecrating a chapel and by seizing Jean le Ferron, who was a tonsured cleric of the Church.

When the Bishop heard of this outrage, he persuaded John V, who hesitated, however, to march against the rebel. So, as one army advanced on Saint-Etienne – which Gilles abandoned in order to take refuge with a small force in the fortified manor of Mâchecoul – another army laid siege to Tiffauges.

Meanwhile, the Bishop hastened his investigations. His activity became extraordinary; he delegated commissioners and prosecutors in all the villages where children had disappeared. He himself left his palace of Nantes, travelled the countryside, taking statements and depositions from the families of the victims. The people finally spoke, and they begged on their knees for the Bishop to protect them. Angered by the atrocities they have revealed, the Bishop swore he would bring about justice.

It took him a month to hear all of their reports. Through the use of letters patent, Jean de Malestroit established publicly the *infamatio* of Gilles, then, when all of the forms of the canonical procedure were completed, he launched the arrest mandate.

In this mandate, presented at Nantes on 13th September in the year of our Lord 1440, the Bishop had inventoried all of the crimes attributed to the Marshal. Then, in an energetic style, he commanded his diocese to march against the murderer and arrest him.

"Thus we urge you each and every one of you, individually,

by these present, to cite immediately and definitively, not counting one upon the other, without discharging the burden upon any other, to summon before us or before the Official of our cathedral church, on Monday of the feast of Exaltation of the Holy Cross, the 19th September, Gilles, the noble baron de Rais, subject to our power and our jurisdiction; and we cite him, ourselves, by these letters to appear before our bar to answer for the crimes he is accused of. Execute these orders, and ensure they are executed."

And the next day, the captain-at-arms Jean Labbé, acting on behalf of the Duke, and Romain Guillaumet, notary, acting on behalf of the Bishop, escorted by a small troop, presented themselves at the château de Mâchecoul.

What was it that occurred deep in the soul of the Marshal? He may have been too weak to stand on a battle field, he could still have defended himself from behind the solid walls of the château – but instead he surrendered!

Roger de Bricqueville and Gilles de Sillé, his trusted advisers, had abandoned him. He remained alone with Prelati, who also attempted – albeit unsuccessfully – to escape. He was, as was Gilles, weighed down with manacles. Romain Guillaumet searched the château from top to bottom. He discovered bloody clothes, badly charred bones and ashes that Prelati has not had time to dump in the moat. Amid condemnation and cries of horror, Gilles and his servants were conducted in Nantes and imprisoned in the Château de la Tour-Neuve.

As soon as Gilles and his accomplices were imprisoned, two courts were organized: one, ecclesiastical, to try Gilles for crimes that were within the Church's jurisdiction, and the other, civil, to try him for crimes pertaining to the state.

The civil court tribunal, which attended the ecclesiastical hearings, effaced itself completely. As a matter of protocol, it subjected Gilles to a brief cross-examination, but it pronounced the death sentence, which the church was reluctant to utter, because the old adage: *Ecclesia abhorret a sanguine*.

Ecclesiastical procedures lasted for one month and eight

days; civil proceedings took forty-eight hours. It seemed that in order to shelter behind the Bishop's robes, the Duke of Brittany has voluntarily subordinated the role of civil justice, which usually stood up for its rights against the encroachments of the ecclesiastical court.

Jean de Malestroit presided over the hearings, he chose for assistants the Bishops of Le Mans, of Saint-Brieuc and of Saint-Lô. In addition to these dignitaries, he surrounded himself with a troop of lawyers who worked in shifts during the endless sessions of the trial. The names of most of them appeared in the pleas, including: Guillaume de Montigné, counsel to the secular court; Jean Blanchet, Bachelor of Laws; Guillaume Groyguet and Robert de la Rivière, licentiates in utroque jure, and Hervé Lévi, Senescal of Quimper. Pierre de l'Hospital, Chancellor of Britanny, who was to preside over the civil hearings, after the canonic judgement, assisted Jean de Malestroit.

The public prosecutor was Guillaume Chapeiron, pastor of St. Nicolas, an eloquent and sophisticated man. Adjunct to him, to relieve him of the fatigue of the readings, were Geoffroy Piprain, Dean of Sainte Marie, and Jacques de Pentcoetdic, Official of the Church of Nantes.

Finally, in connection with the episcopal jurisdiction, the Church had called in the special tribunal of the Inquisition, for the repression of the crime of heresy, which also included the crimes of perjury, blasphemy, sacrilege, and all the crimes of magic. He sat alongside Jean de Malestroit, and was none other than the redoubtable and learned person of Jean Blouyn, of the Order of Saint Dominic, delegated by the Grand Inquisitor of France, Guillaume Mérici, to the post of Vice-Inquisitor of the city and diocese of Nantes.

The Tribunal constituted, the trial opened first thing in the morning, because as is the custom, judges and witnesses must hear evidence on an empty stomach. The testimonies of the parents of the victims were heard, and Romain Guillaumet, acting bailiff, the man who arrested the Marshal at Mâchecoul, read the citation ordering Gilles de Rais to appear.

Gilles was led in and declared disdainfully that he did not

accept the competence of the Tribunal, but, as the canonic procedure demands, the prosecutor immediately rejects this 'in order that by this means the accusation of sorcery is not obstructed,' and petitions for (and obtains) a ruling the objection to be quashed and deemed 'frivolous', therefore null and void in law.

He began to read to the accused the counts of the accusations against him. Gilles suddenly shouted out that Prosecutor was a liar and traitor. Then Guillaume Chapeiron extended his hand towards the court crucifix and swore he was telling the truth and then challenged the marshal to take the same oath. But this man, who had never recoiled from sacrilege, was clearly troubled. He refused to perjure himself before God, and the session concluded for the day with Gilles still vociferating outrageous insults and denunciations against the Prosecutor.

A few days after the preliminaries were completed, the public hearings began. The indictment was read aloud to the accused in front of the people who shuddered as Chapeiron patiently listed the crimes, one by one, and formally accused the Marshal of having practiced witchcraft and sorcery; of having slain little children; of having violated the immunities of Holy Church at Saint Etienne de Mer Morte.

Then after a pause, he resumed his speech and, after leaving aside the murder, he dwelled more on the crimes of which the punishment, prescribed by canonic law, could be pronounced by the Church. He demanded that Gilles be struck with double excommunication, first as an invoker of demons, a heretic, an apostate and a renegade; second as a sodomist and perpetrator of sacrilege.

Gilles, who had listened to this ruthless, scathing and incisive indictment, grew increasingly furious. Finally, he lost control. He insulted the judges, calling them simonists and villains, and he refused to answer any of the questions put to him. The Prosecutor and the advocates remained unimpressed; they simply invited him to present his defense. Again, he denounced and insulted them, then, when called upon to refute them, he remained silent.

So the Bishop and the Inquisitor declared him *absentia* and pronounced against him the sentence of excommunication which was immediately made public. They further agreed that the hearing would continue the next day.

The next day, Gille de Rais appeared again before his judges.

His entered with a bowed head and clasped hands. He had, once again, leaped from one extreme to another; a few hours had sufficed to break the spirit of the fanatic, who now declared he recognized the authority of the magistrates and begged forgiveness for his insults.

They assured him that, for the love of Our Lord, they would forget his insults, and after his prayer, the Bishop and the Inquisitor revoked the sentence of excommunication which they had passed on him the previous day.

The hearing was also taken up with the arraignment of Prelati and his accomplices. Then, based on the authority of the ecclesiastical text which stated that a confession could not be regarded as sufficient if it was *dubia, vaga, generalis, illativa, jocosa,* the Prosecuter asserted that to guarantee the veracity of confessions, Gilles had to be submitted to the 'canonical question', that is, to torture.

The Marshal begged the Bishop to wait until the next day and claimed the right to confess immediately to any judges the Tribunal wished to appoint. He swore that he would repeat his confession before the public and the Court.

Jean de Malestroit granted this request and the Bishop of Saint Brieuc and Pierre de l'Hospital, Chancellor of Britanny, were appointed to hear Gilles in his cell. When he had finished recounting his debaucheries and his murders, they ordered Prelati to be brought.

At the sight of him, Gilles burst into tears. After the interrogation, as they prepared to return the Italian to his cell, Gilles embraced him, saying: "Farewell, François, my friend, we shall never again see each other in this world. I pray God gives you great patience and knowledge, and I hope we meet again in great joy in Paradise. Pray for me, and I shall pray for you."

And Gilles was left alone to consider his crimes, which he would publicly confess at the following day's hearing.

That day was the most solemn day of the trial. The room in which the Tribunal sat was packed, and the multitude sat on the stairs, and filled the surrounding courtyards, blocking the streets and alleyways. From twenty miles around, the peasants had come to see the memorable beast whose name alone was, before his capture, had caused them to close their doors in the evenings, and to comfort their trembling, softly-crying women.

The Tribunal meeting was conducted strictly according to formalities. All of the judges – usually present by proxy during a lengthy hearing – were in attendance.

The courtroom, huge, sombre, supported by heavy Roman pillars, had been refurbished. The ogival wall, with its tapered, vaulted arches which joined, like the sides of abbey mitres, in a point, gave the room the appearance of being cathedral height. The room was lighted by weak, sickly daylight, filtered through narrow leaded windows. The ceiling darkened and the stars, at that height, shone like the heads of steel pins. In the shadows of the vaults, the ermine of the ducal arms appeared in escutcheons that looked like large white dice with black dots.

Suddenly, trumpets sounded, the room was illuminated, the Bishops came in. Their cloth-of-gold mitres flashed like lightning. Their collars were ornately embroidered, and their robes were studded with emeralds. In a silent procession, they advanced, weighed down by their rigid copes, which fell flaring from their shoulders, so they resembled split golden bells. They each carried a crozier, from which hung the maniple, a sort of green veil.

With every step, their clothing sparkled like brazier coals being breathed on. They lit up the room with their jewels, which reflected the pale sun of a rainy October day and dispersed flashes of light to every part of the room, including over the mute spectators.

Outshone by the shimmer of the orphreys and the stones, the costumes of the other judges appeared darker and discordant; the black clothes of the court Officiate, the white and black robe of Jean

Blouyn, the silk robe, the red woollen mantle, the fur-lined scarlet chaperons of the secular justice seemed faded and common by comparison.

The bishops were seated in the front row. They surrounded Jean de Malestroit, who dominated the room from his raised seat.

Under the escort of armed men, Gilles entered. He was broken and gaunt and had aged twenty years overnight. His eyes burned behind seared eyelids. His cheeks trembled. Upon injunction, he began the recital of his crimes.

In a low voice, choked by tears, he recounted his abduction of children, his hideous tactics, and his impetuous murders. Haunted by the vision of his victims, he described their agonies, their cries and their groans. He confessed that he had torn out their hearts through wounds that were enlarged and opened like ripe fruit. And with the look of a somnambulist, he looked at his hands, and then shook them as if were dripping with blood.

The appalled spectators in the courtroom kept a gloomy silence that was punctuated by short, horrified cries. Court officials carried out fainting women, mad with horror.

Gilles seemed to hear nothing, to see nothing. He continued to relate the appalling litany of his crimes. Then his voice became hoarse as he came to the sepulchral violations. He enumerated them all, and divulged every detail. It was so atrocious, so terrible, that beneath their golden caps, the Bishops blanched.

The priests were hardened by the confessions they'd heard, and the prelates were never astonished by any depravity or surprised by the extent of the corruption of any soul. The judges of that era of demonomania and murder had never heard such a horrifying confession, and they all crossed themselves. Appalled, Jean de Malestroit rose and veiled the face of Christ.

They all bowed their heads, and without a word, they listened to the Marshal, who, very agitated and covered in sweat, looked at the crucifix, where Christ's invisible head raised the veil to show the outline of the crown of thorns.

Gilles finished his narrative and broke down completely. Up

to then, he had been standing upright, talking like one in a daze, recounting to himself, aloud, the memories of his unforgettable crimes. When he finished, the strength drained from him. He fell to his knees and, shaken by frightened sobs, he cried: "O God, my Redeemer, I ask your forgiveness and mercy!" Then that ferocious and haughty baron, no doubt the first of his ilk, humiliated himself. He turned to the people and said, weeping: "Parents of those I have so cruelly put to death, give, oh give me the succour of your pious prayers!"

Then, in all its white splendour, the soul of the Middle Ages radiated throughout the room.

Jean de Malestroit left his seat and raised the accused, who was smashing his forehead in despair on the flagstones. The judge in him disappeared, the priest alone remained. He embraced the repentant sinner who was sobbing over his crimes.

A shudder ran through the audience when Jean de Malestroit, standing with Gille's head resting on his chest, said to him: "Pray that the just and terrible wrath of the Almighty be averted. Weep so that your tears purify the blood lust that is in your being."

And everyone in the room knelt down and prayed for the murderer. When those praying were hushed, there was a moment of panic and confusion. Pushed beyond the limits of human endurance by a mixture of out-and-out horror and exasperated pity, the agitated crowd seethed. The Tribunal Judges, silent and nervous, slowly attempted to regain control of themselves, the crowd, and the proceedings.

With a gesture that simultaneously brushed away his tears, the Prosecutor halted the proceedings.

He said that the crimes were "clear and apparent", and that the evidence was incontrovertible, that the Court would now "in good conscience" punish the guilty, and he demanded that the day of passing judgement be fixed. The Court set the date for two days later.

And on that day, the Official of the Church of Nantes, Jacques de Pentcoetdic, read in succession the two sentences. The first, passed by the Bishop and the Inquisitor for the acts coming under their joint jurisdiction, began:

"The Holy name of Christ invoked, we, Jean, Bishop of Nantes, and Brother Jean Blouyn, Bachelor of our Holy Scriptures of the Order of the Preachers of Nantes and delegate of the Inquisitor of heresies for the city and diocese of Nantes, in session of the Tribunal and having before our eyes God alone..."

And, after enumerating the crimes, he concluded:

"We pronounce, decide, and declare that you, Gilles de Rais, cited unto this Tribunal, are heinously guilty of heresy, apostasy, and the invocation of demons; and that for these crimes, you have incurred the sentence of excommunication and all other penalties determined by the law."

The second judgement was given by the Bishop alone, on the crimes of sacrilege and violation of the immunities of the Church, which particularly concerned his authority (and thereby fell under his jurisdiction). It led to the same conclusions and the same pronouncement, and in almost identical form, the same sentence.

Gilles listened, head bowed, to the reading of the judgments. When it was finished, the Bishop and the Inquisitor asked him: "Will you now, now that you admit and loathe your mistakes, your evocations, and your crimes, be reincorporated into the church, your mother?"

And based upon the fervent prayers of the Marshal, they recinded his excommunication and allowed him to participate in the sacraments. God's justice was satisfied, the crime was recognized, punished, but erased by contrition and penitence. Only human justice remained.

The Bishop and the Inquisitor then remanded the culprit to the secular court, where he was charged with the abductions and the murders of children. The court then pronounced the death penalty and the confiscation of his property. Prelati and the other accomplices were sentenced at the same time to be hanged and burned alive.

"Cry to God for mercy!" said Pierre de l'Hospital, who presided over the civil hearings. "And prepare to die in a pure state, with great repentance for having committed such crimes."

The recommendation was unnecessary. Gilles was prepared to face the ordeal without fear. He placed his hope, humbly, eagerly, in the mercy of the Saviour. He prayed for the symbol of his terrestrial expiation, the stake, to redeem him from the eternal flames after his death.

Far from his château, alone in his cell, he opened himself up and examined the cloaca which had for so long been fed the poisoned waters that escaped from the charnal houses of Tiffauges and Mâchecoul. In despair, he sobbed on its shores, despairing of ever being able to drain away the poisoned pool within him.

And then, struck by grace, with a cry of horror and joy, he suddenly saw his soul cleansed with his tears, and dried by the fire of his prayers. The murderer was destroyed; the companion of Jeanne d'Arc had reappeared; the soul of the mystic soared up to God in a state of adoration, in floods of tears!

THE BLOODY COUNTESS

VALENTINE PENROSE

[Chapter IX]

Around 1440, in France, a nobleman of an illustrious family, most handsome and brilliant personally, son of Guy de Laval and Marie de Craon, Dame de la Suze, seldom left his own estate any more, Machecoul Manor, a sad and gloomy building, whose towers still rise up into the blue and grey sky above Poitou. Drawbridge raised, portcullis lowered, doors locked shut. None entered here but the most trusted of domestics. At night a light used to gleam suddenly in one of the tower windows, and such hideous shrieks issued from it that the very wolves in the forest bayed. Nevertheless, the estate of Gilles de Rais was not situated in wooded mountainous country, but rather on stony ground from which the castle walls reared up, their silhouette doleful in the luminous air of the west country. Tiffauges was very ancient. In summer its pinkish walls still flower with a mass of wild carnations. The crypt of Tiffauges still exists, very cool under a vault sustained by half broken columns; in the middle is a rectangular slab. That must have been the altar. As for the towers of Machecoul – towers pure in line – they rise up from a rounded butt of cut grass, formerly surrounded by moats. Dark and dolorous strands of ivy, the leaves, rustling in the wind, ceaselessly beat against the north wall. It was there, in the year 1440, in this unhappy retreat of Machecoul, that Gilles de Rais, Marshal of France, was arrested. Justice in the person of Jean V, Duke of Brittany, had been set in motion by the angry and obstinate behaviour of the lord of Rais in trying to take by force one of his last castles which he had sold to Geoffroy Le Ferron, treasurer of Brittany. Meanwhile, during the two months it lasted, the enquiry into the murders of young children which had been ordered by the Bishop of Nantes, had made great progress; the Marshal had to face the accusation of having evoked the devil and of having bathed in the blood of children which he had sacrificed to rejuvenate himself. The accusation took a more serious turn still when it was learned that, not only had the spilled blood been used as a philtre to maintain youth, but that the victim had been offered as a sacrifice to the devil.

In this era, such a charge constituted one of capital murder. The body was capable of suffering; this was a great pity, particularly when a man was innocent, but after all, death would carry him back to that kingdom of his virtues. And, as Gilles de Rais was to say himself at the end, `Death, it is only a matter of a little pain'. But to use this blood, which as it spilled out carried with it the souls of those who had been sacrificed, to enscribe around the circumference of a magic circle the names of certain minor devils, and to nourish them with this divine stolen substance until they were breathing, whimpered and made their appearance in the form of a black dog, that was absolute evil, the unpardonable sin beside which those erotic practices of Gilles de Rais counted for very little. And what, more than everything, drove the mothers to despair and made them howl with grief, was to learn that the figure of Satan had actually appeared engraved upon the heart of one of their children, and that the right hand of another was anointed with the fat of cursed animals, for Gilles de Rais had ordered that a talisman should be made of it, to prevent his being hurt by steel, water, or fire, as long as he should wear it upon his person.

Gilles had it searched for everywhere, this talisman, when the armed emissaries of the Duke of Brittany entered Machecoul. Poitou, his valet, was to say, `As Jean Labbé came into Machecoul, my master cried out, "Quick, you men, find my black velvet hat with the double brim, for there is the source of my liberty, my honour, and my life".'

It was this hand of a child, dried over glowing carbon which one evening he had himself carried in a fold of his cloak to François Prelati, while the latter was discoursing with the spirits of darkness.

However much they searched, they found nothing. The devil had taken unto himself his own.

The Church insisted on taking the trial in hand. From this moment on, Gilles de Rais was lost. The Bishop of Nantes, Jean de Chateaugiron, and the grand seneschal of Brittany, Pierre de L'Hópital, harassed the Duke with continual requests to obtain the necessary authorization. It was only with great regret that Jean V finally gave the order for the trial of a marshal of France who bore such an illustrious name to commence; for he knew well that 'the spiritual court of the Church is supreme and that it judges according to the crimes, and never according to the involved', as the Bishop himself so solemnly affirmed; and Pierre de L'Hôpital demonstrated that he was far more preoccupied with the crime of magic and witchcraft than with all those others, which were in fact far more abominable.

Gilles had needed gold. Like Erzsébet Báthory, he needed especially to live a life entirely different from the rest of men, because such a life bored him to extinction. He used to pass his time high up in his famous room, in the company of François Prelati, his Italian astronomer; and while the latter traced great red and black circles on the flagstones, Gilles de Rais, in a handsome dark-coloured doublet, drew designs on the walls, rather like coats of arms, representing two heads, two brockets and two crosses. Once, when his valet Poitou, one of the few people who were allowed to enter his master's rooms, came in unheralded, Gilles cried out, 'Get out of here and don't come back, for *he* is coming!' Down below, almost immediately after he got there, Poitou heard a great owl's cry, and then something like the steps of some large beast which might have been a dog or a wolf. There was a shriek, 'Oh! Oh! The Devil!' The Marshal appeared, white as a sheet, and bearing a bloody wound on his cheek. He said, 'Master François may very well have lost his life there.' – 'The Devil, Monseigneur, did he really appear to you?' – 'Yes, he truly did, in the shape of a massive, mangy black dog, with his muzzle dripping blood.'

Magic circles, relating to the planets and their temporal aspect, had been drawn all over the place. Sometimes it was necessary to go far into the night to invoke the demons of hidden treasures. In the meadow of the Risen Stones, in the Machecoul countryside, François Prelati, using a blood-soaked knife, and calling for `Barron', drew such a circle. Then he planted the knife, point upwards and exposed. All that night there was thunderstorm and rain lashed down. Gilles could see nothing; but an immense dog hurled itself against his legs and sent him sprawling. There must have been treasure buried somewhere in that meadow.

Another invocation was made in a place known as Hope Meadow, in a field below Machecoul, close to an isolated farm where *la Picarde*, a prostitute, used to live. This time it was a visitor at the castle, a man called *maître* Jean l'Anglais, who drew the circle, and he had taken the precaution of surrounding it with dried hemp and holly leaves, a barrier which ghosts feared to cross. Despite the preliminary offering of the hearts of five children, nothing came.

At night many things used to happen in these distant farms, around which traces of such great magical circles would remain until they were gradually obliterated in the morning dew. A woman called Perrine Rondeau used to keep an inn of evil repute in the district, a meeting place to which François Prelati and another Italian, the Marquis d'Alombara, frequently repaired. They had rented a first floor room whose luxury, if glimpsed from the landing, would have been in striking contrast with the sordid filth of the rooms below. They used to sleep there with four pretty page boys. Everything went well until that day upon which the Marquis, returning from a journey to Dieppe, brought back with him a young fisherman who was more handsome than all the others. From down below, Perrine heard quarrelling conducted in a very florid Italian. The Marquis hastily removed the pretty fisherman elsewhere to a place of safety. François Prelati, too, used to live shut up with a certain gentleman, Eustache, in another gloomy spot, an isolated little farm which had once been a brothel. When they went to interview him, the place was empty. Nothing was to be found except cinders and ash `of a most evil odour', which was recognised as being that of the remains of children, together with a little bloodstained smock of coarse cloth which had been concealed at the bottom of a trough.

They used all of them to meet frequently at Tiffauges, a residence at once gracious and sinister. There, in a vast chamber above the crypt, they were in the habit of using a book written in blood `to invoke Aliboron'. Charcoal was used to sketch a magical circle on the flagstones, a great circle with signs and crosses all round it. The demonologist would step inside, bearing a certain book full of the names of devils written in red in strange characters. He would read from it, sometimes for as long as two hours, and summon demons who were in no hurry to appear. For Gilles had pledged all to Satan, science, riches, power, but he had wished to part neither with his life nor his soul; and Satan didn't come. One day, however, the latter gave way, demanding simply that some hands and hearts and also eyes of children should be offered up to him. He would overlook the rest. And so he appeared in the form of a great serpent in the large chamber at Tiffauges. On another occasion `Barron' materialised in his favourite guise: a huge black dog which fled away, growling. Meanwhile Henriet and Poitou saw toads and grass-snakes which `seemed to have come up out of hell' slipping out of the room through the crack under the door.

While he was living at Tiffauges, François Prelati had impregnated the place so profoundly with magic that invocations could be accomplished there more easily. He had serious altercations with Gilles whom he reproached with impatience and lack of confidence. One day during a visit to the king's court at Bourges, when he was sick to death of finding himself again and again unsuccessful, had not Gilles thrown a certain vermilion chest sent him by the Italian into a well in the hotel Jacques-Coeur? The chest contained a pouch of black silk, which harboured in its turn a silver-coloured object. When he returned, Prelati had told him that in that act he had sacrificed his happiness. How otherwise could the Devil come and show himself freely? Daily, Gilles heard several masses. And even during the great invocation of the `Savage Hunt', he found the means here and there to interpolate a prayer. One particular time, at the moment of invocation he said an *Ave* and instantly saw a gigantic thing pass across the circle, leaving Prelati half-dead.

A Norman woman, who came to tell his fortune with cards, told him one day that he would never get anywhere 'if he did not pluck his heart away from his orisons and out of his chapel'. Thus Gilles, to please the Devil, obtained more and more right hands for him, more hearts, more locks of hair. He would shut himself up in his lofty room and when he came out of it he was ever sad and down-hearted. A page who was passing by the half-open door caught sight of the instruments of magic, the small furnaces and pincers, the phials of red liquid and a dead hand grasping a bloody dagger. Someone came out. The page was thrown out of the nearest window into the moat where he drowned.

It was because of these stories that, unluckily for Gilles de Rais, his trial was transferred to the tribunal of the Bishop of Nantes.

The woman in grey, so ugly and old, so unpleasant and bad-tempered, Perrine Martin, was purveyor of pages to Milord. She had been seen at dusk in distant hamlets, holding little boys, all of them most handsome, by the hand. At Saint-Etienne-de-Montluc she had come on the wandering little beggar boy, the orphan, Janot, and she had led him away in the direction of Machecoul. This person had been noticed as she passed, this unknown woman, 'vermilion-faced, in a grey dress and a black hood worth scarcely a *sou*', and wearing a linen coat over her dress. One day, at Nantes, she had met a child who appeared to be abandoned; thinking the child's beauty would please her master, she had immediately taken him straight to l'Hôtel de la Suze. Gilles de Rais was great taken with him and sent him forthwith to Machecoul where, it appears, he maintained his 'reserve stock' just as did Erzsébet Báthory at Csejthe.

Sometimes, it was the two valets, Henriet and Poitou, who undertook, by one means or another, the task of attracting young boys to the castle. One day when he made a halt at La Roche-Bernard, Gilles, leaning on Poitou's shoulder at a window, caught a glimpse of a passing boy who pleased him greatly. 'That little fellow has the beauty and grace of an angel!' he said. Nothing more had to be said.

Poitou immediately took leave of his master and spoke with the mother of the boy who entered the Marshal's service as a squire. When he had taken up his post, even a new outfit and a little horse was bought for him. At the inn someone said to Poitou, `you have a nice little page there.' Others shouted, `Don't you believe it! The kid's not for him, he's bound for the gullet of our own good Prince!'

Later on, at Nantes, the little horse was recognised. But it was ridden by someone else. This came to be known at La Roche-Bernard. Perrine Loessard, the mother, questioned some of the Marshal's men-at-arms, when they were passing through the village, asking where her son was. She got the answer, `Don't worry! If he's not at Machecoul, it's because he's at Tiffauges, or else at Pornic. Or somewhere else. Or gone to the Devil.'

Finally, casting aside all prudence, the master began to choose his own victims while playing tennis in the courtyard of the castle. One evening, having noticed an eighteen year-old apprentice tailor who was sewing the Marshal's wife's robes, Gilles began to dream of him.

Gilles de Sillé, a cousin of Gilles de Rais, and Roger de Bricqueville were also involved in this occasion. When they went to order falconer's gloves for hawking, they saw the apprentice, this very pretty little Gandron. They sent him to the castle with a message for Gilles' valet. `And beware!' they urged him, `Don't go by the Upright Stones Valley. The old and the ugly are killed there, but they hold on to the young and the beautiful.'

Even the scullions in the kitchens, when the valets went down there, were not safe. One evening, a handsome lad who was turning the spit was caught sight of through the smoke by one of the Marshal's body servants. On the day after the one following he was gone from the kitchens and he was never seen again there. Nor anywhere else. Of the two Hamelin brothers, one was far more handsome than the other. Gilles chose the former, but killed them both.

It was on almsdays especially that children used to disappear. On such days the drawbridge was lowered and the castle servants distributed alms to the poor: food, a little money, and clothing. When they noticed several children more handsome than the rest, they used to pretend that these had not had enough meat to eat and they would lead them away to the kitchens ostensibly to get them some. However, every trick to appease the curiosity of the local populace had been worked to death; each year they would be astonished at how many young boys had disappeared, even taking into account wolves, black men, sickness, and drownings in the swamps.

And so Gilles de Sillé spread abroad the rumour that the English, who had made a prisoner of his brother, Michel de Sillé, kept on and on demanding a ransom of twenty-four male children, the prettiest to be found. He had sent them away from Machecoul, he said, but seven times the number of local boys had been sent from Tiffauges. The people were certainly most grieved to hear this, but at least they believed they had found a rational explanation, hostages and ransoms being the scourge of the age. Besides, not a single girl was missing from the villages where, just as frequently as their brothers, they would play around the fountain. Not even the most insignificant beggar girl had disappeared.

Only once will Poitou, in his confessions, speak with horror of a `female child, one day when the Master had no boys.'

Anne of Brittany, so prudish, so bigoted, and so circumspect, commanded that the minutes of Gilles de Rais' trial should be deposited in the archives of Nantes.

The companions of Gilles de Rais, his cousin, Gilles de Sillé, and Roger de Bricqueville conducted themselves with great cowardice. At the first hint of trouble, they leapt upon their horses and fled away from Machecoul. No one remained at Gilles' side save his two valets who confessed only in the last resort, `in order that they should no longer antagonise God and be forever precluded from heavenly grace'.

It was mid-September of the year 1440 when they came to arrest the Marshal. On their arrival below the walls of Machecoul, the Captain of the Escort, Jean Labbé and his men demanded that the drawbridge should be lowered for them, who carried arms in the service of the Duke of Brittany. On hearing Labbé's name, Gilles crossed himself, kissed a relic, perhaps a talisman, and said to Gilles de Sillé, `Worthy cousin, this is the moment to turn to God'.

A long time before that his astrologer had predicted that his death would be announced by an abbot; and also that he himself would be a monk in an abbey. Prediction which came true. But it was only as a corpse that Gilles rested in a sepulchre of the Carmelites of Nantes.

Jean Labbé called upon the Marshal to follow him. Henriet and Poitou wished to escort their master. But the others saved themselves by flight on horseback.

Jean V had forbidden any search of the castle, in order to gain time before the evidence became too conclusive. The Marshal mounted his horse and, his lips moving in prayer, followed the man of Brittany. Suddenly, there arose cries of malediction from both sides of the road where it ran through the villages on the way. On arrival at Nantes, instead of heading towards the château de la Tour-Neuve where the Duke was staying, Gilles, to his great astonishment, was conducted to the sinister castle de Bouffay, seat of justice in the Dukedom. Happily, he was not left alone there. Besides his valets, he was permitted to retain his organ-player, even though there was certainly no organ in his prison, as well as an archdeacon, two singers and two choirboys.

From the Archbishop, meanwhile, the command came forbidding him all confession and all communion; and this was most painful for him.

It is incumbent upon or it is a function of the ecclesiastical tribunal to know all of the human soul, and to know the soul by the conduct of the body. For it is essential to know through which derangements of the senses precisely Satan appears in the human being.

To save his soul, Henriet spoke firm. He recounted how, having had to go to Chantocé one evening about eight years previously, he came across the works of Suetonius and Tacitus in the library of Gilles de Rais' uncle. On the instructions of Gilles, who happened to be very bored, Henriet, translating from the Latin, read aloud to his master of the crimes of Tiberius, Caligula, and other

Caesars. That very same night, his blood hot from wines and spices, he found a few victims and committed his first erotic crimes. Afterwards, he confided in his cousin de Sillé and Roger de Bricqueville his friend. During that year, one hundred and twenty children were killed. Henriet repeated what he had said: it had all begun because of the reading.

In order to condemn Gilles de Rais once and for all the ecclesiastical tribunal was looking for the opportunity of charging him with a crime allowing of no appeal for divine mercy. This pagan initiation into the vices of the Caesars of Rome constituted a very satisfactory beginning for a trial relating to witchcraft. They began by having the crucifix veiled under which Henriet, in French and sometimes in Latin, was giving his evidence. From his testimony, his master was appearing as a sumptuous, sensual, and slightly histrionic man. On coming out of the great chamber from his crimes, he would strut about like some great black and violet-plumed bird, relating to the bed pillars and to his assistants the details of the delights he had just experienced. He had to have a background of candles, flames, and tears. Then, suddenly prostrate, he would fall back on the more sordid questions of blood to be washed away and bodies to be disposed of. He was the sensual sadist, the exhibitionist libertine for whom a public was essential. The lords de Sillé and de Bricqueville, were involved just as much as he, or almost, but without bringing to the affairs so much formality, so much wordiness to sensual delight, to remorse. They were all soldiers, cruel, and each, many times eye-witness to the horrors of the sacking of a captured town. But in all this, Gilles alone used to allow himself to be carried away by an extravagant dream of oriental barbarism and the purple of ancient Rome, in which he would plunge and writhe in a spreading lake of blood.

For Gilles de Rais, nothing was left in obscurity. First Henriet and then Poitou, more reticent, were forced to describe in every detail what happened in their master's chamber. They spoke of overspiced meals and aphrodisiac wines, enumerating in minute detail the various sadistic pleasures, the insensate crimes, insisting on the acute pains and immense fatigues they had involved. They spoke of oaths made on pouches of velvet containing heavy talismans, of corpses which had had to be dragged up with hooks from the wells into which they had been thrown: of the hasty transfer by night along the rivers of heavy chests full of dead children with their heads severed from their trunks, `eaten up by worms and rolling about like balls'; of the faggots they had to heap up in the fireplace of the Hôtel de la Suze, at Nantes, and which were shored up by poker-thrusts to make them burn, with thirty-six corpses piled up on top. All of which the Assistant Procurator found hard to believe, for, `Just think what it's like when the fat from a roast drips down on to the charcoal in the kitchen!' But the fire, by dint of constant poking, burned brighter and it took only a few hours to dispose of the whole lot. After much lamentation and when he had prayed for the mercy of God, Seigneur de Rais would stretch himself out upon his bed while the conflagration increased, and with great delight he would inhale the frightful odour of burnt flesh and bones, all the while discoursing upon his sensations.

Eight-hundred children massacred in seven years. A good third of the nights during those seven years, from 1433 to 1440, were spent in murdering, rending, and burning; and the days in carting up and down the bloody and mutilated corpses, in order to hide them dry and charred black here and there, under hay or in odd corners, and in throwing the ash into the water in the moat, and in washing off the blood and other impurities, so as to repeat upon the following night this monstrous mass-murder.

Gilles de Sillé and Poitou had the job of bringing the children to the chamber of the Marshal in the evenings. The pageboys and the choirboys too used to `lend themselves' to `the master's pleasure'; they were showered with expensive gifts to make them hold their tongues.

All this became a veritable routine and, throughout seven years, the same people undertook the same actions with indifference. Henriet would build the fire and prepare the buckets of water to wash the floor. Poitou knew the exact moment when he had to step forward and cut the child's jugular with a neat stroke of the knife, so that the blood would spurt out in just the right manner and soak his master who was meanwhile kissing his victim. They looked without seeing too much, they saw without noticing the intertwined bodies twitching in a corner of the room, and barely heard the stifled moans, for they had first stopped up and gagged the child's mouth so that they wouldn't hear his screams. And whilst Gilles, at the very last moment, made an incision in the boy's neck to make him more `languid' and the better to profit from his final jerks, they used to stand by to remove the body, that their lord might fling himself on to his bed without hindrance and get on with his litanies. Or else they had to keep watch to make sure the children were not left too long hanging from the great hook in the corner of the room. For even in that way Gilles de Rais got pleasure out of them. When it was all over, they were brought down and their necks were severed, and he used to shout to show him the head to see if it was beautiful. On certain days, he was seized with diabolic fury and would require a whole batch of children whom he would abuse first in the most bestial ways and whom he slaughtered afterwards. He used to wallow in seas of blood, would open up his victims and roll himself in them. Sometimes he would kneel before the bodies while they were burning and watch the faces lit up by the leaping flames; he used to love to contemplate the putrefying heads which were conserved in salt in a chest, `the most beautiful ones, to keep them fresh', and he would kiss them on the lips. It was Poitou who used to undertake these macabre curing practices.

Throughout all this butchery and hanging and in the midst of his pleasures Gilles de Rais would never stop murmuring prayers to God and to the Devil simultaneously, and to enjoin his victims to pray for him in heaven. The following day a high mass was conducted for the victims.

There is a mad, or very cunning, letter from the Marshal to the King, in which he confesses that he had to go into retreat at his estates of Rais because, for the Dauphin of France, he had conceived `such passion and unholy lust that one day I might have been driven to slay him'. He begged the King at the same time to grant his plea that he might go into retirement with the Carmelites.

The result was that the King, who knew very well that Gilles wasn't mad, wished to be left out entirely of the criminal proceedings against one of the highest officers of the crown.

On the 24th of October, the prisoner entered the chamber of pleas at the castle de Bouffay. He wore the habit of a Carmelite, and he knelt down and began to pray. Hidden behind an arras, the apparatus for ordinary interrogation had been prepared: racks, wedges, and cords. Gilles believed that the Duke of Brittany was there, listening behind this curtain. Pierre de l'Hôpital called upon him to confess. Then Gilles appealed to the King of France. The grand seneschal cried out to him that his own servants had already admitted everything. The confessions of Henriet and Poitou were read aloud to him. Pale as death, Gilles replied that they had spoken the truth, that he had taken children from their mothers, that he had used them in the manner described, and had sometimes opened them up to look at their entrails and hearts: he described several of them, calling to mind their beauty, and admitted to eight hundred murders in seven years, plus three magical evocations; one in the great room at Tiffauges, another at Bourgneuf-en-Rais, and still another he didn't know where, for it had taken place at night, and by chance.

So unequivocal were the proofs of the crimes of witchcraft and sodomy, which crimes came under ecclesiastical jurisdiction, that the trial was immediately transferred to the tribunal of the Bishop of Nantes. Everything was ready. On the orders of the bishop a herald appeared in the room and called three times upon Gilles de Laval, sire de Rais, to make his appearance at once before the bishop's tribunal.

Gilles did not appeal to the president of Brittany against the legality of the proceedings, but followed his destiny and appeared under escort before the bishop.

The trial lasted only a few hours. The preliminary investigation, carried out in secret, was over. There remained finally the crime of treason against God, and against humanity too: murder, rape, and sodomy. But above all, `sacrilege, impiety, casting evil spells, and other perverse works of devilry, magic, alchemy, and witchcraft.'

Finally, when the bishop was advising him to prepare himself for death, Gilles defended himself: relative by blood and marriage to the Duke of Brittany, supreme officer of the crown of France and principal nobleman of district, he could be judged only by his peers, and with the approval of the King and the Duke of Brittany.

Jean de Chateaugiron answered thus: 'The court of the Church is sovereign and judges according to the crimes, never according to the persons involved. Besides, the duke and the King of France agreed that the judgement should be carried out.' And so Gilles de Rais pulled himself together. 'Gentlemen, pray now that I die a good and saintly death.'

The verdict was: 'Hanged and burned; and, after execution, before the body falls apart and is consumed in the fire, it should be withdrawn and carried in a memorial casket to a church in Nantes designated by the condemned man. Henriet and Poitou shall be burned alive and their cinders thrown into the Loire.'

The following day, the square in front of the castle de Bouffay was packed with people. Gilles appeared all in black, with a hood of velvet and a doublet of black damask trimmed with fur of the same colour. Calmly and firmly, he repeated that he had told the truth.

On the 26th of October, at nine o'clock in the morning, priests, bearing the Holy Sacrament in procession, visited all the churches of Nantes, followed by the people praying for the three criminals. At eleven o'clock, Gilles de Rais, Poitou and Henriet were conducted to the meadow at Biesse on the outskirts of the town, upstream from the bridges of Nantes, on the banks of the Loire. Three gallows had been erected, one higher than the other two. Below, faggots and dry broom had been spread.

The weather was fine. The sky was reflected in the river; the leaves of the poplars and the willows were rustling in the wind as usual. Round about, an immense crowd. Chanting the *De Profundis* slowly, the condemned men arrived; and everyone took up the chorus. The echoing sound of it all reached the Duke, shut away in his castle so that he would not have to accord mercy to the prisoners. The tragic *Requiem* followed the *De Profundis*. Gilles kissed Henriet and Poitou and said, 'There is no sin so great that God will not pardon it if the man who asks it of him is really contrite. Death itself is but a moment of pain.' Then he doffed his hat, kissed the crucifix, and began to utter the prayers for the dying. The executioner adjusted the noose, made Gilles mount the raised platform, and a lighted torch was applied to the faggots. The platform swung down, Gilles de Rais fell; the flames licked upwards around his body which swung to and fro at the end of the taut rope. Then, to the continuous tolling of the cathedral bells, the crowd surrounding the scene of expiation, which towered orange and black against the pale sky, intoned the *Dies Irae*.

Six women clothed and veiled in white and six Carmelite nuns moved forward through the kneeling crowd, bearing a coffin. One of the women was Lady de Rais; the others belonged to the most illustrious houses in Brittany. The hangman cut the rope; the body fell into an iron cradle which had been placed there earlier, and this apparatus was now hoisted from the fire before the body had been consumed, in accordance with the sentence of the tribunal.

The white-veiled ladies bowed low and grasped the six handles of the coffin. The corpse, only very slightly charred, with its red hair and black beard, seemed to be staring through glassy eyes at the light grey-blue sky. The chanting was silent now. The woman at the head gave the word. Slowly, they set off once more with their load towards the Carmelite convent at Nantes.

Right up to the moment of his death Gilles de Rais was polished, elegant, and lyrical. The air, imbued with this death in the meadow of Biesse, circulates amongst the willows and the poplars, into the shimmering tendrils of flame, and floats, transparent screen in front of the water of the river. The atmosphere resounded with bells and the chanting of human voices. Gilles must have felt his heart rending at the thought of leaving this life of ease, for he was in no wise a despairing man. He was sensual, vicious, overwhelmed by great waves of sadism; but he was very much involved in this life, and he tasted its pleasures, indulged in crimes, felt remorse. It cannot be said of him that these heinous crimes of his were uncontrolled; on the contrary, they were meticulously planned. There was nothing gratuitous in his conduct, nothing deranged; his most terrible acts retained something of the colour of the Loire, something of this earth, of this sky, of this water.

Pale grey starred with gold; and if he opened his doublet, a belt of scarlet with a dagger of grey steel hidden in a red sheath. The elegance of a Venusian bird, but evil, and one which, like the peacock, struts around on show, before himself, before the world. He did not belong to that race of men who can plunge irrevocably into chaos. Besides, can a male being ever allow himself to slide down to the ultimate of absolute negative depths? His repenting was a reaffirmation of the manhood of Gilles de Rais.

He and his assistants could still understand each other. The real human terror is not death; it is that primeval chaos bearing the void in its wake. The public repentance of Gilles de Rais, there on the October grass, the fire which glowed red on the leaves of the trees, the fear and the suffering, all this transported him back to the world of the living; for everything that lived reasserted its kinship to him and, in the hour of his last steps, reassured his spirit. The mob understood that he had been evil, a wizard, a murderer, but despite all this, he was flesh and blood like themselves.

THE MARECHAL DE RETZ

SABINE BARING-GOULD

I : THE INVESTIGATION OF CHARGES.

The history of the man whose name heads this chapter I purpose giving in detail, as the circumstances I shall narrate have, I believe, never before been given with accuracy to the English public. The name of Gilles de Laval may be well known, as sketches of his bloody career have appeared in many biographies, but these sketches have been very incomplete, as the material from which they were composed was meagre. M. Michelet alone ventured to give the public an idea of the crimes which brought a marshal of France to the gallows, and his revelations were such that, in the words of M. Henri Martin, "this iron age, which seemed unable to feel surprise at any amount of evil, was struck with dismay."

M. Michelet derived his information from the abstract of the papers relating, to the case, made by order of Ann of Brittany, in the Imperial Library. The original documents were in the library at Nantes, and a great portion of them were destroyed in the Revolution of 1789. But a careful analysis had been made of them, and this valuable abridgment, which was inaccessible to M. Michelet, came into the hands of M. Lacroix, the eminent French antiquarian, who published a memoir of the marshal from the information he had thus obtained, and it is his work, by far the most complete and circumstantial which has appeared, that I condense into the following chapters.

"The most monstrously depraved imagination," says M. Henri Martin, "never could have conceived what the trial reveals." M. Lacroix has been obliged to draw a veil over much that transpired, and I must draw it closer still. I have, however, said enough to show that this memorable trial presents horrors probably unsurpassed in the whole volume of the world's history.

During the year 1440, a terrible rumour spread through Brittany, and especially through the ancient pays de Retz, which extends along the south of the Loire from Nantes to Paimbœuf, to the effect that one of the most famous and powerful noblemen in Brittany, Gilles de Laval, Maréchal de Retz, was guilty of crimes of the most diabolical nature.

Gilles de Laval, eldest son of Gay de Laval, second of his name, Sire de Retz, had raised the junior branch of the illustrious house of Laval above the elder branch, which was related to the reigning family of Brittany. He lost his father when he was aged twenty, and remained master of a vast territorial inheritance, which was increased by his marriage with Catharine de Thouars in 1420. He employed a portion of their fortune in the cause of Charles VII., and in strengthening the French crown. During seven consecutive years, from 1426 to 1433, he was engaged in military enterprises against the English; his name is always cited along with those of Dunois, Xaintrailles, Florent d'Illiers, Gaucourt, Richemont, and the most faithful servants of the king. His services were speedily acknowledged by the king creating him Marshal of France. In 1427, he assaulted the Castle of Lude, and carried it by storm; he killed with his own hand the commander of the place; next year he captured from the English the fortress of Rennefort, and the Castle of Malicorne; in 1429, he took an active part in the expedition of Joan of Arc for the deliverance of Orleans, and the occupation of Jargeau, and he was with her in the moat, when she was wounded by an arrow under the walls of Paris.

The marshal, councillor, and chamberlain of the king participated in the direction of public affairs, and soon obtained the entire confidence of his master. He accompanied Charles to Rheims on the occasion of his coronation, and had the honour of bearing the oriflamme, brought for the occasion from the abbey of S. Remi. His intrepidity on the field of battle was as remarkable as his sagacity in council, and he proved himself to be both an excellent warrior and a shrewd politician.

Suddenly, to the surprise of every one, he quitted the service of Charles VII., and sheathed for ever his sword, in the retirement of the country. The death of his maternal grandfather, Jean de Craon, in 1432, made him so enormously wealthy, that his revenues were estimated at 800,000 livres; nevertheless, in two years, by his excessive prodigality, he managed to lose a considerable portion of his inheritance. Mauléon, S. Etienne de Malemort, Loroux-Botereau, Pornic, and Chantolé, he sold to John V., Duke of Brittany, his kinsman, and other lands and seigneurial rights he ceded to the Bishop of Nantes, and to the chapter of the cathedral in that city.

The rumour soon spread that these extensive cessions of territory were sops thrown to the duke and to the bishop, to restrain the one from confiscating his goods, and the other from pronouncing excommunication, for the crimes of which the people whisperingly accused him; but these rumours were probably without foundation, for eventually it was found hard to persuade the duke of the guilt of his kinsman, and the bishop was the most determined instigator of the trial.

The marshal seldom visited the ducal court, but he often appeared in the city of Nantes, where he inhabited the Hôtel de la Suze, with a princely retinue. He had, always accompanying him, a guard of two hundred men at arms, and a numerous suit of pages, esquires, chaplains, singers, astrologers, &c., all of whom he paid handsomely.

Whenever he left the town, or moved to one of his other seats, the cries of the poor, which had been restrained during the time of his presence, broke forth. Tears flowed, curses were uttered, a long-continued wail rose to heaven, the moment that the last of the marshal's party had left the neighbourhood. Mothers had lost their children, babes had been snatched from the cradle, infants had been spirited away almost from the maternal arms, and it was known by sad experience that the vanished little ones would never be seen again.

But on no part of the country did the shadow of this great fear fall so deeply as on the villages in the neighbourhood of the Castle of Machecoul, a gloomy château, composed of huge towers, and surrounded by deep moats, a residence much frequented by Do Retz, notwithstanding its sombre and repulsive appearance. This fortress was always in a condition to resist a siege: the drawbridge was raised, the portcullis down, the gates closed, the men under arms, the culverins on the bastion always loaded. No one, except the servants, had penetrated into this mysterious asylum and had come forth alive. In the surrounding country strange tales of horror and devilry circulated in whispers, and yet it was observed that the chapel of the castle was gorgeously decked with tapestries of silk and cloth of gold, that the sacred vessels were encrusted with gems, and that the vestments of the priests were of the most sumptuous character. The excessive devotion of the marshal was also noticed; he was said to hear mass thrice daily, and to be passionately fond of ecclesiastical music. He was said to have asked permission of the pope, that a crucifer should precede him in processions. But when dusk settled down over the forest, and one by one the windows of the castle became illumined, peasants would point to one casement high up in an isolated tower, from which a clear light streamed through the gloom of night; they spoke of a fierce red glare which irradiated the chamber at times, and of sharp cries ringing out of it, through the hushed woods, to be answered only by the howl of the wolf as it rose from its lair to begin its nocturnal rambles.

On certain days, at fixed hours, the drawbridge sank, and the servants of De Retz stood in the gateway distributing clothes, money, and food to the mendicants who crowded round them soliciting alms. It often happened that children were among the beggars: as often one of the servants would promise them some dainty if they would go to the kitchen for it. Those children who accepted the offer were never seen again.

In 1440 the long-pent-up exasperation of the people broke all bounds, and with one voice they charged the marshal with the murder of their children, whom they said he had sacrificed to the devil.

This charge came to the ears of the Duke of Brittany, but he pooh-poohed it, and would have taken no steps to investigate the truth, had not one of his nobles insisted on his doing so. At the same time Jean do Châteaugiron, bishop of Nantes, and the noble and sage Pierre de l'Hospital, grand-seneschal of Brittany, wrote to the duke, expressing very decidedly their views, that the charge demanded thorough investigation.

John V., reluctant to move against a relation, a man who had served his country so well, and was in such a high position, at last yielded to their request, and authorized them to seize the persons of the Sire de Retz and his accomplices. A serjent d'armes, Jean Labbé, was charged with this difficult commission. He picked a band of resolute fellows, twenty in all, and in the middle of September they presented themselves at the gate of the castle, and summoned the Sire do Retz to surrender. As soon as Gilles heard that a troop in the livery of Brittany was at the gate, he inquired who was their leader? On receiving the answer "Labbé," he started, turned pale, crossed himself, and prepared to surrender, observing that it was impossible to resist fate.

Years before, one of his astrologers had assured him that he would one day pass into the hands of an Abbé, and, till this moment, De Retz had supposed that the prophecy signified that he should eventually become a monk.

Gilles de Sillé, Roger de Briqueville, and other of the accomplices of the marshal, took to flight, but Henriet and Pontou remained with him.

The drawbridge was lowered and the marshal offered his sword to Jean Labbé. The gallant serjeant approached, knelt to the marshal, and unrolled before him a parchment sealed with the seal of Brittany.

"Tell me the tenor of this parchment?" said Gilles de Retz with dignity.

"Our good Sire of Brittany enjoins you, my lord, by these presents, to follow me to the good town of Nantes, there to clear yourself of certain criminal charges brought against you."

"I will follow immediately, my friend, glad to obey the will of my lord of Brittany: but, that it may not be said that the Seigneur de

Retz has received a message without largess, I order my treasurer, Henriet, to hand over to you and your followers twenty gold crowns."

"Grand-merci, monseigneur! I pray God that he may give you good and long life."

"Pray God only to have mercy upon me, and to pardon my sins."

The marshal had his horses saddled, and left Machecoul with Pontou and Henriet, who had thrown in their lot with him.

It was with lively emotion that the people in the villages traversed by the little troop, saw the redoubted Gilles de Laval ride through their streets, surrounded by soldiers in the livery of the Duke of Brittany, and unaccompanied by a single soldier of his own. The roads and streets were thronged, peasants left the fields, women their kitchens, labourers deserted their cattle at the plough, to throng the road to Nantes. The cavalcade proceeded in silence. The very crowd which had gathered to see it, was hushed. Presently a shrill woman's voice was raised:—

"My child! restore my child!"

Then a wild, wrathful howl broke from the lips of the throng, rang along the Nantes road, and only died away, as the great gates of the Chateau de Bouffay closed on the prisoner.

The whole population of Nantes was in commotion, and it was said that the investigation would be fictitious, that the duke would screen his kinsman, and that the object of general execration would escape with the surrender of some of his lands.

And such would probably have been the event of the trial, had not the Bishop of Nantes and the grand-seneschal taken a very decided course in the matter. They gave the duke no peace till he had yielded to their demand for a thorough investigation and a public trial.

John V. nominated Jean de Toucheronde to collect information, and to take down the charges brought against the marshal. At the same time he was given to understand that the matter was not to be pressed, and that the charges upon which the marshal was to be tried were to be softened down as much as possible.

The commissioner, Jean de Toucheronde, opened the

investigation on the 18th September, assisted only by his clerk, Jean Thomas. The witnesses were introduced either singly, or in groups, if they were relations. On entering, the witness knelt before the commissioner, kissed the crucifix, and swore with his hand on the Gospels that he would speak the truth, and nothing but the truth: after this he related all the facts referring to the charge, which came under his cognizance, without being interrupted or interrogated.

The first to present herself was Perrine Loessard, living at la Roche-Bernard.

She related, with tears in her eyes, that two years ago, in the month of September, the Sire de Retz had passed with all his retinue through la Roche-Bernard, on his way from Vannes, and had lodged with Jean Collin. She lived opposite the house in which the nobleman was staying.

Her child, the finest in the village, a lad aged ten, had attracted the notice of Pontou, and perhaps of the marshal himself, who stood at a window, leaning on his squire's shoulder.

Pontou spoke to the child, and asked him whether he would like to be a chorister; the boy replied that his ambition was to be a soldier.

"Well, then," said the squire, "I will equip you."

The lad then laid hold of Pontou's dagger, and expressed his desire to have such a weapon in his belt. Thereupon the mother had ran up and had made him leave hold of the dagger, saying that the boy was doing very well at school, and was getting on with his letters, for he was one day to be a monk. Pontou had dissuaded her from this project, and had proposed to take the child with him to Machecoul, and to educate him to be a soldier. Thereupon he had paid her clown a hundred sols to buy the lad a dress, and had obtained permission to carry him off.

Next day her son had been mounted on a horse purchased for him from Jean Collin, and had left the village in the retinue of the Sire de Retz. The poor mother at parting had gone in tears to the marshal, and had entreated him to be kind to her child. From that time she had been able to obtain no information regarding her son. She had watched the Sire de Retz whenever he had passed through La Roche Bernard, but had never observed her child among his pages. She had questioned several of the marshal's people, but they had laughed at her; the only answer she had obtained was: "Be not afraid. He is either at Machecoul, or else at Tiffauges, or else at Pornic, or somewhere." Perrine's story was corroborated by Jean Collin, his wife, and his mother-in-law.

Jean Lemegren and his wife, Alain Dulix, Perrot p. 194 Duponest, Guillaume Guillon, Guillaume Portayer, Etienne de Monclades, and Jean Lefebure, all inhabitants of S. Etienne de Montluc, deposed that a little child, son of Guillaume Brice of the said parish, having lost his father at the age of nine, lived on alms, and went round the country begging.

This child, named Jamet, had vanished suddenly at midsummer, and nothing was known of what had become of him; but strong suspicions were entertained of his having been carried off by an aged hag who had appeared shortly before in the neighbourhood, and who had vanished along with the child.

On the 27th September, Jean de Toucheronde, assisted by Nicolas Chateau, notary of the court at Nantes, received the depositions of several inhabitants of Pont-de-Launay, near Bouvron: to wit, Guillaume Fourage and wife; Jeanne, wife of Jean Leflou; and Richarde, wife of Jean Gandeau.

These depositions, though very vague, afforded sufficient cause for suspicion to rest on the marshal. Two years before, a child of twelve, son of Jean Bernard, and another child of the same age, son of Ménégué, had gone to Machecoul. The son of Ménégué had returned alone in the evening, relating that his companion had asked him to wait for him on the road whilst he begged at the gates of the Sire de Retz. The son of Ménégué said that he had waited three hours, but his companion had not returned. The wife of Guillaume Fourage deposed that she had seen the lad at this time with an old hag, who was leading him by the hand towards Machecoul. That same evening this hag passed over the bridge of Launay, and the wife of Fourage asked her what had become of little Bernard. The old woman neither stopped nor answered further than by saying he was well provided for. The boy had not been seen since. On the 28th September, the Duke of Brittany joined another commissioner, Jean Couppegorge, and a second notary, Michel Estallure, to Toucheronde and Chateau.

The inhabitants of Machecoul, a little town over which the Sire de Retz exercised supreme power, appeared now to depose against their lord. André Barbier, shoemaker, declared that last Easter, a child, son of his neighbour Georges Lebarbier, had disappeared. He was last seen gathering plums behind the hotel Rondeau. This disappearance surprised none in Machecoul, and no one ventured to comment on it. André and his wife were in daily terror of losing their own child. They had been a pilgrimage to S. Jean d'Angely, and had been asked there whether it was the custom at Machecoul to eat children. On their return they had heard of two children having vanished—the son of Jean Gendron, and that of Alexandre Châtellier. André Barbier had made some inquiries about the circumstances of their disappearance, and had been advised to hold his tongue, and to shut his ears and eyes, unless he were prepared to be thrown into a dungeon by the lord of Machecoul.

"But, bless me!" he had said, "am I to believe that a fairy spirits off and eats our little ones?"

"Believe what you like," was the advice given to him; "but ask no questions." As this conversation had taken place, one of the marshal's men at arms had passed, when all those who had been speaking took to their heels. André, who had run with the rest, without knowing exactly why he fled, came upon a man near the church of the Holy Trinity, who was weeping bitterly, and crying out,—"O my God, wilt Thou not restore to me my little one?" This man had also been robbed of his child.

Licette, wife of Guillaume Sergent, living at La Boneardière, in the parish of S. Croix de Machecoul, had lost her son two years before, and had not seen him since; she besought the commissioners, with tears in her eyes, to restore him to her.

"I left him," said she, "at home whilst I went into the field with my husband to sow flax. He was a bonny little lad, and he was as good as he was bonny. He had to look after his tiny sister, who was a year and a half old. On my return home, the little girl was found, but she could not tell me what had become of him. Afterwards we found in the marsh a small red woollen cap which had belonged to my poor darling; but it was in vain that we dragged the marsh, nothing was found more, except good evidence that he had not been drowned. A hawker who sold needles and thread passed through Machecoul at the time, and told me that an old woman in grey, with a black hood on her head, had bought of him some children's toys, and had a few moments after passed him, leading a little boy by the hand."

Georges Lebarbier, living near the gate of the châtelet de Machecoul, gave an account of the manner in which his son had evanesced. The boy was apprenticed to Jean Pelletier, tailor to Mme. de Retz and to the household of the castle. He seemed to be getting on in his profession, when last year, about S. Barnabas' Day, he went to play at ball on the castle green. He never returned from the game.

This youth and his master, Jean Pelletier, had been in the habit of eating and drinking at the castle, and bad always laughed at the ominous stories told by the people.

Guillaume Hilaire and his wife confirmed the statements of Lebarbier. They also said that they knew of the loss of the sons of Jean Gendron, Jeanne Rouen, and Alexandre Châtellier. The son of Jean Gendron, aged twelve, lived with the said Hilaire and learned of him the trade of skinner. He had been working in the shop for seven or eight years, and was a steady, hardworking lad. One day Messieurs Gilles de Sillé and Roger de Briqueville entered the shop to purchase a pair of hunting gloves. They asked if little Gendron might take a message for them to the castle. Hilaire readily consented, and the boy received beforehand the payment for going—a gold angelus, and he started, promising to be back directly. But he had never returned. That evening Hiliare and his wife, observing Gilles de Sillé and Roger de Briqueville returning to the castle, ran to them and asked what had become of the apprentice. They replied that they had no notion of where he was, as they had been absent hunting, but that it was possible he might have been sent to Tiffauges, another castle of De

Retz.

Guillaume Hilaire, whose depositions were more grave and explicit than the others, positively asserted that Jean Dujardin, valet to Roger de Briqueville had told him he knew of a cask secreted in the castle, full of children's corpses. He said that he had often heard people say that children were enticed to the château and then murdered, but had treated it as an idle tale. He said, moreover, that the marshal was not accused of having any hand in the murders, but that his servants were supposed to be guilty.

Jean Gendron himself deposed to the loss of his son, and he added that his was not the only child which had vanished mysteriously at Machecoul. He knew of thirty that had disappeared.

Jean Chipholon, elder and junior, Jean Aubin, and Clement Doré, all inhabitants of the parish of Thomage, deposed that they had known a poor man of the same parish, named Mathelin Thomas, who had lost his son, aged twelve, and that he had died of grief in consequence.

Jeanne Rouen, of Machecoul, who for nine years had been in a state of uncertainty whether her son were alive or dead, deposed that the child had been carried off whilst keeping sheep. She had thought that he had been devoured of wolves, but two women of Machecoul, now deceased, had seen Gilles de Sillé approach the little shepherd, speak to him, and point to the castle. Shortly after the lad had walked off in that direction. The husband of Jeanne Rouen went to the château to inquire after his son, but could obtain no information. When next Gilles de Sillé appeared in the town, the disconsolate mother entreated him to restore her child to her. Gilles replied that he knew nothing about him, as he had been to the king at Amboise.

Jeanne, widow of Aymery Hedelin, living at Machecoul, had also lost, eight years before, a little child as he had pursued some butterflies into the wood. At the same time four other children had been carried off, those of Gendron, Rouen, and Macé Sorin. She said that the story circulated through the country was, that Gilles de Sillé stole children to make them over to the English, in order to obtain the ransom of his brother who was a captive. But she added that this report was traced to the servants of Sillé, and that it was propagated by them.

One of the last children to disappear was that of Noël Aise, living in the parish of S. Croix.

A man from Tiffauges had said to her (Jeanne Hedelin) that for one child stolen at Machecoul, there were seven carried away at Tiffauges.

Macé Sorin confirmed the deposition of the widow Hedelin., and repeated the circumstances connected with the loss of the children of Châtellier, Rouen, Gendron, and Lebarbier.

Perrine Rondeau had entered the castle with the company of Jean Labbé. She had entered a stable, and had found a heap of ashes and powder, which had a sickly and peculiar smell. At the bottom of a trough she had found a child's shirt covered with blood.

Several inhabitants of the bourg of Fresnay, to wit, Perrot, Parqueteau, Jean Soreau, Catherine Degrépie, Gilles Garnier, Perrine Viellard, Marguerite Rediern, Marie Carfin, Jeanne Laudais, said that they had heard Guillaume Hamelin, last Easter, lamenting the loss of two children.

Isabeau, wife of Guillaume Hamelin, confirmed these depositions, saving that she had lost them seven years before. She had at that time four children; the eldest aged fifteen, the youngest aged seven, went together to Machecoul to buy some bread, but they did not return. She sat up for them all night and next morning. She heard that another child had been lost, the son of Michaut Bonnel of S. Ciré de Retz.

Guillemette, wife of Michaut Bonnel, said that her son had been carried off whilst guarding cows.

Guillaume Rodigo and his wife, living at Bourg-neuf-en-Retz, deposed that on the eve of last S. Bartholomew's day, the Sire do Retz lodged with Guillaume Plumet in his village.

Pontou, who accompanied the marshal, saw a lad of fifteen, named Bernard Lecanino, servant to Rodigo, standing at the door of his house. The lad could not speak much French, but only bas-Breton. Pontou beckoned to him and spoke to him in a low tone. That evening, at ten o'clock, Bernard left his master's house, Rodigo and his wife being absent. The servant maid, who saw him go out, called to him that the supper table was not yet cleared, but he paid no attention to what she said. Rodigo, annoyed at the loss of his servant, asked some of the marshal's men what had become of him. They replied mockingly that they knew nothing of the little Breton, but that he had probably been sent to Tiffauges to be trained as page to their lord.

Marguerite Sorain, the chambermaid alluded to above, confirmed the statement of Rodigo, adding that Pontou had entered the house and spoken with Bernard. Guillaume Plumet and wife confirmed what Rodigo and Sorain had said.

Thomas Aysée and wife deposed to the loss of their son, aged ten, who had gone to beg at the gate of the castle of Machecoul; and a little girl had seen him drawn by an offer of meat into the château.

Jamette, wife of Eustache Drouet of S. Léger, had sent two sons, one aged ten, the other seven, to the castle to obtain alms. They had not been seen since.

On the 2nd October the commissioners sat again, and the charges became graver, and the servants of the marshal became more and more implicated.

The disappearance of thirteen other children was substantiated under circumstances throwing strong suspicion on the inmates of the castle. I will not give the details, for they much resemble those of the former depositions. Suffice it to say that before the commissioners closed the inquiry, a herald of the Duke of Brittany in tabard blew three calls on the trumpet, from the steps of the tower of Bouffay, summoning all who had additional charges to bring against the Sire de Retz, to present themselves without delay. As no fresh witnesses arrived, the case was considered to be made out, and the commissioners visited the duke, with the information they had collected, in their hands.

The duke hesitated long as to the steps he should take. Should he judge and sentence a kinsman, the most powerful of his vassals, the bravest of his captains, a councillor of the king, a marshal of France?

Whilst still unsettled in his mind as to the course he should pursue, he received a letter from Gilles de Retz, which produced quite a different effect from that which it had been intended to produce.

MONSIEUR MY COUSIN AND HONOURED SIRE,
It is quite true that I am perhaps the most detestable of all sinners, having sinned horribly again and again, yet have I never failed in my religious duties. I have heard many masses, vespers, etc., have fasted in Lent and on vigils, have confessed my sins, deploring them heartily, and have received the blood of our Lord at least once in the year.

Since I have been languishing in prison, awaiting your honoured justice, I have been overwhelmed with incomparable repentance for my crimes, which I am ready to acknowledge and to expiate as is suitable.

Wherefore I supplicate you, M. my cousin, to give me licence to retire into a monastery, and there to lead a good and exemplary life. I care not into what monastery I am sent, but I intend that all my goods, &c., should be distributed among the poor, who are the members of Jesus Christ on earth... Awaiting your glorious clemency, on which I rely, I pray God our Lord to protect you and your kingdom.

He who addresses you is in all earthly humility,
FRIAR GILLES,
Carmelite in intention.

The duke read this letter to Pierre de l'Hospital, president of Brittany, and to the Bishop of Nantes, who were those most resolute in pressing on the trial. They were horrified at the tone of this dreadful communication, and assured the duke that the case was so clear, and the steps taken had been so decided, that it was impossible for him to allow De Retz to escape trial by such an impious device as he suggested. In the meantime, the bishop and the grand-seneschal had set on foot an investigation at the castle of Machecoul, and had found numerous traces of human remains. But a complete examination could not be made, as the duke was anxious to screen his kinsman as much as possible, and refused to authorize one.

The duke now summoned his principal officers and held a council with them. They unanimously sided with the bishop and de l'Hospital, and when John still hesitated, the Bishop of Nantes rose and said: "Monseigneur, this case is one for the church as much as for your court to take up. Consequently, if your President of Brittany does not bring the case into secular court, by the Judge of heaven and earth! I will cite the author of these execrable crimes to appear before our ecclesiastical tribunal."

The resolution of the bishop compelled the duke to yield, and it was decided that the trial should take its course without let or hindrance.

In the meantime, the unhappy wife of Gilles de Retz, who had been separated from him for some while, and who loathed his crimes, though she still felt for him as her husband, hurried to the duke with her daughter to entreat pardon for the wretched man. But the duke refused to hear her. Thereupon she went to Amboise to intercede with the king for him who bad once been his close friend and adviser.

II : THE TRIAL

On the 10th October, Nicolas Chateau, notary of the duke, went to the Château of Bouffay, to read to the prisoner the summons to appear in person on the morrow before Messire de l'Hospital, President of Brittany, Seneschal of Rennes, and Chief Justice of the Duchy of Brittany.

The Sire de Retz, who believed himself already a novice in the Carmelite order, had dressed in white, and was engaged in singing litanies. When the summons had been read, he ordered a page to give the notary wine and cake, and then he returned to his prayers with every appearance of compunction and piety.

On the morrow Jean Labbé and four soldiers conducted him to the hall of justice. He asked for Pontou and Henriet to accompany him, but this was not permitted.

He was adorned with all his military insignia, as though to impose on his judges; he had around his neck massive chains of gold, and several collars of knightly orders. His costume, with the exception of his purpoint, was white, in token of his repentance. His purpoint was of pearl-grey silk, studded with gold stars, and girded around his waist by a scarlet belt, from which dangled a poignard in scarlet velvet sheath. His collar, cufs, and the edging of his purpoint were of white ermine, his little round cap or chapel was white, surrounded with a belt of ermine—a fur which only the great feudal lords of Brittany had a right to wear. All the rest of his dress, to the shoes which were long and pointed, was white.

No one at a first glance would have thought the Sire do Retz to be by nature so cruel and vicious as he was supposed to be. On the contrary, his physiognomy was calm and phlegmatic, somewhat pale, and expressive of melancholy. His hair and moustache were light brown, and his beard was clipped to a point. This beard, which resembled no other beard, was black, but under certain lights it assumed a blue hue, and it was this peculiarity which obtained for the Sire do Retz the surname of Blue-beard, a name which has attached to him in popular romance, at the same time that his story has undergone strange metamorphoses.

But on closer examination of the countenance of Gilles de Retz, contraction in the muscles of the face, nervous quivering of the mouth, spasmodic twitchings of the brows, and above all, the sinister expression of the eyes, showed that there was something strange and frightful in the man. At intervals he ground his teeth like a wild beast preparing to dash upon his prey, and then his lips became so contracted, as they were drawn in and glued, as it were, to his teeth, that their very colour was indiscernible.

At times also his eyes became fixed, and the pupils dilated to such an extent, with a sombre fire quivering in them, that the iris seemed to fill the whole orbit, which became circular, and sank back into the head. At these moments his complexion became livid and cadaverous; his brow, especially just over the nose, was covered with deep wrinkles, and his beard appeared to bristle, and to assume its bluish hues. But, after a few moments, his features became again serene, with a sweet smile reposing upon them, and his expression relaxed into a vague and tender melancholy.

"Messires," said he, saluting his judges, "I pray you to expedite my matter, and despatch as speedily as possible my unfortunate case; for I am peculiarly anxious to consecrate myself to the service of God, who has pardoned my great sins. I shall not fail, I assure you, to endow several of the churches in Nantes, and I shall distribute the greater portion of my goods among the poor, to secure the salvation of my soul."

"Monseigneur," replied gravely Pierre de l'Hospital: "It is always well to think of the salvation of one's soul; but, if you please, think now that we are concerned with the salvation of your body."

"I have confessed to the father superior of the Carmelites," replied the marshal, with tranquillity; "and through his absolution I have been able to communicate: I am, therefore, guiltless and purified."

"Men's justice is not in common with that of God, monseigneur, and I cannot tell you what will be your sentence. Be ready to make your defence, and listen to the charges brought against you, which M. le lieutenant du Procureur de Nantes will read."

The officer rose, and read the following paper of charges, which I shall condense:

"Having heard the bitter complaints of several of the inhabitants of the diocese of Nantes, whose names follow hereinafter (here follow the names of the parents of the lost children), we, Philippe do Livron, lieutenant assesseur of Messire le Procureur de Nantes, have invited, and do invite, the very noble and very wise Messire Pierre de l'Hospital, President of Brittany, &c., to bring to trial the very high and very powerful lord, Gilles de Laval, Sire de Retz, Machecoul, Ingrande and other places, Councillor of his Majesty the King, and Marshal of France:

"Forasmuch as the said Sire de Retz has seized and caused to be seized several little children, not only ten or twenty, but thirty, forty, fifty, sixty, one hundred, two hundred, and more, and has murdered and slain them inhumanly, and then burned their bodies to convert them to ashes:

"Forasmuch as persevering in evil, the said Sire, notwithstanding that the powers that be are ordained of God, and that every one should be an obedient subject to his prince, . . . has assaulted Jean Leferon, subject of the Duke of Brittany, the said Jean Leferon being guardian of the fortress of Malemort, in the name of Geoffrey Leferon, his brother, to whom the said lord had made over the possession of the said place:

"Forasmuch as the said Sire forced Jean Leferon to give up to him the said place, and moreover retook the lordship of Malemort in despite of the order of the duke and of justice:

"Forasmuch as the said Sire arrested Master Jean Rousseau, sergeant of the duke, who was sent to him with injunctions from the said duke, and beat his men with their own staves, although their persons were under the protection of his grace:

"We conclude that the said Sire de Retz, homicide in fact and in intent according to the first count, rebel and felon according to the second, should be condemned to suffer corporal punishment, and to pay a fine of his possessions in lands and goods held in fief to the said nobleman, and that these should be confiscated and remitted to the crown of Brittany."

This requisition was evidently drawn up with the view of saving the life of the Sire de Retz; for the crime of homicide was presented without aggravating circumstances, in such a manner that it could be denied or shelved, whilst the crimes of felony and rebellion against the Duke of Brittany were brought into exaggerated prominence.

Gilles de Retz had undoubtedly been forewarned of the course which was to be pursued, and he was prepared to deny totally the charges made in the first count.

"Monseigneur," said Pierre de l'Hospital, whom the form of the requisition had visibly astonished: "What justification have you to make? Take an oath on the Gospels to declare the truth."

"No, messire!" answered the marshal. "The witnesses are bound to declare what they know upon oath, but the accused is never put on his oath."

"Quite so," replied the judge. "Because the accused may be put on the rack and constrained to speak the truth, an' please you."

Gilles de Retz turned pale, bit his lips, and cast a glance of malignant hate at Pierre de l'Hospital; then, composing his countenance, he spoke with an appearance of calm:

"Messires, I shall not deny that I behaved wrongfully in the case of Jean Rousseau; but, in excuse, let me say that the said Rousseau was full of wine, and he behaved with such indecorum towards me in the presence of my servants, that it was quite intolerable. Nor will I deny my revenge on the brothers Leferon: Jean had declared that the said Grace of Brittany had confiscated my fortress of Malemort, which I had sold to him, and for which I have not yet received payment; and Geoffrey Leferon had announced far and wide that I was about to be expelled Brittany as a traitor and a rebel. To punish them I re-entered my fortress of Malemort.—As for the other charges, I shall say nothing about them, they are simply false and calumnious."

"Indeed exclaimed Pierre de l'Hospital, whose blood boiled with indignation against the wretch who stood before him with such effrontery. "All these witnesses who complain of having lost their children, lied under oath!"

"Undoubtedly, if they accuse me of having anything to do with their loss. What am I to know about them, am I their keeper?"

"The answer of Cain!" exclaimed Pierre de l'Hospital, rising from his seat in the vehemence of his emotion. "However, as you solemnly deny these charges, we must question Henriet and Pontou."

"Henriet, Pontou!" cried the marshal, trembling; "they accuse me of nothing, surely!"

"Not as yet, they have not been questioned, but they are about to be brought into court, and I do not expect that they will lie in the face of justice."

"I demand that my servants be not brought forward as witnesses against their master," said the marshal, his eyes dilating, his brow wrinkling, and his beard bristling blue upon his chin: "a master is above the gossiping tales and charges of his servants."

"Do you think then, messire, that your servants will accuse you?"

"I demand that I, a marshal of France, a baron of the duchy, should be sheltered from the slanders of small folk, whom I disown as my servants if they are untrue to their master."

"Messire, I see we must put you on the rack, or nothing will be got from you."

"Hola! I appeal to his grace the Duke of Brittany, and ask an adjournment, that I may take advice on the charges brought against me, which I have denied, and which I deny still."

"Well, I shall adjourn the case till the 25th of this month, that you may be well prepared to meet the accusations."

On his way back to prison, the marshal passed Henriet and Pontou as they were being conducted to the court. Henriet pretended not to see his master, but Pontou burst into tears on meeting him. The marshal held out his hand, and Pontou kissed it affectionately.

"Remember what I have done for you, and be faithful servants," said Gilles de Retz. Henriet recoiled from him with a shudder, and the marshal passed on.

"I shall speak," whispered Henriet; "for we have another master beside our poor master of Retz, and we shall soon be with the heavenly one."

The president ordered the clerk to read again the requisition of the lieutenant, that the two presumed accomplices of Gilles de Retz might be informed of the charges brought against their master. Henriet burst into tears, trembled violently, and cried out that he would tell all. Pontou, alarmed, tried to hinder his companion, and said that Henriet was touched in his head, and that what he was about to say would be the ravings of insanity.

Silence was imposed upon him.

"I will speak out," continued Henriet and yet I dare not speak of the horrors which I know have taken place, before that image of my Lord Christ; "and he pointed tremblingly to a large crucifix above the seat of the judge.

"Henriet." moaned Pontou, squeezing his hand, "you will

destroy yourself as well as your master."

Pierre de l'Hospital rose, and the figure of our Redeemer was solemnly veiled.

Henriet, who had great difficulty in overcoming his agitation, than began his revelations.

The following is the substance of them:

On leaving the university of Angers, he had taken the situation of reader in the house of Gilles de Retz. The marshal took a liking to him, and made him his chamberlain and confidant.

On the occasion of the Sire de la Suze, brother of the Sire de Retz, taking possession of the castle of Chantoncé, Charles de Soenne, who had arrived at Chantoncé, assured Henriet that he had found in the oubliettes of a tower a number of dead children, some headless, others frightfully mutilated. Henriet then thought that this was but a calumny invented by the Sire de la Suze.

But when, some while after, the Sire de Retz retook the castle of Chantoncé and had ceded it to the Duke of Brittany, he one evening summoned Henriet, Pontou, and a certain Petit Robin to his room; the two latter were already deep in the secrets of their master. But before confiding anything to Henriet, De Retz made him take a solemn oath never to reveal what he was about to tell him. The oath taken, the Sire de Retz, addressing the three, said that on the morrow an officer of the duke would take possession of the castle in the name of the duke, and that it was necessary, before this took place, that a certain well should be emptied of children's corpses, and that their bodies should be put into boxes and transported to Machecoul.

Henriet, Pontou, and Petit Robin went together, furnished with ropes and hooks, to the tower where were the corpses. They toiled all night in removing the half-decayed bodies, and with them they filled three large cases, which they sent by a boat down the Loire to Machecoul, where they were reduced to ashes.

Henriet counted thirty-six children's heads, but there were more bodies than heads. This night's work, he said, bad produced a profound impression on his imagination, and he was constantly haunted with a vision of these heads rolling as in a game of skittles, and clashing with a mournful wail.

Henriet soon began to collect children for his master, and was present whilst he massacred them. They were murdered invariably in one room at Machecoul. The marshal used to bathe in their blood; he was fond of making Gilles do Sillé, Pontou, or Henriet torture them, and he experienced intense pleasure in seeing them in their agonies. But his great passion was to welter in their blood. His servants would stab a child in the jugular vein, and let the blood squirt over him. The room was often steeped in blood. When the horrible deed was done, and the child was dead, the marshal would be filled with grief for what he had done, and would toss weeping and praying on a bed, or recite fervent prayers and litanies on his knees, whilst his servants washed the floor, and burned in the huge fireplace the bodies of the murdered children. With the bodies were burned the clothes and everything that had belonged to the little victims.

An insupportable odour filled the room, but the Maréchal do Retz inhaled it with delight.

Henriet acknowledged that he had seen forty children put to death in this manner, and he was able to give an account of several, so that it was possible to identify them with the children reported to be lost.

"It is quite impossible," said the lieutenant, who had been given the cue to do all that was possible to save the marshal—"It is impossible that bodies could be burned in a chamber fireplace."

"It was done, for all that, messire," replied Henriet. "The fireplace was very large, both at the hotel Suze, and also at Machecoul; we piled up great faggots and logs, and laid the dead children among them. In a few hours the operation was complete, and we flung the ashes out of the window into the moat."

Henriet remembered the case of the two sons of Hamelin; he said that, whilst the one child was being tortured, the other was on its knees sobbing and praying to God, till its own turn came.

"What you have said concerning the excesses of Messire de Retz," exclaimed the lieutenant du procureur, "seems to be pure invention, and destitute of all probability. The greatest monsters of iniquity never committed such crimes, except perhaps some Cæsars of old Rome."

"Messire, it was the acts of these Cæsars that my Lord of Retz desired to imitate. I used to read to him the chronicles of Suetonius, and Tacitus, in which their cruelties are recorded. He used to delight in hearing of them, and he said that it gave him greater pleasure to hack off a child's head than to assist at a banquet. Sometimes he would seat himself on the breast of a little one, and with a knife sever the head from the body at a single blow; sometimes he cut the throat half through very gently, that the child might languish, and he would wash his hands and his beard in its blood. Sometimes he had all the limbs chopped off at once from the trunk; at other times he ordered us to hang the infants till they were nearly dead, and then take them down and cut their throats. I remember having brought to him three little girls who were asking charity at the castle gates. He bade me cut their throats whilst he looked on. André Bricket found another little girl crying on the steps of the house at Vannes because she had lost her mother. He brought the little thing—it was but a babe—in his arms to my lord, and it was killed before him. Pontou and I had to make away with the body. We threw it down a privy in one of the towers, but the corpse caught on a nail in the outer wall, so that it would be visible to all who passed. Pontou was let down by a rope, and he disengaged it with great difficulty."

"How many children do you estimate that the Sire de Retz and his servants have killed?"

"The reckoning is long. I, for my part, confess to having killed twelve with my own hand, by my master's orders, and I have brought him about sixty. I knew that things of the kind went on before I was admitted to the secret; for the castle of Machecoul had been occupied a short while by the Sire do la Sage. My lord recovered it speedily, for he knew that there were many children's corpses hidden in a hayloft. There were forty there quite dry and black as coal, because they had been charred. One of the women of Madame de Retz came by chance into the loft and saw the corpses. Roger de Briqueville wanted to kill her, but the maréchal would not let him."

"Have you nothing more to declare?

"Nothing. I ask Pontou, my friend, to corroborate what I have said."

This deposition, so circumstantial and detailed, produced on the judges a profound impression of horror. Human imagination at this time had not penetrated such mysteries of refined cruelty. Several times, as Henriet spake, the president had shown his astonishment and indignation by signing himself with the cross. Several times his face had become scarlet, and his eyes had fallen; he had pressed his hand to his brow, to assure himself that he was not labouring under a hideous dream, and a quiver of horror had run through his whole frame.

Pontou had taken no part in the revelation of Henriet; but when the latter appealed to him he raised his head, looked sadly round the court, and sighed.

"Etienne Cornillant, alias Pontou, I command you in the name of God and of justice, to declare what you know."

This injunction of Pierre do l'Hospital remained unresponded to, and Pontou seemed to strengthen himself in his resolution not to accuse his master.

But Henriet, flinging himself into the arms of his accomplice, implored him, as he valued his soul, no longer to harden his heart to the calls of God; but to bring to light the crimes he had committed along with the Sire do Retz.

The lieutenant du procureur, who hitherto had endeavoured to extenuate or discredit the charges brought against Gilles do Retz, tried a last expedient to counterbalance the damaging confessions of Henriet, and to withhold Pontou from giving way.

"You have heard, monseigneur," said he to the president, "the atrocities which have been acknowledged by Henriet, and you, as I do, consider them to be pure inventions of the aforesaid, made out of bitter hatred and envy with the purpose of ruining his master. I therefore demand that Henriet should be put on the rack, that he may be brought to give the lie to his former statements."

"You forget," replied de l'Hospital, "that the rack is for those who do not confess, and not for those who freely acknowledge their crimes. Therefore I order the second accused, Etienne Cornillant, alias Pontou, to be placed on the rack if he continues silent. Pontou! will you speak or will you not?"

"Monseigneur, he will speak!" exclaimed Henriet. Oh, Pontou, dear friend, resist not God any more."

"Well then, messeigneurs," said Pontou, with emotion; "I will satisfy you; I cannot defend my poor lord against the allegations of Henriet, who has confessed all through dread of eternal damnation."

He then fully substantiated all the statements of the other, adding other facts of the same character, known only to himself.

Notwithstanding the avowal of Pontou and Henriet, the adjourned trial was not hurried on. It would have been easy to have captured some of the accomplices of the wretched man; but the duke, who was informed of the whole of the proceedings, did not wish to augment the scandal by increasing the number of the accused. He even forbade researches to be made in the castles and mansions of the Sire de Retz, fearing lest proofs of fresh crimes, more mysterious and more horrible than those already divulged, should come to light.

The dismay spread through the country by the revelations already made, demanded that religion and morality, which had been so grossly outraged, should be speedily avenged. People wondered at the delay in pronouncing sentence, and it was loudly proclaimed in Nantes that the Sire de Retz was rich enough to purchase his life. It is true that Madame de Retz solicited the king and the duke again to give pardon to her husband; but the duke, counselled by the bishop, refused to extend his authority to interfere with the course of justice; and the king, after having sent one of his councillors to Nantes to investigate the case, determined not to stir in it.

III : THE SENTENCE AND EXECUTION

On the 24th October the trial of the Maréchal de Retz was resumed. The prisoner entered in a Carmelite habit, knelt and prayed in silence before the examination began. Then he ran his eye over the court, and the sight of the rack, windlass, and cords made a slight shudder run through him.

"Messire Gilles de Laval," began the president; "you appear before me now for the second time to answer to a certain requisition read by M. le Lieutenant du Procureur de Nantes."

"I shall answer frankly, monseigneur," said the prisoner calmly; "but I reserve the right of appeal to the benign intervention of the very venerated majesty of the King of France, of whom I am, or have been, chamberlain and marshal, as may be proved by my letters patent duly enregistered in the parliament at Paris—"

"This is no affair of the King of France," interrupted Pierre de l'Hospital; "if you were chamberlain and marshal of his Majesty, you are also vassal of his grace the Duke of Brittany."

"I do not deny it; but, on the contrary, I trust to his Grace of Brittany to allow me to retire to a convent of Carmelites, there to repent me of my sins."

"That is as may be; will you confess, or must I send you to the rack?"

"Torture me not!" exclaimed Gilles de Retz "I will confess all. Tell me first, what have Henriet and Pontou said?"

"They have confessed. M. le Lieutenant du Procureur shall read you their allegations."

"Not so," said the lieutenant, who continued to show favour to the accused; "I pronounce them false, unless Messire de Retz confirms them by oath, which God forbid!"

Pierre de l'Hospital made a motion of anger to check this scandalous pleading in favour of the accused, and then nodded to the clerk to read the evidence.

The Sire do Retz, on hearing that his servants had made such explicit avowals of their acts, remained motionless, as though thunderstruck. He saw that it was in vain for him to equivocate, and that he would have to confess all.

"What have you to say?" asked the president, when the confessions of Henriet and Pontou had been read.

"Say what befits you, my lord," interrupted the lieutenant du procureur, as though to indicate to the accused the line he was to take: "are not these abominable lies and calumnies trumped up to ruin you?"

"Alas, no!" replied the Sire do Retz; and his face was pale as death: "Henriet and Pontou have spoken the truth. God has loosened their tongues."

"My lord! relieve yourself of the burden of your crimes by acknowledging them at once," said M. do l'Hospital earnestly.

"Messires!" said the prisoner, after a moment's silence: "it is quite true that I have robbed mothers of their little ones; and that I have killed their children, or caused them to be killed, either by cutting their throats with daggers or knives, or by chopping off their heads with cleavers; or else I have had their skulls broken by hammers or sticks; sometimes I had their limbs hewn off one after another; at other times I have ripped them open, that I might examine their entrails and hearts; I have occasionally strangled them or put them to a slow death; and when the children were dead I had their bodies burned and reduced to ashes."

"When did you begin your execrable practices?" asked Pierre de l'Hospital, staggered by the frankness of these horrible avowals: "the evil one must have possessed you."

"It came to me from myself,—no doubt at the instigation of the devil: but still these acts of cruelty afforded me incomparable delight. The desire to commit these atrocities came upon me eight years ago. I left court to go to Chantoncé, that I might claim the property of my grandfather, deceased. In the library of the castle I found a Latin book—Suetonius, I believe—full of accounts of the cruelties of the Roman Emperors. I read the charming history of Tiberius, Caracalla, and other Cæsars, and the pleasure they took in watching the agonies of tortured children. Thereupon I resolved to imitate and surpass these same Cæsars, and that very night I began to do so. For some while I confided my secret to no one, but afterwards I communicated it to my cousin, Gilles de Sillé, then to Master Roger de Briqueville, next in succession to Henriet, Pontou, Rossignol, and Robin." He then confirmed all the accounts given by his two servants.

He confessed to about one hundred and twenty murders in a single year.

"An average of eight hundred in less than seven years!" exclaimed Pierre de l'Hospital, with a cry of pain: "Ah! messire, you were possessed! "

His confession was too explicit and circumstantial for the Lieutenant du Procureur to say another word in his defence; but he pleaded that the case should be made over to the ecclesiastical court, as there were confessions of invocations of the devil and of witchcraft mixed up with those of murder. Pierre de l'Hospital saw that the object of the lieutenant was to gain time for Mme. de Retz to make a fresh attempt to obtain a pardon; however he was unable to resist, so he consented that the case should be transferred to the bishop's court.

But the bishop was not a man to let the matter slip, and there and then a sergeant of the bishop summoned Gilles de Laval, Sire do Retz, to appear forthwith before the ecclesiastical tribunal. The marshal was staggered by this unexpected citation, and he did not think of appealing against it to the president; he merely signed his readiness to follow, and he was at once conducted into the ecclesiastical court assembled hurriedly to try him.

This new trial lasted only a few hours.

The marshal, now thoroughly cowed, made no attempt to defend himself, but he endeavoured to bribe the bishop into leniency, by promises of the surrender of all his lands and goods to the Church, and begged to be allowed to retire into the Carmelite monastery at Nantes.

His request was peremptorily refused, and sentence of death was pronounced against him.

On the 25th October, the ecclesiastical court having pronounced judgment, the sentence was transmitted to the secular court, which had now no pretext upon which to withhold ratification.

There was some hesitation as to the kind of death the marshal was to suffer. The members of the secular tribunal were not unanimous on this point. The president put it to the vote, and collected the votes himself; then he reseated himself, covered his head, and said in a solemn voice:—

"The court, notwithstanding the quality, dignity, and nobility of the accused, condemns him to be hung and burned. Wherefore I admonish you who are condemned, to ask pardon of God, and grace to die well, in great contrition for having committed the said crimes. And the said sentence shall be carried into execution to-morrow morning between eleven and twelve o'clock." A similar sentence was pronounced upon Henriet and Pontou.

On the morrow, October 26th, at nine o'clock in the morning, a general procession composed of half the people of Nantes, the clergy and the bishop bearing the blessed Sacrament, left the cathedral and went round the city visiting each of the principal churches, where masses were said for the three under sentence.

At eleven the prisoners were conducted to the place of execution, which was in the meadow of Biesse, on the further side of the Loire.

Three gibbets had been erected, one higher than the others, and beneath each was a pile of faggots, tar, and brushwood.

It was a glorious, breezy day, not a cloud was to be seen in the blue heavens; the Loire rolled silently towards the sea its mighty volumes of turbid water, seeming bright and blue as it reflected the brilliancy and colour of the sky. The poplars shivered and whitened in the fresh air with a pleasant rustle, and the willows flickered and wavered above the stream.

A vast crowd had assembled round the gallows; it was with difficulty that a way was made for the condemned, who came on chanting the De profundis. The spectators of all ages took up the psalm and chanted it with them, so that the surge of the old Gregorian tone might have been heard by the duke and the bishop, who had shut themselves up in the château of Nantes during the hour of execution.

After the close of the psalm, which was terminated by the Requiem æternam instead of the Gloria, the Sire de Retz thanked those who had conducted him, and then embraced Pontou and Henriet, before delivering himself of the following address, or rather sermon:

"My very dear friends and servants, be strong and courageous against the assaults of the devil, and feel great displeasure and contrition for your ill deeds, without despairing of God's mercy. Believe with me, that there is no sin, however great, in the world, which God, in his grace and loving kindness, will not pardon, when one asks it of Him with contrition of heart. Remember that the Lord God is always more ready to receive the sinner than is the sinner to ask of Him pardon. Moreover, let us very humbly thank Him for his great love to us in letting us die in full possession of our faculties, and not cutting us off suddenly in the midst of our misdeeds. Let us conceive such a love of God, and such repentance, that we shall not fear death, which is only a little pang, without which we could not see God in his glory. Besides we must desire to be freed from this world, in which is only misery, that we may go to everlasting glory. Let us rejoice rather, for although we have sinned grievously here below, yet we shall be united in Paradise, our souls being parted from our bodies, and we shall be together for ever and ever, if only we endure in our pious and honourable contrition to our last sigh." Then the marshal, who was to be executed first, left his companions and placed himself in the hands of his executioners. He took off his cap, knelt, kissed a crucifix, and made a pious oration to the crowd much in the style of his address to his friends Pontou and Henriet.

Then he commenced reciting the prayers of the dying; the executioner passed the cord round his neck, and adjusted the knot. He mounted a tall stool, erected at the foot of the gallows as a last honour paid to the nobility of the criminal. The pile of firewood was lighted before the executioners had left him.

Pontou and Henriet, who were still on their knees, raised their eyes to their master and cried to him, extending their arms,—

"At this last hour, monseigneur, be a good and valiant soldier of God, and remember the passion of Jesus Christ which wrought our redemption. Farewell, we hope soon to meet in Paradise!

The stool was cast down, and the Sire de Retz dropped. The fire roared up, the flames leaped about him, and enveloped him as be swung.

Suddenly, mingling with the deep booming of the cathedral bell, swelled up the wild unearthly wail of the Dies iræ.

No sound among the crowd, only the growl of the fire, and the solemn strain of the hymn:

Lo, the Book, exactly worded,
Wherein all hath been recorded;
Thence shall judgment be awarded.

When the Judge his seat attaineth,
And each hidden deed arraigneth,
Nothing unavenged remaineth.

What shall I, frail man, be pleading?
Who for me be interceding?
When the just are mercy needing.

King of Majesty tremendous,
Who dost free salvation send us,
Fount of pity! then befriend us.

Low I kneel, with heart-submission;
See, like ashes, my contrition—
Help me in my last condition!

Ah I that day of tears and mourning!
From the dust of earth returning,
Man for judgment must prepare him!
Spare, O, God, in mercy spare him!
Lord, who didst our souls redeem,
Grant a blessed requiem!

AMEN.

Six women, veiled, and robed in white, and six Carmelites advanced.

bearing a coffin.

It was whispered that one of the veiled women was Madame de Retz, and that the others were members of the most illustrious houses of Brittany.

The cord by which the marshal was hung was cut, and he fell into a cradle of iron prepared to receive the corpse. The body was removed before the fire had gained any mastery over it. It was placed in the coffin, and the monks and the women transported it to the Carmelite monastery of Nantes, according to the wishes of the deceased.

In the meantime, the sentence had been executed upon Pontou and Henriet; they were hung and burned to dust. Their ashes were cast to the winds; whilst in the Carmelite church of Our Lady were celebrated with pomp the obsequies of the very high, very powerful, very illustrious Seigneur Gilles de Laval, Sire de Retz, late Chamberlain of King Charles VII., and Marshal of France!

GILLES DE RAIS

GEORGES BATAILLE

I : GILLES DE RAIS

This evening, I am going to talk to you about Gilles de Rais. The history of Gilles de Rais is interesting from more than one point of view. In particular, it touches here on local history. Gilles de Rais lived at Tiffauges for a long time, some of his domains were in the area of present-day Vendée, others in the neighbouring region. However, I must apologise for, or at least warn you from the outset about the very singular nature of this figure. I believe that there are few more horrible characters in the whole of history. He was a great lord, but in other respects he compares with famous criminals of modern times. Some of you may recall a butcher from Hanover named Haarman who was sentenced in 1924 for the sadistic murder of eight young people. Well, Gilles de Rais was a sort of butcher of Hanover writ large. It is difficult to estimate the number of his victims but apparently there were at least 200. Gilles de Rais also recalls another very famous figure, the Marquis de Sade. The Marquis de Sade is famous for having written novels the heroes of which, like the owner of Tiffauges, indulge in the pleasure of killing. Moreover, it is the Marquis de Sade who gives his name to the aberration, sadism, of which Gilles de Rais is a terrifying example. However, it must be said that the Marquis de Sade merely described such abominations in books. He was never incriminated with any murder. The most one can say is that he sometimes committed minor acts of cruelty, the victims of which quickly recovered. It is a curious thing, but it has recently been discovered that Sade was a captain of the Burgundy cavalry regiment at Fontenay-le-Comte—a fact of which, I am sure, you were unaware. But he did not stay here for long. Immediately upon his arrival, the major who was standing in for Lieutenant-Colonel Comte de Saigues, the commanding officer of the regiment, placed him under arrest, doubtless for the simple reason that shortly before, Sade had been found guilty of abusing some poor woman. Sade complained to the Comte de Saigues who reversed the major's decision (this major was doubtless a certain M. de Malherbe). In any event, the matter was quickly resolved. Sade received a promotion and became a captain in the cavalry. But although his destiny was more long-lived and less tragic than Gilles de Rais's, it was no less troubled. He spent more than thirty years in prison. Though probably in error, he was almost sentenced to death on two occasions.

[...]

At this point, I must eliminate a quite bizarre hypothesis according to which Gilles de Rais is said to have been not only a brilliant soldier and criminal but one of the most cultivated and intelligent men of his age. He is alleged to have retired to the solitude of his manorial residences to lead the life of a kind of Doctor Faust *avant la lettre*. This point of view was advanced by Huysmans. The novel,[1] a large part of which Huysmans devoted to the account of the Maréchal de Rais' life and death, is of undoubted literary value, but the hypothesis that I have just outlined in no way deserves our attention. Though actually a remarkably intelligent man, Gilles de Rais sometimes appears exceptionally naïve, but we have no evidence of a disinterested taste in things of the mind. Huysmans was perhaps taken in by a passion for church hymns and ceremonies which he himself is known to have been steeped in. Gilles de Rais's education was doubtless not rudimentary. He knew latin. But there is little to say about his interest in books. All we know is that he must have possessed a *Suetone* and we have the titles of four manuscripts that he disposed of: a *Valerius-Maximus*, Ovid's *Metamorphosis* and two copies of *The City of God* by St. Augustine, one in French, the other in latin. This proves nothing. We have no cause to look for interests above and beyond what is known to us from verified documents.

II : SEXUAL LIFE – WAR

It appeared tame possible to situate the vices of Gilles de Rais in an ensemble of traditional cruelties and drinking bouts. Besides, we are informed, albeit imperfectly, on the actual development of his vices.

I have already spoken of the confessions Giles de Rais himself made that "iniquitously... since the beginning of his youth," he had committed "high and enormous crimes." I have also cited what the trial said afterwards: that the origin of these crimes is attributed by the guilty party "to the bad management he had received in his childhood, when, unbridled, he applied himself to whatever pleased him, and pleased himself with every illicit act." From here it is difficult to become more explicit. From a vague tradition to begin with (we have to imagine the occasional stories: "this fellow's son did this, that one did something else"), violent habits, at least of precocious irregularity, could have thus perpetuated themselves. However, two distinct aspects are implicated in the confessions.

In the first place, during his childhood, inasmuch as it seems on account of the bad management of the grandfather, the grandson must have practiced the various illicit acts that were accessible to him slyly and unchecked. As we have seen, he was eleven years old in September 1415 upon the death of his father (which followed several months after the death of his mother). Still, the tutelage of the grandfather had a sense of total freedom for the child. But it was then a question of reprehensible acts – of unquestionably sexual, perhaps sadistic, perversions – but not of crimes.

The crimes, properly speaking the "high and enormous crimes," date from the "beginning of his youth:"

On this point we cannot be more specific.

On the date of the first child murders, the trial gives two contradictory indications.

According to the bill of indictment, it all began around 1426, fourteen years before the trial: invocations of demons and murders of children. But according to the guilty party's confessions, which coincide with the first testimonies of the victims' parents, the first murders dated only from the year of the grandfather's death, that is from 1432.

The year 1426 would correspond to the beginning of his youth: twenty-two years old. This is the date, moreover, when the campaign into the Maine region begins. Gilles has asked, as of 1424, to take control of the administration of all his goods. In 1426, taking the field, he revels in an increased freedom in addition to his complete personal power.

One conjecture would resolve the difficulty; the "high and enormous crimes" of the beginning of his youth would be separate from the series of child murders that, as of 1432, must have had a certain continuity and given way to a sort of "fixation": the same procedure, same ceremony, finally, more and more, the same participants. As early as the "beginning of his youth" there would have only been, regarding the words crime and enormity, the conjury of demons and maybe those cruel brutalities that could then be associated with war.

It is doubtful in my opinion that this reveler who took so much pleasure in spilling blood would not, from the first campaign, have profited from war.

We ought not to lose sight of precisely what we know of Gilles de Rais, or what we know of the wars of this period.

We ought never to forget that in this period of incessant wars, the scenes of slaughter in towns and burning villages had a sort of banality to them. Pillage was then the inevitable means of feeding a voracious soldiery. In every sense, it is certain that war stimulated greed.

I cannot evoke these fundamental aspects of human life any better than by recalling how the King of Spain, Philippe II, vomited from his horse during the pillage of Saint-Quentin. But far from vomiting, Gilles evidently found some pleasure in watching the wretches be disemboweled. Faced with the spectacles of war, this pederast must have had occasions to bind his sexual excitement to these butcheries.

As for these butcheries, and the banality of these butcheries, we can refer to the text of the Archbishop of Reims, Juvénal des Ursins (in his Epistles of 1439 and 1440). The prelate contends that not only were such offenses an act of the enemy, but of "no one allied to the King"; locating their indispensable provisions in a village, the soldiers "seized men, women, and children, without distinguishing between age or sex, raping the women and girls; they killed husbands and fathers in the presence of their wives and daughters; they took wet nurses, leaving their babies who died for lack of nourishment; they seized and shackled pregnant women who, in their chains, gave birth to their offspring, which were left to die unbaptized, and they were then going to throw mother and child into the river; they took priests, monks, men of the Church, laborers, shackled them in various manners and thus tormented, beat them, by which certain of them died mutilated, others enraged or out of their senses... They... imprisoned them .... they put them in irons..., in pits, in disgusting places full of vermin, they left them.. . to die of hunger. Many died of it. And God knows the tyrannies that they did! They roasted one another; they pulled each other's teeth out, others were beaten with big sticks; they were never set free before having given more money than they possessed..." In 1439, one of Gilles de Rais' captains just missed being hanged for acts of this very nature. But after 1427 Gilles himself probably had very few occasions in which to participate in these sadistic scenes; after the first campaign, he could have only fought two times: first, beside Joan of Arc, who was violently opposed to lawlessness; and second, in 1432 at Lagny, where it is probable that things did not drag on.

In any case, nothing proves that Gilles took part in actual butcheries. We only know that, at Lude, he insisted on hanging French prisoners who had fought with the English and who could have passed for having betrayed their country. It is likely that other captains, more anxious for money, would have preferred a ransom. In his own way Gilles also appreciated money, but he refused to appear to prize it.

'Whatever the case, it is difficult to believe that, while he was making war in 1427, the "high and enormous crimes" of the "beginning of his youth" were far removed from the bedlam that the passing men-at-arms brought on. We will see that the sight of human blood and bodies cut open fascinated him. Later he must have only been interested in privileged victims, in children. His curiosity and excitement, however, could have been exhibited earlier on coarser occasions. He would have not spoken of crime, if crime itself had not cruelly intervened; if at that time he had done his killing with a taste for cruelty. It is not certain, but it is believable, and after everything has been said on the subject, it is probable. Doubtless he could have been speaking of crime when referring to invocations of the demon; without a doubt, these began during this period. But the murders which followed from 1432 on, did they have no antecedent? The abuse of children, it seems to me, had a greater chance of degenerating into murder if Rais at some point had had the opportunity to begin amusing himself with blood.

In speaking of this period (he is speaking of this period, apparently, if he is speaking of his youth), he says that he, "for his pleasure and according to his will, had done whatever evil he could"; he also says that at that time he had put "his hope and intention into the illicit and dishonest acts and things that he did." The opportunity to take pleasure in butchery was too good to pass up.

III : SEXUAL LIFE – THE MURDERS

A description of the monster's sexual deviations does not, by itself, constitute the hallucinatory aspect of Gilles de Rais' life; it is, at the same time, the best known aspect. We are familiar with it not only by Lord de Rais' confessions, but by his valets' depositions. From various sides, the trial accumulates an abundance of suffocating details. Twice rather than once, what we come to know only rarely – the tastes, the fantasies, the caprices, the preferences of the monster – were noted with a meticulousness which defies decency. From 1432 on, each of Rais' residences had a room worthy of the cruel imaginings of Sade, where pleasure was fused to the jerks of dying bodies. There was such a room reserved for horror in the enormous fortress at Champtocé. Maybe his grandfather had just died there? Maybe he finished dying a little later on? The practice of murdering began the year that this grandfather died. Right from the start, surrounded by his companions,

Gilles abandoned himself to sensual pleasure. Things were arranged so that if he wanted to do the killing, he could do so himself. Or if he preferred, he prevailed upon Guillaume de Sillé or Roger de Briqueville, his accomplices and cousins, who came from noble families ruined by the war. Often Gilles did the killing himself, in the presence of Sillé and Briqueville; but if it was needed, one of these brigands would lend a hand. All of them lived at the master's expense; the master paid, but first they procured for him that which he desired. To begin with, the company gave themselves up to excess; they gorged
3 themselves on fine food and strong drink – but it seems the fanatics never abandoned Gilles to the solitude of blood.

After 1432, Champtocé probably had stopped being used; the house of La Suze at Nantes, the castles at Tiffauges and at Machecoul very quickly took over. Later the participants of these feasts were also completely changed; others entered into the secrets. At first there apparently were singers from the chapel: André Buchet from Vannes and Jean Rossignol of La Rochelle, both of whom apparently had the voices of homosexual angels, and both of whom Gilles made into canons of Saint-Hilaire-de-Poitiers. There was Hicquet de Brémont and Robin Romulart (or 'Petit Robin"), who apparently died at the end of 1439. Finally, two valets going by the names of Poitou and Henriet made it into these bloody barracks. Other, younger singers, spared by the master, were used on the days when new victims could not be found; persuaded to keep quiet, they were probably introduced into the secrets... These libidinous abodes at Machecoul and Tiffauges were terrifying.. . Filled with people, they were terrifying. Even if we forget the frivolity of sorcerers who sought the Devil and priests who sang the Office, they were terrifying.

These fortresses had the feeling of diabolical traps. They closed around those children imprudently waiting for alms at their portal. The greatest number of the juvenile victims were taken by this trickery. In this monstrous lawlessness was a suffocating preparation for the worst. Occasionally Giles himself chose, sometimes he requested Sues or others to choose. Once the child was brought into Gilles' room, things abruptly began. Taking his "virile member" in hand, Gilles "rubbed" it, "erected" it, or "stretched" it on the belly of his victim, introducing it between his thighs. He rubbed himself "on the bellies of the... children..., he took great delight, and got so excited that the sperm, criminally and in a way it ought not, spurted onto the bellies of the said children." With each child Gilles only came once or twice, whereupon "he killed them or had them killed."

But it was rare for the orgy to begin without the child first being abused. To begin with, there was a sort of strangling: the poor wretches were put on an abominable apparatus. Gilles wanted to "prevent their cries" and avoid their being heard. "Sometimes he suspended them by his own hand, sometimes he had others suspend them by the throat with cords and rope, in his room, on a peg or small hook." Thus, with their necks extended, they were reduced to death rattles.

At this moment, a comedy could intervene. Giles, halting the suspension, had the child let down; then he caressed and cajoled him, assuring him that he had not wanted to "harm" him or "hurt him," but that, on the contrary, he only wanted "to have fun" with him. If he had at last silenced him, he could then have his way with him, but the appeasement did not last.

Having drawn violent pleasure from the victim, he killed him or had him killed. But often Gilles' enjoyment combined with the child's death. He might cut – or cause to be cut – a vein in the neck, when the blood spurted, Gilles would come. Occasionally, at the decisive moment, he wanted the victim to be in the languor of death. Or further, he had him decapitated; from then on the orgy lasted "as long as the bodies were warm." Occasionally, after decapitation, he sat on the belly of the victim and delighted in watching him die like this; he sat at an angle, the better to see his last tremblings.

He occasionally varied the method of killing. Here is what he himself said on the subject: –Sometimes he inflicted, sometimes the accomplices inflicted "various types and manners of torment; sometimes they severed the head from the body with dirks, daggers, and knives, sometimes they struck them violently on the head with a cudgel or other blunt instruments." He specifies that the punishment of suspension was added to these torments. When interrogated, the valet Poitou enumerates the manner of killing as follows: "Sometimes beheading or decapitating them, sometimes cutting their throats, sometimes dismembering them, and sometimes breaking their necks with a cudgel." He said also that there was a "sword dedicated to their execution, commonly called a braquemard" (p. 220).

But we are not at the end of this voyage to the limits of the worst.

Here is what we know from Henriet the valet. Gilles boasted in his presence of taking "greater pleasure in murdering the.. . children, in seeing their heads and members separated, in seeing them languish and seeing their blood, than he did in knowing them carnally" (p. 231). Thus he expressed, before the Marquis de Sade, the principle of libertines inured in vice.

What we know of the search for the "most beautiful heads" leads us to the aberration. We learn of it from the monster himself: when at last the children were lying dead, he embraced them, "and he gave way to contemplating those who had the most beautiful heads and members, and he had their bodies cruelly opened up and delighted at the sight of their internal organs" (p. 190). Henriet, who, of the two valets, reports it with the minutest of details, is for his own part not ignorant of this delirious aspect.

According to him, Gilles "delighted" in looking at the severed heads, and he showed them to him, the witness, and to Etienne Corrillaut . asking them which of the said heads was the most beautiful of those he was showing them, the head severed at that very moment, or that from the day before, or another from the day before that, and he often kissed the head that pleased him most, and delighted in doing so" (p. 231). In Gilles' eyes, mankind was no more than an element of voluptuous turmoil; this element was entirely at his sovereign disposal, having no other meaning than a possibility for more violent pleasure, and he did not stop losing himself in that violence.

No sexual confession is more pathetic, as it exceeds all bounds in the will to horrify.

The following words do away with the possibility of not trembling:

–"And very often," he said, "when the said children were dying, he sat on their bellies and delighted in watching them die thus, and with the said Corrillaut and Henriet he laughed at them..." (p. 190).

Finally, Lord de Rais – who in order to excite his senses as much as possible had gotten drunk – went out like a light. The servants cleaned the room, washing up the blood, and while the master slept, burned the cadaver in the fireplace. Long logs and a quantity of faggots allowed them to rapidly reduce it to ashes. They took pains to burn the clothes one by one, wanting, as they said, to avoid the stench.

The whole order of the feast had taken place according to plan: it did not correspond to the impulses of passion. Designed to serve the sensual pleasure of one sole man, it passed without anguish: these children of seven to twenty died with no more fuss than a kid goat.

If there was tragedy, it was not unceasing. Rather, what is the more remarkable in these horrors is the indifference of the participants.

They could not have conceived of the feeling that this unbending severity assumes for us: terror and indignation beyond bounds ... In his day, Gilles de Rais was a very important man, and the little beggars whose throats he cut were worth no more than the horses.

It is difficult for us to evaluate the distance that then separated the man (magnified by birth and fortune) who did the crushing from the insect crushed between two stones.

More than a century later in Hungary; an eminent lady was killing her servants with no more difficulty than Gilles had killing children. This great lady, Erszebeth Bathory; was related to royalty, and she was not pursued until after having yielded to a desire to kill daughters of the lesser nobility; Gilles de Rais himself was not distressed until after a long pause, and that was not until after absurd blunders; probably public rumor finally grew to such a point that one could not easily close one's eyes. Without friends, without support, Gilles was unable to shake off the hostility and the general weariness. But with skill and moderation, his crimes would not have been profoundly shocking; without any other reason, one's first impulse might have been to close one's eyes.

TWO MONSTERS EXTRAORDINARY

R. L. MASTERS

"As it is very difficult to become a saint, one may do what is almost equally satisfying and become a satanist – the other of the two possible extremes. The diabolist may be proud to be worth in crime what the saint is worth in virtue."
–J-K Huysmans

Many sex-driven monsters stalk the pages of history, but probably none seriously challenge Gilles de Rais, Marshal of France and murderer of eight hundred boys, and Countess Elisabeth Bathory, murderess of six hundred girls, for the title of history's most remarkable erotic criminals.

De Rais is known popularly, and erroneously, as the original Bluebeard (a name that must be reserved for Comorre the Cursed, among whose victims were four of his wives: one slain by poisoning, one by strangulation, one by burning, and one by bludgeoning). Countess Bathory is known in France as *la comtesse hongroise sanguinaire*, and in Germany as *Die Blutgräfin*. For the most part, and curiously, she has escaped the attention of English-language authors. Both are eternally infamous less for the formidable numbers of their victims – about which estimates vary – than for the sexual pleasure they derived from the slaughter of their helpless victims.

Countess Bathory is also of especial interest because she is a woman. Female sadists and mass-murderers have been less frequent than male ones, though perhaps only because women have less often attained to positions of power where large-scale crimes were possible.

Yet even if one takes the highest estimate of Countess Bathory's victims – about six hundred and fifty – she is not, from a numerical standpoint, history's champion butcheress. That distinction must be granted to the "witch" Catherine la Voisin, who may have been involved in the slaughter of more than fifteen hundred children and infants.

More than one hundred forty children were named in the bill of particulars against the Abbé Guibourg, who sacrificed most of them on behalf of Madame de Montespan's desire to become the wife as well as the mistress of Louis XIV. The Voisin-Guibourg-Montespan case, which also involved many of the most prominent persons in France, may have contained elements of vampirism. The blood of the slain child was collected in a chalice and then either drunk or poured over the naked body of the person for whom the magical ceremony was being celebrated. Moreover, the blood, bones, and entrails, and sometimes the brains of the slain babes were used in the preparation of love potions. The story sounds preposterous, but there is an abundance of substantiating evidence. Infants and children were easy to obtain at the time. It is said that a woman called la Chaufrein, one of Guibourg's mistresses, could supply an infant for the price of only one crown.

There is no evidence that la Voisin was a sadist. Her motivation was monetary. But for examples of female sex pleasure of a sadistic sort we are not at all lacking. The nymphomaniac Messalina, for example, ordered men systematically masturbated until they succumbed to permanent impotence or even died. While amusing herself in this way, she reclined on a luxurious couch, fingering her genitals and inviting her companions to do the same.

Zoe, the wife of a Chinese emperor, is said to have copulated with her husband while observing executions of criminals and slaves. She was also stimulated by witnessing tortures, and if her husband was not available for coitus would masturbate while watching – as Theodora, wife of Justinian, is said to have done while observing the making of eunuchs. The famed Lady Hamilton is said to have experienced great erotic stimulation while watching the executions at

Naples.

A great favorite of the Marquis de Sade – as were all sex criminals and human monsters – was Zingua, queen of Angola in southwestern Africa. This wanton and ferocious Negro monarch declared, according to De Sade, "a law which established the *vulgivaguability* of women: one which, that is to say, made their cunts as universally free to be fucked as the air is to be breathed."

"A chapter of this same edict," De Sade notes with approval, "made it incumbent upon women to take the measures necessary to thwart pregnancy; evidence having been adduced thereof, disobedience was punished capitally: the culprit was ground to pulp in a mortar." (*Juliette*, Vol. 1)

Queen Zingua's edict was not to be taken as lightly handed down. On one occasion, she invoked the penalty throughout her kingdom, and every pregnant girl and woman under thirty years of age was ground or pounded to death.

This queen, whose law of *vulgivaguability* the champion of all vice so much admired, was a formidable nymphomaniac. But hers was the kiss of death, for every man she copulated with was afterward executed before her eyes, thus providing her with pleasure a second time. In this, she reminds us of the famous prostitute who once resided at Kabul, in Afghanistan. It was this harlot's boast that no man who had lain with her would ever lie with another woman. Nor was it an idle boast, for each man arising from her side was seized and castrated on the spot. She is said to have possessed a collection of male genitalia unrivaled anywhere on this earth. Whether Queen Zingua was also a collector of such treasures, neither De Sade nor any other source reveals.

But blood-letting, whenever it could be arranged, was almost as raging a passion with Queen Zingua of Angola as was sexual intercourse. And sometimes the two could be pleasurably combined:

Thus, brawny warriors with glistening black hides were ordered to fight to the death for her pleasure, after which the victor became, for the moment, her lover. Afterwards, of course, he was overpowered and murdered on the Queen's orders.

In these instances, it was a man's honour and reward to please her thrice: once by slaying his opponent in combat; once upon the royal couch; and at last, by affording her the pleasure of witnessing his own painful death.'

But none of these women approaches, so far as depth and sophistication of sadistic sexual perversion is concerned, Elisabeth Bathory, the Bloody Countess.

The blood of six hundred, perhaps more, girls and young women stained her hands, her lips, her entire voluptuous body – for she bathed in this warm and viscous fluid, seeking thus to preserve her famous beauty. The scent of death, torture, and innumerable lesbian orgies hovered about her: a sinister perfume. And even when she was caught in the midst of a murderous debauch, no executioner's axe could touch her white and still lovely throat, for she was the Countess Bathory, widow of Hungary's great "Black Hero", cousin to the Prime Minister himself, kin of princes and kings, bishops and cardinals, judges and governors.

Castle Csejthe, its massive grey stones arranged in walls and towers, turrets and battlements, dominated from its bleak hilltop the thatch-roofed village below. The peasants of northwestern Hungary's county of Nyitra climbed the path to the sombre fortress only when imperiously summoned, and then with a fearful reluctance. The Counts Nadasdy, who occupied Castle Csejthe, were traditionally cruel and without mercy, liberal where the lash and the dungeons were concerned, tight-fisted in dispensing rewards to those who toiled endlessly to work their lands.

It was to this feudal chateau, already of hateful reputation, that twenty-one-year-old Count Ferencz Nadasdy, destined for greatness as a warrior, brought his bride, the fifteen-year-old Countess Elisabeth Bathory, already renowned as a prototype of the Hungarian style of beauty: astonishingly white flesh, almost translucent, through which one could see clearly the delicate blue veins beneath; long, shimmering, silken hair, black as the plumage of the raven; sensual, scarlet lips; great dark eyes, capable of doe-like tenderness, but sometimes igniting into savage anger, and at others glazing over with the abandoned somnolence of intense sexual passion.

Who can say what course the lives of this pair might have taken had the young Count Nadasdy remained at home, with his ardent and beautiful young wife, instead of galloping off to win on bloody battlefields the acclaim of all Hungary? They were well matched: the same tigerish desires drove them, the same streak of barbarous cruelty surged in their blood. Even Elisabeth's consuming interest in witchcraft, sorcery, and diabolism was one they shared. That despite all separations, all the tests to which it was put, their love for one another endured, is testimonial enough to the powerful bond that linked them.

If the taint of traditional savagery marred the bloodstream of the noble Nadasdy line, no less was it true that hereditary forces found their culmination in the monstrous passions of Elisabeth Bathory. Hers was a curious heritage, wherein distinction and even greatness resided side by side with psychosis, brutality, and extremes of corruption.

Kings and cardinals, bishops and judges, sheriffs and governors bore proudly the name of Bathory. The prime minister of Hungary, Gyorgy Thurzo, was Elisabeth's cousin. The great Sigismund Bathory, Prince of Transylvania, was her kinsman. One of the greatest of Hungary's military leaders, Sigismund was both a genius and a madman, noted for the savagery and instability of his temperament. An aunt, one of the most distinguished ladies of the royal court, was a witch and a lesbian, a notorious corruptor of young girls. An uncle, equally distinguished, was a sorcerer, an alchemist, a witch, and a worshipper of the Devil. Elisabeth's own brother, handsome and brilliant like all the Bathorys, was a satyr, a monster of depravity, whose lusts were so overwhelming and barbaric that neither child nor withered crone could be considered safe from his unremitting and twisted cravings.

As if this heritage were not sufficient, the Countess Elisabeth was exposed from infancy to the vicious teachings of her nurse, Ilona Joo, a woman steeped in black magic, witchcraft, and satanism. Never, throughout her life, was Elisabeth to know freedom from this malign influence: an influence paid its full due by the Hungarian tribunal, which burned the hag alive after putting her to the torture, while others of the Countess' entourage were merely beheaded.

Left in the castle by her warrior husband, Elisabeth, her sexuality fully aroused by the virile Nadasdy, grew ever more lonely and more frustrated. The magic of Ilona Joo could not relieve her anguish. Gradually, she accumulated around her other witches, alchemists, and sorcerers: Darvula, a strange female creature who had practiced her witchcraft in the depths of the forest; Johannes Uvary, alchemist and black magician, servant and plotter of tortures; Thorko, sorcerer and favorite of Nadasdy, who sometimes accompanied his master into battle, meanwhile formulating evil spells for the Count to send home by courier-tokens of his affection – to his beloved young countess; Dorottya Szentes, witch, lesbian, and sadist; and others of similar qualifications and predilections.

It was still not enough. Elisabeth summoned to the castle a pale young nobleman whose strange black eyes flashed in a head made even more cadaverous by long dark hair that hung thin and lifeless to his shoulders. He was reputed to be a vampire, and perhaps it was this that fanned to flames Elisabeth's smoldering passion. The pair eloped – it was her only infidelity – but soon she returned, alone. Forgiven by Nadasdy, who could understand the overwhelming force of passions no less demanding than his own, Elisabeth absorbed herself again in witchcraft and – since no man save her husband would again know her embraces – in other practices aimed at easing the aching her body knew in the long lonely nights. With her two personal maids, Barsovny and Otvos, carefully chosen for their youth, their beauty, and their unscrupled ardour, Elisabeth abandoned herself to all the possible pleasures one woman may know in the arms of another. For a time this, and the occasional visits of her husband, were sufficient to fend off her evil destiny. But always in Elisabeth's ear were the whispers of the crone Ilona Joo, hinting of other, far more perverse, more dangerous, more monstrous pleasures. Long before she succumbed, Elisabeth knew that one day she would put into practice the evil her old nurse suggested. As fully as Ilona Joo, perhaps more fully than the old woman or any other member of her corrupt household, Elisabeth craved the descent into evil. If she delayed, it was from prudence, a fear of the consequences, and not from any want of desire or absence of depravity sufficient to the dark deeds contemplated. For ten years following her marriage the Countess had failed to conceive, though Nadasdy, strongly desirous of a male heir, strove manfully. At length, the bevy of witches, alchemists, black magicians, and sorcerers was instructed to take a hand in the matter. Perhaps they were successful. At any rate, shortly after her twenty-sixth birthday Elisabeth gave birth to a child, who was followed in quick succession by three others. For a time, the Countess was absorbed by her maternal role. Like a typical mother, she dispatched loving notes to Nadasdy, returned to the wars, advising him of the doings and health of the children. Indeed, up until Nadasdy's death, when she was almost forty, Elisabeth seems to have resisted the more extreme urgings of Ilona Joo and the others. But once her husband, who had been a true lover and companion, was gone, Elisabeth at last cast off all restraints.

Strange and fearful whisperings began to be heard in the village, and at night the peasants locked themselves in their houses and listened in terror to the anguished and agonized screams that sometimes drifted down to them from the hilltop. Despite all precautions, children disappeared, as did young girls, even some of the younger women. Occasionally people came to the village, inquiring after travelers – girls and women – who had last been seen in that vicinity. The peasants were not helpful in such cases. The less said, they surmised, the better.

The maids and former lesbian lovers of the Countess, Barsovny and Otvos, were assigned the roles of procurers and kidnappers. If they could not tempt girls and women to the castle with promises of jobs, they drugged them, beat them into insensibility or submission, or otherwise overpowered them. For no less than eleven years the terrified peasants watched from behind their curtained windows and shuddered as the carriage, drawn by black horses and illuminated by moonlight, descended from Castle Csejthe to roam the countryside in search of new victims. On its sides the carriage bore the emblems of the Nadasdys and the Bathorys: symbols of power no mere policeman would ever dare to challenge.

It was not for the indulgence of her lesbian pleasures only that the Countess required this endless flow of children, girls, and women, not one of whom ever managed to escape the castle alive. Even in middle age, Elisabeth was still a remarkably beautiful woman, seeming far younger than her years. Still, time was beginning to take its toll. It could not be denied – not, at least, by the vain Elisabeth herself. Then, one day, around the time of her husband's death, there occurred an incident that determined to a degree the nature of all the horrors to follow.

Striking one of her maids for some act of carelessness, the Countess noted that where the blood she had drawn fell upon her skin the flesh seemed whiter, younger, softer than before. Obtaining more blood, she bathed her beautiful face in it. Sure enough, or so it seemed, the blood restored the youthful texture and vibrancy to her flesh. After that, she was not long in concluding that complete and regular submersion in blood would restore her entire body to the full bloom of youthful loveliness. It was to appease this requirement, as well as her sadistic and lesbian ones, that Barsovny and Otvos scoured the countryside by night, luring, abducting, and overpowering new victims for their insatiable mistress.

Ilona Joo and other witches, magicians, and sorcerers had long been insisting to the Countess that only human sacrifices would enable them to achieve the desired results with their magic. For the alchemical experiments, skulls and other bones, especially those of small children, were urgently needed. Further, all in the castle, from the Countess on down to her lowliest cohort, seem to have been capable of deriving intense erotic pleasure from sadistic orgies of torture and murder. Thus there was nothing but enthusiasm when it became apparent that Elisabeth's blood baths would also make possible the fulfillment and indulgence of the other needs.

In the dungeons beneath the castle, girls and women were chained to the walls and fed like cattle being fattened for market. The fatter they were, thought the Countess, the more blood in their veins; and the healthier, the better the cosmetic effects of their blood when she immersed herself in her gory baths.

The delicacy of the Countess' flesh was such, she thought, that it could not be subjected to drying by coarse towels. Emerging from her tub, covered with human blood from head to toe, she had herself licked by girls, carefully chosen for their beauty and, above all, for the softness of their tongues. If such a girl became ill or otherwise displayed her disgust, horrible tortures and a speedy death awaited her – as each was firmly advised before being admitted into the Countess' bloody presence. If, however, a girl reacted as if with pleasure to the experience, and especially if she lingered long and lovingly between Elisabeth's ceaselessly voracious thighs, she might gain the Countess' favour. Such favour might mean a deferral of the death sentence for a considerable length of time, though it seldom did. The Countess soon wearied of those she exploited for her pleasure, however obliging they might be. And not infrequently she took a particular delight in inflicting the most cruel tortures of all upon precisely those who for a time had been her favourites.

Some of the tortures inflicted by Elisabeth and the others upon their victims are a matter of record, preserved in still-existing (at last word) records pertaining to her trial. At that trial, Ilona Joo and Thorko, along with others, testified that hundreds of girls had been, over the years, kept in the dungeons and milked there, by means of incisions, of their blood, as if they were a kind of human dairy herd. The Countess, these accomplices turned witnesses declared, not only bathed in this blood, but she also drank it, as did some of the others.

Human sacrifices were made, in the course of magical and alchemical experiments and rituals and other practices. Girls were bound with ropes, and these were twisted until they cut into the flesh, after which the veins were opened with scissors, and the blood, as a result of the "tourniquets", spurted forth under great pressure, drenching the walls of the torture chamber as well as the eager bodies of the torturers. Girls were beaten with whips and their flesh slit with knives. Sometimes they were flayed, and after this "frozen" in tubs of icy water. The victims were also, it was testified, forced to hold in their hands metallic objects heated until they glowed. Paper was placed at their toes, and then set afire. Some of the tortures described were "so revolting" that even at that time, when torture was commonplace as a punishment and in the questioning of accused persons, the judges found themselves scarcely able to believe that such things could be. (Eisler insists, taking his information from Von Elsberg by way of another writer, that most of the victims were brought to the Countess' bed and there "bitten to death". But apparently a great many died in other ways, as the trial testimony indicates.)

Rumours of these tortures and murders and reports of kidnappings had reached the ears of the authorities, and even come to the attention of King Matthias of Hungary, years before any action was taken. It was most difficult to proceed against the Countess, whose distinguished family had powerful friends everywhere. Her cousin, the prime minister, was by no means eager to confirm his suspicions about what was going on at Csejthe. But despite all this, it was at last and reluctantly decided that an investigation would have to be undertaken. Once this decision had been made, the inquiry was placed under the personal direction of Prime Minister Thurzo, who took with him to the village the governor of the province. There, they conferred with the village priest, who had lodged a lengthy and specific complaint, as well as with numerous villagers who insisted that the castle was the residence of a vampire. They were more nearly correct in this than either Thurzo or his chief assistant, the governor, suspected.

The raid on Castle Csejthe was conducted on New Year's Eve, when it was hoped the raiding party would be able to approach the castle undetected. This proved to be the case, and the raiders, Prime Minister Thurzo, the governor, the priest, and numerous soldiers and policemen, gained the summit of the hill unnoticed. There, they found the massive doors of the castle ajar, and were able simply to walk in. Grisly surprises awaited them.

In the great hall, not far from the door, lay the pale, lifeless body of a young girl, the blood completely drained from her body.

Sprawled grotesquely and pitiably on the floor, a few paces away, lay another girl, still alive. Her body had been pierced repeatedly with some kind of sharp instrument, and a great deal of blood had obviously been removed. Yet a little further on, chained to a pillar, was the body of another murdered girl. She had been burned, savagely whipped, and her blood drained from her body.

Hastening to the dungeons below, which the prime minister recalled from childhood visits to the castle, the party found several dozen children, girls, and women, many of whom had been bled repeatedly by the Countess and her household. Others had not yet been molested, and were fat and in excellent health, for all the world like animals ready to be shipped off to the slaughterhouse.

Still, the party of raiders went unnoticed. After freeing the captives from their chains, they made their way to the second floor of the castle. There, they surprised the Countess and the others in the midst of a drunken and depraved orgy, details of which are said to have been too awful to be described. The celebrants were easily overpowered and taken into custody, Countess Bathory being confined in her apartment in the castle under heavy guard, and the others taken away to a nearby jail.

The trial court was convened as quickly as possible, with Theodosius de Szulo of the Royal Supreme Court presiding. The seriousness of the case and the high position of Elisabeth Bathory are emphasized by the fact that no less than twenty other judges, all of prominence, were on hand to assist Szulo.

The corpses, skeletons, and other human remains found by the raiders at Csejthe, along with a mass of additional evidence including testimony of the liberated prisoners, eliminated all possibility that pleas of "not guilty" might reasonably be entered. Instead, having been caught red-handed (an accurate description here if anywhere!), the murderous crew of witches and sorcerers, diabolists and alchemists, competed to see who could provide the court with the most detailed and horrifying testimony, each hoping, by such enthusiastic and unreserved cooperation, to win clemency. Some of that testimony has already been summarized, and to repeat more of it would shed no further light on the case.

Present in the courtroom were all the accused except one: the principal defendant, Elisabeth Bathory. She was permitted to remain in her apartment at the castle, where she was kept under heavy guard at all times. *In absentia*, she was announced convicted along with the rest. All were held to be guilty of at least eighty murders, the number of identifiable cadavers actually found. There were strong indications, however, that the real number of victims was in excess of three hundred, and possibly as high as six hundred and fifty.

After due consideration of the roles played by each of the defendants, the court announced the following sentences, which were without exception carried out.

Ilona Joo: Her fingers will be torn off one by one, after which torture she will be burned alive and her ashes strewn.

Doryotta Szentes: The fingers will be torn off one by one, to be followed by burning alive. (It is not clear why Szentes was singled out to share with Ilona Joo the more extreme punishment.)

Johannes Ujvary, Thorko, Darvula, Barsovny, Otvos: All will have their heads struck from their bodies by the executioner.

Following the solemn reading of these grim sentences, Judge Szulo at once declared the special tribunal adjourned. The reader will note, no doubt, that in reading the sentences Judge Szulo omitted the name of Countess Elisabeth Bathory.

This was not done lightly. King Matthias II of Hungary, whose father had been a wedding guest at the ceremony uniting Elisabeth and Count Nadasdy, was personally interested in the case and, despite many close ties with the Bathorys and the Nadasdys, favoured execution. Only the strenuous efforts of Prime Minister Thurzo, who convinced the King of Elisabeth's insanity – and perhaps brought other pressures to bear – saved her from sharing the fate of her childhood nurse and lifelong mentor, Ilona Joo.

In Elisabeth's apartment at Castle Csejthe, the stone masons went to work. Her windows were walled up, save for tiny slits in the stone, left for ventilation. The same was done with the entrance to the apartment, with the exception that there was left an aperture through which food might be passed in to the prisoner. Inside this heavily walled apartment, never to be seen again in life, was Countess Elisabeth Bathory, still a strikingly beautiful and strangely youthful woman, though she was nearing her fiftieth birthday.

The Countess lived for four more years in her solitary confinement, never attempting to communicate with anyone, never uttering a sound that could be heard by the guards always stationed outside the slit-like aperture in the massive stone wall that imprisoned her. Her death, detected only when the food plates went for a long time untouched, is believed to have occurred on the 1st of August, 1614. She was fifty-four.

Unfortunately, those who examined Elisabeth Bathory's body after her death do not tell us whether she had grown old and withered in those four years of her confinement or whether she retained her beauty and her curiously youthful appearance. The reader's fancy will have to supply this missing detail. Found among her belongings was, however, strange little document, written, according to its date, on the eve of her arrest.

It was, William Seabrook (in *Witchcraft*) tells us, an invocation to the Devil, who is beseeched by the Countess to send her ninety-nine cats. They are to tear out the hearts of King Matthias, Prime Minister Thurzo, and other officials she knew or believed were preparing to take action against her. The village priest, when this document was revealed, felt inspired to disclose that on the occasion of the raid, cats did in fact attack him. There were six of them, he said, and some mice as well; but when he gave chase, after being severely scratched and bitten, they vanished into thin air. But why did the "Supreme Commander of Cats" send only six, when ninety-three more had been requested? Was the Devil short of cats on that occasion?

More interesting, probably, is another question raised by the document. It indicates, as is plausible, that the Countess knew that Castle Csejthe was about to be raided. Why, knowing this, did she fail to take any action to protect herself, such as disposing of the captives and removing as much as possible of the other damning evidence?

Why were there not, as was customary, sentinels posted to warn the Countess that a large party was approaching up the road?

The sadist and lust-murderer Peter Kürten once observed that "there arrives for every criminal that moment beyond which he cannot go." Was it Elisabeth Bathory herself, guilt-ridden and craving punishment, who unbarred the castle doors so that the raiders could enter, and who saw to it that they would find corpses strewn along their path and a drunken orgiastic revel at its end? But we will never know about that.

The story of Gilles de Rais is well known, and there are a good many book-length studies of his life readily available, so we will summarize much more briefly and with less biographical detail the facts surrounding the crimes of which he was guilty.

Today, even the most heinous and atrocious misdeeds committed by individuals must seem slight, almost trivial, when compared to the monstrous infamies perpetrated by nations. Nonetheless, we are still not too calloused to shudder at the evil slaughters and debaucheries of Gilles de Rais.

Born in 1404, Gilles became heir, at the age of eleven, to the greatest fortune in the whole of France. When he was sixteen, he further increased his riches by marrying the immensely wealthy Catherine de Thouars.

By the time he was scarcely more than twenty, Gilles, a youth of "rare elegance and startling beauty", had taken his place at the side of Joan of Arc, as her chief lieutenant: a post he occupied by order of his friend, King Charles VII. Here he served with such distinction as to be awarded the title of Marshal of France.

Historians have long pondered how it could be that Gilles, heroic soldier and protector of Joan of Arc, renowned for his mysticism and even his piety, should have suddenly in later years become the most fiendish, satanic, and murderous of men. There is much to suggest that it was precisely the death of Saint Joan that set him upon this terrible course.

Previous to his assumption of the role of Joan's guardian and lieutenant, there was, so far as is known, no suggestion of sexual abnormality in Gilles' behaviour. He married, and his wife conceived a child. Like other powerful men of his time had many mistresses, with whom he behaved in the usual and then-accepted manner. But once he had begun to ride at the right arm of Saint Joan, these mistresses were cast aside, his carousings were abandoned, and the mystical-ascetic side of his nature seemed to come to the fore.

There is good reason to believe that Gilles de Rais was the lover of Joan of Arc – though quite likely the relationship was never physically consummated. (The sexual organs of Saint Joan seem to have been much explored. We are assured that a medical examination yielded indisputable proof, presumably a hymen, that she was a virgin at the time of her trial; but we are also told that she was the victim of a "faulty womb structure," such as could have explained her "hysteria", which in turn could account for her visions, the voices she heard, and her other mental abnormalities.) The capture of Joan plunged Gilles de Rais into a rage and anguish almost psychotic in its intensity. An attempt on his part to rescue her from her captors proved abortive, and Joan was burned. After this, Gilles separated from his wife, never had sexual intercourse with another woman, and embarked upon a career of crime and sacrilege perhaps unequaled in the annals of human infamy. It seems altogether likely that in so doing he was lashing out defiantly and with inexhaustible fury at the God who had permitted his beloved Joan to be tortured and slain.

Returning home, after Joan's death, Gilles shut himself up in his castle at Tiffauges. There, he surrounded himself with courtiers – sycophants and freeloaders – squandering immense sums on lavish entertainments, in every way behaving like a man locked in mortal combat with despair and an overwhelming loneliness. So great were his expenditures that even his enormous fortune was soon seriously depleted; and he was reduced to selling off, bit by bit, his vast ancestral holdings of land.

Pondering his declining fortunes, Gilles turned to alchemy – to the alchemist's dream of converting base metals into gold. Soon he had established extensive laboratories in a wing of his castle, and there he laboured feverishly, scarcely pausing to eat or sleep, and assisted by alchemists and magicians imported from all over Europe. But he laboured in vain. The alchemists fleeced him of large sums of money and then disappeared, stealing away in the night. The magic of the magicians produced nothing magical. The prophecies of his astrologers – that "very soon" he would be successful in his efforts – all came to naught.

Disgusted, Gilles dismissed all but a few of his favourites and imported a fresh crop of adepts, alchemists, and other charlatans. They proved a more sinister lot than their predecessors, and were not long in persuading Gilles that only by enlisting the aid of the Devil would he be able to obtain the gold he desired, while only by committing the most abominable crimes would he be able to interest the Devil in his cause.

Gilles' first crime was committed under the able tutelage of the most sadistic and persuasive member of his retinue, the sorcerer Prelati. In Prelati's chambers in the castle, Gilles seized a young boy, slit his throat, severed his wrists, cut out his heart, and ripped the eyes from their sockets. The boy's blood he saved for the purpose of writing down pacts and evocations.

No gold was transmuted from base metals; the Devil did not appear to Gilles de Rais, Marshal of France; but he no longer cared. He had discovered what was henceforth to be the consuming passion of his life: the torture and murder of children. Hereafter, wherever he went the children would disappear, never to be seen again. When all was done, the number of his victims would be placed in the hundreds: more than eight hundred, some authorities maintain.

Not until 1440, many years later, was Gilles to stand trial for his crimes. Meanwhile, how did he make use of the years left to him? His own confession, and the confessions of his followers, taken at the trial, inform us as to the fate that awaited the children who fell into his hands.'

Gilles himself recounted how he delighted in visiting a room where a child had been suspended from a hook by one of his confederates. Seeing the child's plight, Gilles would at once feign horror, cut the ropes, take the boy tenderly on his knee and dry his tears, assuring him that all was now well and that he would soon be safely returned to his mother. Then, once he had gained the child's trust and affection, he would produce a knife and cut the child's throat – after which he would violate the corpse.

Etienne Corillaut, one of Gilles' personal attendants, testified that Gilles, "...in order to practice his debauches with said children, against the use of nature, first with licentious passion [would] take his penis in his hand, rub it so it became erect and sticking out, and then place it between the thighs or legs of the said children, and rub his said virile member on the belly of the said children with much gratification, heat and libidinous excitement, until he emitted his sperm on their stomachs."

(After which, of course, the children were murdered and dismembered, the blood and portions of the remains being saved for magical purposes, the rest tossed down a sewer or otherwise disposed of.)

This same Corillaut also testified that Gilles, "...after having had an orgasm on the stomach of the said children, holding their legs between his, had considerable pleasure in watching the heads of the children separated from their bodies. Sometimes he made an incision behind the neck to make them die slowly, at which he would become greatly excited, and while they were bleeding to death he would sometimes masturbate on them until they were dead, and sometimes he did this after they had died and while their bodies were still warm... In order to stifle the cries of the children when he wished to have relations with them, he would first put a rope around their necks, and hang them up three feet off the floor in a corner of the room, and just before they were dead he would cause them to be taken down, telling them they would not utter a word, and then he would excite his member, holding it in his hand, and afterwards have his emissions on their stomachs. When he had done this, he would have their heads separated from their bodies. Sometimes he would ask, when they were dead, which of these children had the most beautiful head."

As regards this latter item, it was testified that it was one of

Gilles' pleasures to have these heads of children stuck on upright rods. A professional beautician, a member of his entourage, would then be called in, and the child's hair would be exquisitely curled, its lips and cheeks rouged, and so on.

When enough heads were accumulated and thus prepared, Gilles would hold a kind of beauty contest, with everyone voting on which head was the most beautiful – after which the "winner" might again be put to necrophiliac use.

It is said that Gilles, after the commission of crimes of vampirism and necrophilia (the drinking of blood and sexual use of corpses), would fall into a deep slumber, almost a coma, and it is interesting to note that both Sergeant Bertrand and Henri Blot, two other vampires and necrophiles, also fell into such slumbers just after the completion of their assaults on dead bodies – Blot, in fact, being captured when he fell into such a sleep at the very side of the cadaver he had dug up and ravished in a public cemetery. This curious phenomenon has been noted in other cases as well.

But to return to Gilles de Rais: the testimony quoted above gives sufficient insight into the nature and depravity of his crimes, so that it would serve no useful purpose to provide the reader with further recitals of his villainies. It should be kept in mind, however, that hundreds – not just a few – of children were thus horribly misused and slaughtered, and that the suffering inflicted upon these little innocents' was only slightly greater than that to which their parents were subjected: a first time when their children were wrenched from their bosoms, a second time when they learned the awful truth of what had befallen their loved ones.

Gilles, when finally brought to trial and forced to listen to a near-endless recounting of his crimes, made a formal repentance and was granted by the tribunal the mercy of being strangled before being burnt – and further, he was never actually burnt at all, since his family was allowed to retrieve his body once it had been suspended over the flames in token obedience to the sentence of the court. He was given Christian (Catholic) burial in a nearby Carmelite churchyard.

As for his confederates, some of them equally as guilty as

Gilles, or almost so, many of them were never punished at all, while even the blood-stained Prelati, Gilles' chief accomplice, remained in prison only a few months and was then pardoned. It is thought likely by some historians that this was their reward for testifying against their master – and that both ecclesiastical and civil authorities were far more interested in obtaining Gilles' money and properties, which were still considerable, than in punishing him for his crimes.

JOAN OF ARC & GILLES DE RAIS

MARGARET MURRAY

These two personages – so closely connected in life and dying similar deaths, yet as the poles asunder in character – have been minutely studied from the historical and medical. points of view, and in the case of Joan from the religious standpoint also. But hitherto the anthropological aspect has been disregarded. This is largely due to the fact that these intensive studies have been made of each person separately, whereas to obtain the true perspective the two should be taken together. This individual treatment is probably owing to the wide divergence of the two characters; the simplicity and purity of the one is in marked contrast with the repulsive attributes of the other. Yet anthropologically speaking the tie between the two is as strongly marked as the contrast of character.

I : JOAN OF ARC

The case of Joan is easily studied, as the documents are accessible. Anatole France has realized that behind Joan there lay some unseen power, which Charles VII feared and from which he unwillingly accepted help. M. France sees in this power a party in the Church, and in his eyes the Church was a house divided against itself. Though agreeing with the view that Joan was the rallying-point of a great and powerful organization, I see in that organization the underlying religion which permeated the lower orders of the people in France as in England; that religion which I have set forth in the foregoing chapters. The men-at-arms, drawn from the lower orders, followed without hesitation one whom they believed to have been sent by their

God, while the whole army was commanded by Marshal Gilles de Rais, who apparently tried to belong to both religions at once.

The questions asked by the judges at Joan's trial show that they were well aware of an underlying organization of which they stood in some dread. The judges were ecclesiastics, and the accusation against the prisoner was on points of Christian faith and doctrine and ecclesiastical observance. It was the first great trial of strength between the old and the new religions, and the political conditions gave the victory to the new, which was triumphant accordingly. 'We have caught her now', said the Bishop of Beauvais, and she was burned without even the formality of handing her over to the secular authorities. After the execution, the judges and counsellors who had sat in judgement on Joan received letters of indemnity from the Great Council; the Chancellor of England sent letters to the Emperor, to the kings and princes of Christendom, to all the nobles and towns of France, explaining that King Henry and his Counsellors had put Joan to death through zeal for the Christian Faith and the University of Paris sent similar letters to the Pope, the Emperor, and the College of Cardinals. Such action can hardly be explained had Joan been an ordinary heretic or an ordinary political prisoner. But if she were in the eyes of the great mass of the population not merely a religious leader but actually the incarnate God, then it was only natural for the authorities who had compassed her death, to shelter themselves behind the bulwark of their zeal for the Christian religion, and to explain to the heads of that religion their reasons for the execution. On the other hand, the belief that Joan was God Incarnate will account, as nothing else can, for the extraordinary supineness of the French, who never lifted a finger to ransom or rescue Joan from the hands of either the Burgundians or the English. As God himself or his voluntary substitute she was doomed to suffer as the sacrifice for the people, and no one of those people could attempt to save her.

In comparing the facts elicited at the trial with the Dianic Cult as set out in the previous chapters, the coincidences are too numerous to be merely accidental. I do not propose to enter into a detailed discussion of the trial, I only wish to draw attention to a few points in this connexion.

The questions put to Joan on the subject of fairies appear to the modern reader to be entirely irrelevant, though much importance was evidently attached to her answers by the Court. She could not disprove, though she denied, the popular rumour that 'Joan received her mission at the tree of the Fairy-ladies' (*Iohanna ceperat factum suum apud arborem Dominarum Fatalium*), and she was finally forced to admit that she had first met the 'Voices' near that spot. Connexion with the fairies was as damning in the eyes of the Bishop of Beauvais and his colleagues as it was later in the eyes of the judges who tried John Walsh and Aleson Peirson.

The names of Christian saints, given to the persons whom Joan called her 'Voices', have misled modern writers; but the questions showered upon her show that the judges had shrewd suspicions as to the identity of these persons. That the 'Voices' were human beings is very clear from Joan's own testimony: 'Those of my party know well that the Voice had been sent to me from God, they have seen and known this Voice. My king and many others have also heard and seen the Voices which came to me... I saw him [St. Michael] with my bodily eyes as well as I see you.' She refused to describe I St. Michael'; and bearing in mind some of the descriptions of the Devil in later trials, it is interesting to find that when the judges put the direct question to her as to whether I St. Michael' came to her naked, she did not give a direct answer. Later the following dialogue took place If the devil were to put himself in the form or likeness an angel, how would you know if it were a good or an evil angel?' asked the judges. Again Joan's reply was not direct: 'I should know quite well if it were St. Michael or a counterfeit.' She then stated that she had seen him many times before she knew him to be St. Michael; when a child she had seen him and had been afraid at first. Pressed for a description, she said he came ' in the form of a true honest man' [tres vray preudomme, forma unius verissimi probi hominis]. The accounts of the trial prove that Joan continually received advice from the 'saints'. The person whom she called 'St. Katherine' was obviously in the castle and able to communicate with the prisoner; this was not difficult, for the evidence shows that there was a concealed opening between Joan's room and the next. It was in the adjoining room, close to the opening, that the notaries sat to take down Joan's words when the spy Loyseleur engaged her in conversation; and it was evidently through this opening that 'St. Katherine' spoke when she awoke Joan 'without touching her', and again when Joan could not hear distinctly what she said 'on account of the noise in the castle'. A remark of Joan's that 'she often saw them [the Voices] among the Christians, they themselves unseen', is noteworthy for the use of the word Christian, suggesting that the 'Voices' were of a different religion. The remark should also be compared with the account given by Bessie Dunlop as to her recognizing Thom Reid when those about him did not know him; and with the statement by Danaeus that I among a great company of men, the Sorcerer only knoweth Satan, that is present, when other doo not know him, although they see another man, but who or what he is they know not'.

The points of mortal sin, of which Joan finally stood accused, were the following: 1, The attack on Paris on a feast day; 2, taking the Horse of the Bishop of Senlis; 3, leaping from the tower of Beaurevoir; 4, wearing male costume; 5, consenting to the death of Franquet d'Arras at Lagny.

Of these the most surprising to modern ideas is the one referring to costume, yet it was on this that the judges laid most stress. Even the severest of sumptuary laws has never made the wearing of male dress by a woman a capital crime; yet, though Joan had recanted and had been received into the Church, the moment that she put on male attire she was doomed on that account only. Whether she donned it by accident, by treachery, by force, or out of bravado, tile extraordinary fact remains that the mere resuming of male garments was the signal for her death without further trial. On the Sunday she wore the dress, on the Monday she was condemned, on the Tuesday the sentence was communicated to her, on the Wednesday she was burned, as an 'idolator, apostate, heretic, relapsed'. If, as I suppose, she were a member of the Dianic Cult, the wearing of male attire must have been, for her, an outward sign of that faith, and the resuming of it indicated the relapse; the inscription on the high cap, which she wore at her execution, shows that the judges at least held this opinion. Throughout the trial questions were poured upon her as to her reasons for wearing the dress, and she acknowledged that she wore it, not by the advice of a human man [per consilium hominis mundi] . . . 'Totum quod feci est per praeceptum Domimi, et si aliam praeciperet assumere ego assumerem, postquam hoc esset per praeceptum Dei.' Asked if she thought she would have been committing mortal sin by wearing women's clothes, she answered that she did better in obeying and serving her supreme Lord, who is God. She refused to wear women's dress except by command of God: 'I would rather die than revoke what God has made me do.'

On her letters were placed sometimes the words Jhesus Maria or a cross. 'Sometimes I put a cross as a sign for those of my party to whom I wrote so that they should not do as the letters said.' Though the mark was merely a code-signal to the recipient of the letter, it seems hardly probable that a Christian of that date would have used the symbol of the Faith for such a purpose. She also consistently refused to take an oath on the Gospels, and was with difficulty persuaded to do so on the Missal. When she was asked whether she had ever blasphemed [blasphemaverit] God, she replied that she had never cursed the Saints [maledixit Sanctum vel Sanctam]. When pressed whether she had not denied [denegaverit] God, she again refused a direct answer, saying that she had not denied the Saints [denegaverit Sanctum nec Sanctam].

The general feeling towards her among the Christian priesthood is shown by the action of Brother Richard. When he first entered her presence 'he made the sign of the cross and sprinkled holy water, and I said to him, Approach boldly, I shall not fly away.'

Another point to be noted is her answer that she learned the Paternoster, Ave Maria, and Credo from her mother, thus proving that she was not of a witch-family. According to Reginald Scot it was sufficient evidence to condemn a woman to death as a witch if her mother had been a witch before her. At the same time, however, Joan refused to say the Paternoster except in confession, when the priest's lips would have been sealed if she had proved herself not to be a Christian. She was very urgent to confess to the Bishop of, Beauvais, but he was too wary to be caught.

She first heard the 'Voices' at the age of thirteen, the usual time for the Devil and the witch to make 'paction'. One of her followers, Pierronne, was burnt as a witch, avowing to the last that she had spoken with God as friend with friend, and describing the costume of her Deity with a detail which shows the reality of the occurrence. If also there is any weight to be attached to certain names—as seems likely after studying the lists given above—then we have in this history four of the chief witch-names; Joan, the daughter of Isabel, and the two saints Katherine and Margaret. These coincidences may be small, but there are too many of them to be ignored.

There is evidence from Joan's own words that she felt herself divine and also that she knew her time was limited, but she never realized till the last that th end meant death; this, however, the 'Voices' knew and it was for this that they were preparing her. At the beginning of the trial, 'she said she had come from God, and had nothing to do here, asking to be sent back to God from whom she came [dixit quod venit ex parte Dei, et non habet quid negotiari quidquam, petens ut remitteretur ad Deum a quo venerat]. 'Many times she said to him [the King], I shall live a year, barely longer. During that year let as much as possible be done.' The 'Voices' told her she would be taken before the feast of St. John, and that thus it must be, and that she must not be troubled but accept willingly and God would help her. They also said it was necessary for her to be captured: 'Receive all willingly, care not for thy martyrdom, thou shalt come at last to the kingdom of paradise.' On the fatal Tuesday when she learned her doom, flesh and spirit quailed at the prospect of the agony to come, and she cried out that her 'Voices' had deceived her, for she had thought that in her imprisonment she had already suffered the promised martyrdom. Yet within twenty-four hours she went to the stake with courage unquenched, acknowledging that her 'Voices' were from God. Like John Fian nearly two centuries later, her spirit had sunk at first, and again like Fian she endured to the end, dying a martyr to the God who had exploited her confidence and simplicity and whom she had served so well. To her de Lancre's words might well apply, 'The witches are so devoted to his service that neither torture nor death can affright them, and they go to martyrdom and to death for love of him as gaily as to a festival of pleasure and public rejoicing.'

The ashes were collected and thrown into running water; a common rite, in religions of the Lower Culture, after the sacrifice of the Incarnate God. It is also worth noting that Rouen was one of the French cities in which there was still a living tradition of human sacrifice.

II : GILLES DE RAIS

Like Joan of Arc, Gilles de Rais was tried and executed as a witch and in the same way, much that is mysterious in this trial can also be explained by the Dianic Cult.

On the mother's side he descended from Tiphaine de Champtocé, and on the father's from Tiphaine de Husson; this latter was the niece of Bertrand du Guesclin, and called after du Guesclin's wife, who was a fairy woman. The name Tiphaine appears to come from the same root as Fein, Finn, and Fian, all of which meant 'fairy' in Great Britain, and probably in Brittany as well. There is therefore a strong suggestion of a strain of fairy blood, and with that blood there may also have descended to Gilles many of the beliefs and customs of the dwarf race.

The bond between Gilles and Joan was a very close one. She obtained permission from the King to choose whom she would for her escort; her choice at once fell on Gilles, for she would naturally prefer those of her own faith. He held already a high command in the relieving, force, and added the protection of Joan as a special part of his duties. Later on, even after he had reached the high position of Marshal of France, he still continued those duties, remaining with her all day when she was wounded at the assault on Paris. It is an interesting point also that Charles VII granted permission to both these great leaders to bear the royal arms on their escutcheons. It seems incredible that a soldier of Gilles's character and standing should have made no move to rescue Joan by ransom or by force, when she was captured. She was not only a comrade, she was especially under his protection, and it is natural for us to think that his honour was involved. But if he regarded her as the destined victim, chosen and set apart for death, as required by the religion to which both he and she belonged, he could do nothing but remain inactive and let her fate be consummated. If this is so, then the 'Mystery of Orleans ', of which he was the author, would be a religious play of the same class as the mystery-plays of the Christians.

The extraordinary prodigality and extravagance of Gilles may have been due, as is usually suggested, to profligacy or to madness, but it may equally well have been that he took seriously the belief that as the Incarnate God—or at any rate as a candidate for that honour—he must give to all who asked. He rode a black horse, as also did Joan and the 'Devils' of later centuries; and on two separate occasions he attempted to enter into a compact with the 'Devil'. He could not decide to which religion he would belong, the old or the new, and his life was one long struggle. The old religion demanded human sacrifices and he gave them, the new religion regarded murder as mortal sin and he tried to offer expiation; openly he had Christian masses and prayers celebrated with the utmost pomp, secretly he followed the ancient cult; when he was about to remove the bodies of the human victims from the castle of Champtocé, he swore his accomplices to secrecy by the binding oaths of both religions; on the other hand members of the old faith, whom he consulted when in trouble, warned him that as long as he professed Christianity and practised its rites they could do nothing for him.

An infringement of the rights of the Church brought him under the ecclesiastical law, and the Church was not slow to take advantage of the position. Had he chosen to resist, his exalted position would have protected him, but he preferred to yield, and like Joan he stood his trial on the charge of heresy. The trial did not take long; he was arrested on September 14, and executed on October 26. With him were arrested eight others, of whom two were executed with him.

Seeing that thirteen was always the number of witches in a Coven, it is surely more than an accidental coincidence that nine men and women, including Gilles, were arrested, two saved themselves by flight, and two more who had played a large part in the celebration of the rites of the old religion were already dead. Thus even as early as the middle of the fifteenth century the Coven of thirteen was in existence.

Gilles was charged with heresy before a Court composed of ecclesiastics only, and like Joan he was willing to be tried for his faith. He announced that he had always been a Christian, which may be taken to mean that there was some doubt as to whether he was not a heathen. He suddenly gave way to a curious outburst against the authority of the Court, saying that he would rather be hanged by the neck with a lace than submit to them as judges. This can only be understood by comparing his reference to 'hanging with a lace' with the method by which Playfair in 1597, John Stewart in 1618, and John Reid in 1697, met their deaths.

The sudden change of front in this haughty noble may be accounted for by the excommunication which was decreed against him, but this explains neither his passionate haste to confess all, and more than all, of which he was accused, nor his earnest and eager desire to die. How much of his confession was true cannot be determined now, but it is very evident that he was resolved to make his own death certain. His action in this may be compared with that of Major Weir in 1670, who also was executed on his own voluntary confession of witchcraft and crime. Gilles's last words, though couched in Christian phraseology, show that he had not realized the enormity of the crimes which he confessed: 'We have sinned, all three of us', he said to his two companions, 'but as soon as our souls have left our bodies we shall all see God in His glory in Paradise.' He was hanged on a gibbet above a pyre, but when the fire burned through the rope the body was snatched from the flames by several ladies of his family, who prepared it for burial with their own hands, and it was then interred in the Carmelite church close by. His two associates were also hanged, their bodies being burned and the ashes scattered.

On the spot where Gilles was executed his daughter erected a monument, to which came all nursing mothers to pray for an abundance of milk. Here again is a strong suggestion that he was regarded as the Incarnate God of fertility. Another suggestive fact is the length of time – nine years – which elapsed between the death of Joan and the death of Gilles. This is a usual interval when the Incarnate God is given a time-limit.

It required twenty-five years before an action of rehabilitation could be taken for Joan. In the case of Gilles, two years after the execution the King granted letters of rehabilitation for that 'the said Gilles, unduly and without cause, was condemned and put to death'.

An intensive study of this period might reveal the witch organization at the royal Court and possibly even the Grand-master to whom Joan owed allegiance, the 'God' who sent her. Giac, the King's favourite, was executed as a witch, and Joan's beau duc, the Duke d'Alençon, was also of the fraternity.

PART II

FROM GILLES DE RAIS TO BLUEBEARD

MATEI CAZACU

More than a century ago, the abbé Eugène Bossard published a voluminous work entitled *Gilles de Rais, Maréchal de France, alias Bluebeard (1404-1440),* (Paris, H. Champion, 1886), in which he wrote:

"Children of the people of the Vendée in the area around Tiffauges, we were lulled to sleep by the murmur of ancient tales; and to listen today to the voices of this race, all we need do is commune with ourselves, look inside our souls, and lend an ear to the beloved voices that sing in the depths of our memories and filled our childhood with poetry: they all tell us in unisson that Bluebeard, the bogeyman of our youth, was not Gilles de Rais, – these voices are not so knowledgeable – but the terrible lord of Tiffauges; we can at least admire the accuracy of these voices! For no one ever made the mistake of giving that vulture an area in the Vendée that was not his: no one says that he was ever the lord of Mortagne or of Clisson. Yet, the ruined châteaux of Mortagne and Clisson cast their shadows over the Sèvre, just like Tiffauges which is situated between them, close to but equidistant from each of them. These memories from one's youth belong to everyone; they are the same everywhere; everywhere they have the same precision and the same clarity, not only among children in and around Tiffauges, but also among those of the Loire valley above which sits Champtocé and those of the marshy plain that extends around Machecoul. There is not a mother or a nursemaid who gets the

places wrong in the tales they tell about Bluebeard: the ruins of the châteaux of Tiffauges, Champtocé, la Verrière, Machecoul, Pornic, Saint-Etienne-de-Mer-Morte and Pouzauges, which all belonged to Gilles de Rais, are named in these tales as the places where Bluebeard lived.

But these childhood memories are merely the youthful echo of the memories of old age. Having listened to them in days long gone, trembling with excitement, we have enjoyed hearing them again, now that we feel safe from the terrors of old. Now, it is astonishing the extent to which all local traditions agree. We interviewed many old men in and around Tiffauges, Machecoul or Champtocé; their stories are unanimous: it was either the lord of Tiffauges, or the lord of Machecoul, or the lord of Champtocé who was and still is for everyone the true Bluebeard; and listening to them speak, we thought to ourselves how strange it is that men of the same age, separated by great distances, often ignorant for the most part of the faraway châteaux with which their story may have some connection, share a unanimity that they do not even suspect. We said to ourselves how remarkable it is that they still have memories of this man who was both unique and multiple – unique in his person, multiple by virtue of the titles he bore: at one and the same time, the lord of Champtocé, the lord of Machecoul, and the lord of Tiffauges, in a word, Gilles de Rais.

With the secret intention of shaking their conviction and undermining their beliefs, how many times have we attempted to throw their memories into confusion and force them to adopt an opinion that was not ours! – 'You are mistaken', we would say, 'Bluebeard was neither lord of Champtocé, nor lord of Machecoul, nor lord of Tiffauges.' To some we would say, 'He lived at Mortagne or Clisson', to others, 'Champtoceaux'; and to yet others, some well-known ruin of the area. Everywhere, there was first the same surprised reaction, soon followed by the same air of incredulity and the same response. Try it yourself if you chance to visit those parts, tell the inhabitants all you know of the life of Gilles de Rais: that he only ever had one wife, that his wife outlived him, that he massacred a host of children. They will believe you, as they will regard you, quite rightly, as scholars who have leafed their way through large volumes; but a conviction will persist that all your knowledge and all your assertions will never shake, which is that, for the people of the Vendée, Bluebeard lived at Tiffauges, for the people of Angers, at Champtocé, for the people of Brittany, at Machecoul. We must believe them, for they know better than anyone, better than all the books, better than all the old manuscripts. They learnt it from their forebears who had themselves learnt it from theirs, and in this way, they will take you back in just a few steps to the 16th century and even to the 15th century which were so full of the memories of Gilles de Rais and his cruelty. The murderous beast left such strong traces of his presence among these populations! What mortal dread struck all their hearts! In our own hearts a long shudder of terror lingers on, passed down to us from age to age, from father to son, like some hereditary flaw. Thus, this tradition is everywhere the same and remains constant today."[1]

The learned abbé had interviewed aged men and women, and fought against the claims of historians who sought the origins of fairy-tales in India and identified Bluebeard with the god, Indira, or else, with the god, Bès with the blue beard, and even with Jupiter, and traced back the origins of the tale to Eve's apple or Pandora's box, if not to Lohengrin's wife or to Psyche and her lamp.

Let us say right away that the faith of the erudite Breton is today confirmed by a century of patient research on fairy-tales, both in France and throughout the world. In the great lists of tales compiled by Anti Aarne[2] and Stith Thompson[3], *Bluebeard* was recorded as no. T312A, with one version, T312B, which is found only in the centre of France (vallée de la Nièvre and le Berry, three examples in all).

Of the 39 known versions of the tale numbered T312A, Paul Delarue has recorded 13 in Brittany and in the Vendée, 3 in Poitou, 3 in Guienne, 3 Basque versions and one in the Pyrenees, in all 23 versions in the West and the South-west of France. To these are added 4 versions in the Centre of France, 2 in Canada (in Laval), one in

Louisiana, and 4 in Guadeloupe, all of these, of course, separate from the Perrault fairy-tale[4].

The conclusion to be drawn from the study of this variation is that Bluebeard is a tale specific to Brittany and the West of France, and is not found anywhere else (the centre being the only exception), not in Ile-de-France, Champagne, Alsace, the Dauphiné, nor the South of France.

The hero of the tale is, in 19 cases, Bluebeard, in two cases, the devil and a "rich man", and there is a single instance each of Blackbeard, Redbeard, Greenbeard, the Turkish Prince Frimelgus, King Comorrus, a giant, an ogre of the forest, an ogre, a man, a gentleman dressed in gold, a lord, a handsome rider, Brazen-Face, and finally, the Beast with a long tail.

It should be noted first and foremost that, of the four versions recorded in Guadeloupe, two call the hero Bluebeard, and the other two the devil.

The Canadian versions were recorded in Laval, whose population did in fact originate from the region of France that is Gilles de Rais's domain.

Finally, the Louisiana version also calls the hero Bluebeard because of his blue suit.

Bluebeard must therefore be considered a typically Breton tale, whose theme persisted in an area, when all is said and done, limited to the West and Centre of France.

Another factor that must be taken into account is that none of the tales or ballads related to Bluebeard gives this name to our hero. The German and Dutch tales, and those from other countries, are all translations or imitations of the Perrault fairy-tale, which means that the name, Bluebeard is uniquely French.[5]

In other respects, *Fitchers Vogel* ("The Bird With The Strange Plumage"), recorded by the brothers Grimm in 1812 at Kassel, belongs to a different type, the T311, which has elements in common with Bluebeard, but which is nonetheless considered a separate tale.[6]

The same can be said of the ballad, *Renaud The Woman-*

Slayer, widespread throughout France, and notably Brittany, in the form, *The Marquis de Coatredrez* and *The Daughter of du Guesclin*.[7]

In Brittany, the tale of Bluebeard has been recorded in the Vendée (six versions, including three in Le Coudrais, in the commune (parish) of Monsireigne; in Velluire, in the canton of Fontenay-Le-Comte; in Le Boupère and in La Verrie), in Ille-et-Vilaine (four versions in Ercé-près-Liffré, Bréal-sous-Montfort, Redon and Goulet, in the commune of En-Pleine-Fougère), in the Côtes du Nord (two versions in Plouaret and in Saint-Glen), in the Morbihan (Vannes), in Finistère (Prat and Pléeur).

It is noteworthy that these tales have been recorded in localities neighbouring or near to the properties that Roland Villeneuve identifies as Gilles de Rais's: "From his father and the Montmorency-Lavals, he inherited Blaison, Chemillé, La Mothe-Achard, Ambrières and Saint-Aubin-de-Fosse-Louvain, all fiefdoms of Anjou, Maine, Poitou, and Brittany. The inheritance that his father had received from Jeanne la sage (Joan the wise) made him master in turn of the seigniories of Machecoul, Saint-Etienne-de-Mer-Morte, Pornic, Prinçay and Vue, as well as the Isle of Bouin. From his mother's side and from Jean de Craon, he inherited the sumptuous de la Suze mansion in Nantes, now destroyed, but where he committed so many crimes; the seigniories of Briollay, Champtocé, Ingrandes, La Bénate, Le Loroux-Botereau, Sénéché, Bourgneuf and La Voulte. Finally, his marriage to the sole heiress of the lords of Thouars brought him Tiffauges, which became his favourite residence, Pouzauges, Chabanais, Confolenc, Savenay, Lambert, Gretz-sur-Maine and Chateaumorant."[8]

The mapping of Gilles de Rais's properties and of the places where the tale has been recorded (not to mention the oral traditions reported by abbé Bossard) coincide to an astonishing degree, a coincidence which is backed up by the mapping of the places of origin of the children who disappeared and whose deaths he would be charged with at the 1440 trial.[9]

One final problem arises with regard to the confusion between Gilles de Rais, the rapist and child-murderer, and Bluebeard, the murderer of seven wives. This confusion is already apparent in Enguerrand de Monstrelet (around 1400-1453), who speaks of child-murders and murders of pregnant women[10], and a century later, in the work of Jean Bodin who wrote:

"And in fact the baron de Raiz (who was sentenced at Nantes and executed as a sorcerer) having confessed to the murders of eight little children, and admitted that he still intended to kill the ninth and sacrifice him who was his own son to the Devil, a child that he had deliberately killed in the mother's womb to pay greater homage to Satan..."[11]

The explanation for this displacement of meaning from children to wives is in our view related to the very nature of collective memory which operates according to categories and not individual cases, as Mircea Eliade points out:

"...the memory of an historical event or of a real-life character does not endure for more than two or three centuries in the memory of the people. This is due to the fact that the collective memory does not easily retain 'individual' events and 'authentic' figures. It functions by means of different structures, categories instead of events, archetypes instead of historical characters. The historical figure is absorbed into its mythical model (hero, etc.), while the event is integrated into the category of mythical acts (fighting the monster, brothers at war, etc.)."[12]

Now, in this collective perspective, children are asexual beings *par excellence*, and cannot, therefore, constitute the object of sexual abuse or relations. This explains the appearance of women as victims, for in the great index of themes of the popular tale, Stith Thompson even records bearded children, but never a child who has been raped or subjected to other forms of sexual abuse or relations. We may therefore assume that Gilles de Rais was poured into the mould of Bluebeard, the wife-murderer (the theme of the initiation of the young spouse) in Brittany, the Vendée and in the West of France in general. This "identification" was facilitated by the existence of Gilles de Rais's châteaux, visible elements which allowed story-tellers to latch onto a local building, and so to keep the story alive.

The tenacity with which this identification has persisted in Brittany, the Vendée, Anjou and Haut-Poitou until modern times, a tenacity recorded since abbé Bossard right up to recent folklorists[13], is such as to prove abbé Bossard right when he says in his conclusion that "first of all, this legend is one of those popular creations from which Perrault found inspiration; next, that Bluebeard is still the name, not only of a man who killed his wives, but also of a cruel and formidable nobleman, of *the most terrible of men*, – in a word, of Gilles de Rais."[14]

Notes

1. pp. 411-413.
2. A. Aarne, *The Types of the Folktale*, Helsinki, 1928, s.v.
3. S. Thompson, *Motif-Index of Folk Literature*, Helsinki, 1932-1936, 6 volumes.
4. P. Delarue, Le conte populaire français, I, Paris, 1957, pp. 191-196. A version recorded at La Buratière, a hamlet adjoining Le Coudrais in the Commune of Monsireigne (between Pouzauges and Chantonnay, both properties of Gilles de Rais's) clearly indicates that Bluebeard is the lord of Tiffauges, the principal residence of Gilles de Rais. Cf. Ariane de Felice, *Enquêtes sur les traditions orales du Bas-Poitou, 1942-1943-1945*, manuscript, cited by P. Delarue, op. cit., I, p. 193, n° 15.
5. J. Bolte and G. Polivka, *Anmerkungen zu den Kinder- und Hausmärchen der Brüder Grimm*, I, Leipzig, 1913, pp. 404-407.
6. Idem, *ibidem*, I, pp. 398-412.
7. Fr. Holz, *Die Mädchenräuberballade*, Heidelberg, 1929, records 120 versions, of which 23 in France.
8. Roland Villeneuve, *Gilles de Rays*; new edition revised by the author, Brussels, Bibliothèque Marabout, 1973, p. 66.
9. The minutes of the trial were published in an edition by René de Mauldre in an appendix to abbé Bossard's book, together with other important records; Georges Bataille has provided a translation with commentary, *Le Procès de Gilles de Rais*, Paris, Jean-Jacques Pauvert, 1972.
10. *Chroniques d'Enguerrand de Monstrelet...*, II, Paris, 1572, p. 1713.
11. *De la Démonomanie des sorciers*, Paris, 1580, p. 188.

12. *Le mythe de l'éternel retour. Archétypes et répétition*, Paris, Gallimard, 1949, p. 74 et seq. (Les Essais, XXXIV).

13. See the tales of Bluebeard recorded by Ariane de Félice between 1942-1945, in P. Delarue, *op. cit.*, I, p. 193; by Geneviève Massignon, *Contes de l'Ouest (Brière, Vendée, l'Angoumois)*, Paris, 1954, p. 171, no. 19; p. 259; by Alix de la Chapelle d'Apchier, *Un vent sauvage souffle sur la montagne*, Paris, 1947, p. 149.

14. p. 410.

THE PASSIONS OF GILLES DE RAIS

PHILIPPE RELIQUET

"I would have preferred to contemplate the Maréchal de Retz's breeches than Madame Anne of Brittany's heart; there was more passion in the first than greatness in the second."
–Gustave Flaubert, *Over the Fields and the Beaches*

Contemporary interest in Gilles de Rais is surprising at a time when one might think that everything has been said or written about a character identified in sufficient detail by the minutes of the trial, and on the subject of whom it seems unlikely that fresh discoveries may be made.

And yet, this criminal figure keeps on reappearing in many different guises: as the object of attention of a novelist (Tournier, *Gilles et Jeanne*), of a musician (Philippe Boesmans, *La Passion de Gilles*, libretto by Pierre Mertens, directed at La Monnaie by Daniel Mesguisch), of a playwright (Cormann, *La Plaie et le Couteau*), while new editions of texts and studies continue to appear.

One of the reasons (is reason the right word?) for such interest five hundred and fifty years after the trial, one hundred years after his exhumation, is no doubt to be found in the mixture of passions experienced and inspired by the character.

I : GILLES, MAN OF PASSION

"I have been driven by my imagination alone... I only ever wished to satisfy my desires."

Is it not tempting to contrast the art of extravagance, such as it was practised by a figure haunted by excess and the very unboundedness of the passions, with our own times, which are both fascinated by the imaginary and yet filled with disillusion?

A passion for luxury in a century of misery, thrown in the face of an impoverished King and errant paupers, ostentatious passions that made him also the object of desire, envy and doubtless pillage, with the same avidity with which he put his wealth on display.

Passions bordering on the prodigality that drove him to strip himself bare, to squander his astonishing fortune in proportions that made him the source of torment for his family and whipped up a storm among his heirs (whose *Memoir* is a precious source for discovering the extent of his possessions and their dispersal).

Passion for gold, for lost gold, for gold to be regained by the obsessive methods borrowed from alchemy, whatever the abuses of which Gilles was victim, whatever his misfortunes.

Passion for men, too, which brought him to the frenzy of his last years, to the perhaps tender delirium of his relationship with Prelati to whom he said an emotional goodbye on 21st October 1440, five days before his execution: " Adieu, Françoys, my friend! We shall never see each other again in this world... we shall see each other again in the great joy of paradise!"[1]

And of course, the criminal passions expressed in this avowal: "Alas! monseigneur, you torment yourself and me as well (...) I have told you greater things than this, enough to send ten thousand men to their deaths."

And, combined with all of these, other passions still, including the compulsion to force events as much as to force others, and, I believe, the mad passion of self-destruction, of losing his way in the quicksands of crime, in the labyrinths of confession, in the twisting paths to redemption.

II : THE PASSION: THE MARTYRDOM OF GILLES DE RAIS

"Perhaps at bottom, Christianity even requires the existence of crime and horror, which it needs in a sense in order to pardon them."

–Georges Bataille, *The Trial of Gilles de Rais*

An old soldier cursed by the fates, the maréchal de Rais lived his final moments like a Passion, symbolically inspired – without any sacreligious intent – by the Passion of Christ, in the hope of obtaining pardon and redemption.

Gilles thus felt an imperative need to assume his crimes before his judges, but above all, before his victims – relatives, friends – and before his accomplices: he accepts responsibility for all crimes, his own, those of his accomplices, those of humanity gone astray and suffering in its sinfulness.

After his outrageous avowal, it is he who asks to process ostentatiously in front of all the people – like an ascent to Golgotha.

It is he who asks, indeed begs to be allowed to die at the same time (and between?) his two accomplices, Henriet and Poitou, two new thieves whom he will exhort like Christ on Golgotha: "In death, I can lend them my support and assure them they will be saved when they leave this world, for I hope (...) that, having been the cause of the offences that have led to their deaths, I shall, through my words and example, be the cause of their salvation."

His wish was granted. Gilles was allowed to play the role he had requested, processing through the streets and climbing up to the place of execution, in a piece of theatre which in part repeated that of the Passion (of Joan of Arc's Passion, too), an edifying, troubling, redemptive act. This occurred at his request, shaping the way he was viewed by his contemporaries, as well as by successive generations. Abbé Bossard sees Gilles "by a miraculous metamorphosis (becoming) an apostle and a proselyte."[2]

III : CONTEMPORARY PASSIONS

"Neither the Neros of the Empire, nor the tyrants of Lombardy could offer anything comparable; we would be bound to add all that covers the Dead Sea and, into the bargain, all the sacrifices made to those execrable gods who devoured children."

–Jules Michelet, *History of France*

It is clear that, even today, much passion is still provoked by the subject of Gilles de Rais.

What is this passion which gripped Sade in the 18th century, Michelet and Huysmans in the 19th century, Klossowski, Tournier, Mertens and others in the 20th century?

We might think that it is fright or horror, a sort of curiosity mixed with a repellence inspired by the macabre, as with horror films. This would be only a partial explanation.

The true history of the maréchal de Rais has also given rise to passions in the legal arena, where some have sought to deny facts, others to provoke critical reactions which have never been backed up by the production of significant "new facts". Let us forget them.

It seems to me that the real passion is that engendered by the very personality of de Rais, this nobleman who was "exceptionally moulded by nature" in the rather strong terms used by Sade (*The Misfortunes of Virtue*) – the inspiration for which Sade is, in part, suspected of having drawn from the description of depravities at the trial, the minutes of which he may have had access to.

The contemporary fascination for Sade perhaps springs from the same urges: to say the unsayable, the unavowable, to reflect upon the transgression of all rules, which is furious, horrible and superb at the same time. De Rais is also the Duke of Blangis as seen by Buñuel in *L'Age d'Or*: a monstrous product of the unconscious.

Of an unconscious that is both individual and collective: the 20th century, century of Hitler and of Pol Pot, of the Shoah and "ethnic cleansing" has taught us emphatically that there are many de Rais' among us, potential murderers that require our vigilance, and call upon our humanist values to oppose.

A passion for de Rais, now frightful and anxious, because we know the awful potential of human nature. A passion that is perhaps more of a wake-up call than a disease: de Rais, the man of passion, who died in a Passion, incites passions whose meaning, five hundred and fifty years after his death is also a salutary one.

Notes

1. Transcribed in Old French and also in Latin in the minutes of the trial.
2. *Gilles de Rais, maréchal de France dit Barbe-Bleue*, 1885.

ALCHEMY IN THE TIME OF DE RAIS

SYLVAIN MATTON

"Item, he spontaneously confessed that he had received the sacrament of baptism and renounced the devil and all his works, but that he had never summoned evil spirits, nor caused them to be summoned, nor offered any sacrifice to these spirits, nor caused any sacrifice to be offered to them; and that he had obtained a certain book on the art of alchemy and on the conjuring of demons from a certain knight of Anjou, who was in prison for heresy at that time, that he had read this book several times, had had it publicly read aloud in Angers in a certain room before an audience of several individuals; that he had spoken with said knight then in prison concerning the practice of said art of alchemy and the conjuring of demons; he declared that he had returned said book to said knight and that he had not kept it long. Moreover, the said Gilles de Rais, the accused, confessed that he had practised said art of alchemy for a certain time and had caused it to be practised by certain Lombards named Antoine[1] *and François*[2], *and by a certain goldsmith of Paris*[3], *and that while practising this art and causing it to be practised, he had frozen and caused to be frozen mercury, which he declared to be quicksilver, and that he had conducted several other experiments concerning this art, that he believed he was achieving results with said art, if it had not been for the arrival of the Lord Dauphin of Viennois to said place of Tiffauges where he had had ovens built and prepared for the exercise of said art. The Lord Dauphin was opposed to these practices and the ovens were demolished on his arrival. As for the other facts contained and detailed in the list of charges, the above-named Gilles de Rais, the*

accused, denied that they were true; he similarly denied having summoned evil spirits as mentioned in the list of charges"[4].

This extract from Gilles de Rais's confession, in which he acknowledges having practised the "art of alchemy" but denies ever having conjured demons, clearly raises the problem of the status of alchemy in relation to sorcery and the magic arts with which it is too often confused today. Doubtless such confusion was already current in the Middle Ages, although this depended on the social milieu. It is understandable that there was some confusion in the popular imagination between the figure of the magician or sorcerer and that of the alchemist with his strange instruments, his 'athanor' or still and his retorts, his mysterious experiments on substances no less mysterious, his books written in a language that contained significant elements of allegory and enigma. But these things were viewed quite differently by scholars who, even if they did not believe in the possibility of the transmutation of metal, were far from all contemptuous of the art of alchemy. However, this art must always be seen in the context of a certain cultural marginality. Not introduced into the West until the 12th century, via translations into latin of alchemical texts from arabic (the first of which by Robert of Chester in 1144 is said to have been the *Morienus*), alchemy posed an embarrassing epistemological problem by virtue of its very novelty, that is, how could it be incorporated into an existing system of arts and sciences? Rejecting the option of resolving the problem by ignoring it purely and simply, medieval scholars found the most diverse solutions, according to the interest shown in the subject. As J.-M. Mandosio has convincingly demonstrated, the prevailing tradition (as exemplified by the Dominicans Vincent de Beauvais, Robert Kilwardby, Albertus Magnus or Thomas Aquinas) looked upon alchemy, the mechanical art, as "an empirical savoir-faire the theory of which can be demonstrated only by means of a physics deriving from a wholly different level of knowledge". But against this tradition, a certain Roger Bacon, a Franciscan, judged that alchemy "constitutes the base upon which are constructed natural philosophy and medecine, bereft of any solid basis were it not for the 'validation' provided by experimental alchemy, thanks to theoretical alchemy, 'which speculates about all inanimate things and the complete generation of these realities from the elements'". Consequently, for Bacon, the practice of alchemy no longer "needed the support of external physical theories, since it gives rise in itself to the theory which it simultaneously verifies"[5].

We can see, therefore, that even reduced to the status of a mechanical art subordinated to physics, alchemy was far from condemned by the scholastics. Moreover, what could it be reproached with? In order to condemn alchemy, it was first of all up to those who judged that the creation of the philosopher's stone was impossible to realise to demonstrate it, and to show in what ways it was intrinsically opposed to the truths of natural philosophy and of religion. In order to do this, the opponents of alchemy had recourse to a fundamental objection put forward by Avicenne in his *De congelatione et conglutinatione lapidum*, a text that was all the more important in that it was frequently annexed to Book IV of Aristotle's *Treatise on Meteorology*, and was very often taken to be Aristotle's work[6]. Summed up in the famous formula, *Sciant artifices alkimie species metallorum mutare non posse*, this objection states that natural phenomena belonging to different species cannot be changed into other such phenomena, either naturally or artificially: a cat cannot be changed into a dog, or a stone into a tree, etc., except by God Himself. Man can only act upon the accidents of things, not on their essence. Reference was then made to the famous *Canon Episcopi* (*Decree* of Gratien, cause 26, question 5, canon 12) which asserted: "Whosoever believes in the possibility of changing a creature into a better one or transforming it into another species or a different but similar one, except by the Creator Himself, is an infidel and worse than a pagan". Alchemists will not, therefore, be able to make real gold from a base metal like lead: the latter will remain lead, it will just have the appearance of gold. Thus, alchemists can at best be imitators only, and at worst, forgers.

To this objection, alchemists responded in general that it was worthless to the extent that metals do not differ according to species but only in terms of perfection. Metals, they would say, are formed in the entrails of the earth in a manner analagous to that of living beings: they are born and grow, develop to reach their final, perfect form, that of gold. Thus, base metals are simply metals that have not yet attained their state of perfection which is their natural end, that of gold, a little like a fruit that has not yet ripened, a child who has not attained the full maturity of adulthood. The legitimate role of the alchemist is simply, therefore, by faithfully imitating nature, to have base metals resume their interrupted development and to accelerate their progess towards their state of perfection, or even to reinitiate the whole process of their genesis starting from their *materia prima*.

This defence of alchemy was sufficiently convincing to win the support of almost all medieval jurists. Their conclusions were echoed in the 16th century by the famous jurist, François Hotman, who under the anagrammatical pseudonym of Thomas Arfoncinus, gave an account of the problem. "To the question posed", he writes, "I shall briefly respond: whereas the common opinion of doctors is vindicatory (as agreed by specialists), it follows that alchemy is lawful. This proposition is true because Oldrade, Baldeschi de Pérouse, Jean Andreae, Panormitain, André de Isernia, Alberic de Rosate, Albert Brunus, Guido Papa and many other jurists in both civil and canon law confirm it. Only Ange de Chivasso in his *Somme angélique* opposes this view. But apart from the fact that the authority of a single doctor is worthless in the face of a general consensus, there was, as we know, a great expert in canon law, Jérôme Zanetin, who very precisely refuted all his arguments one by one (cf. *De accus.*). This, then, is the very solid basis formed by the authority of great and illustrious doctors and jurists, not to mention the authority of Thomas Aquinas who, in two or three places, very clearly endorses alchemy."[7]

These jurists were indeed agreed that the *Episcopi* canon was not applicable to alchemists since the latter were not claiming to change one species into another; and that, therefore, they could legitimately exercise their art, which was both useful and praiseworthy, according to Oldrade, provided of course that they did not step over its boundaries and did not commit the two crimes tempting those who fail in their quest for the philosopher's stone: becoming forgers and, worse still, drifting into the conjuring of demons.

But only the bad alchemists, who had gone astray, were involved in these crimes, those whom the adherents themselves called "puffers and blowers" and "sophists". Thus, one does not come across any texts in classical alchemical literature that concern "both the art of alchemy and the conjuring of demons" like the one Gilles de Rais is alleged to have obtained "from a certain knight of Anjou". The alchemist who does not commit these crimes remains unassailable, a view after all shared by one of the most ferocious adversaries of alchemists, the Inquisitor of Catalogne-Aragon, Nicolas Eymerich (1320-1399), the author of a famous *Manual of Inquisitors* and of a special treatise entitled *Against Alchemists*[8]. The transmutation of metals, he explains in this work, is absolutely impossible, so that if someone claims to know how to achieve it, he must necessarily be a liar and a thief. The alchemist's efforts are therefore vain. Thus, unable to obtain what he desires, driven by his culpable lust for wealth, in the end he either "asks for the help of the demon, invoking and imploring him, praying to him and sacrificing to him, expressly or tacitly"[9], or devotes himself to the manufacture of counterfeit money. This is why, Eymerich concludes, alchemy is condemned by the decree of Pope John XXII entitled *Spondent quas non exhibent*, to be found in the compilation of *Extravagantes communes* (5.6.1). However, as jurists observed, this decree, (perhaps forged by Eymerich himself) does not concern alchemy as a whole but just the crime of forgery which, moreover, owes its title to it.

Thus, contrary to received ideas, the Church never condemned the art of alchemy, and the interdictions that were put in place against the practice of the art by some ecclesiastical authorities (for example, within a religious order) had no general legitimacy, any more than did the interdictions pronounced outside their own jurisdiction by the civil powers (who were anxious to preserve any potential transmutations for themselves), such as the royal edict that led Gilles de Rais to destroy his ovens when the Dauphin came to

Tiffauges.

In confessing that he had devoted himself to the art of alchemy, but "that he had never summoned evil spirits, nor caused them to be summoned, nor sacrificed nor caused to be sacrificed anything whatsoever to these spirits", Gilles de Rais was not, therefore, taking much of a risk.

Notes

1. Antoine de Palerme. Cf. *Cahiers Gilles de Rais*, no 2, p. 29.
2. François Prelati. Cf. *Cahiers Gilles de Rais*, no 2, p. 30.
3. This is the goldsmith Jean Petit, who is not to be confused with Jean Petit the public notary at Nantes. Cf. *Cahiers Gilles de Rais*, no 2, p. 29.
4. *Procès de Gilles de Rais, Documents précédés d'une introduction de Georges Bataille*, Club français du livre, Paris, 1959, pp. 217-218.
5. J.-M. Mandosio, "La place de l'alchimie dans les classifications des sciences et des arts à la Renaissance", *Chrysopœia*, IV (1990-1991), pp. 199-282, this ref. p. 207 & 210.
6. Cf. E.J. Holmyard and D.C. Mandeville, *Avicennae "De congelatione et conglutinatione lapidum" being sections of the "Kitâb al-Shifâ'", The Latin and Arabic texts edited with an English translation of the latter and with critical notes*, Paris, 1927.
7. Text published by J.Ch. Fanianus in his *De iure artis Alchemiæ veterum auctorum et præsertim iuriconsultorum iudicia et responsa ad quæstionem: An alchemia sit ars legitima*, Bâle (Basel), 1576, reprinted in *Theatrum chemicum*, 1659 ed., I, pp. 59-60. Most of the texts quoted by F. Hotman are reproduced by Fanianus. The identification of Thomas Arfoncinus was made by Carlos Gilly. An original hand-written version of the text, dated 1574, was published by F. Secret, "Un document oublié sur François Hotman and alchemy", *Bibliothèque d'Humanisme et Renaissance*, XLII (1980), pp. 435-446. On alchemy and the law, see J.-P. Baud, *Le Procès de l'Alchemie*, Strasbourg, 1983.
8. See our edition and translation of this text, "Le traité *Contre les alchimistes* de Nicolas Eymerich", *Chrysopœia*, I (1987), pp. 93-136.
9. *Directorium inquisitorum*, III, 1578 ed., p. 295. See also *Contra alchimistas*, op. cit., p. 132.

THE MYSTERY OF ORLEANS

MICHEL ROUSSE

Gilles de Rais is profoundly a man of his time and, more than many of his contemporaries high up in the social hierarchy, he devoted exceptional energies to the theatre (only René d'Anjou compares with him in this respect). Most extraordinarily of all, perhaps, he himself became a dramatic character.

Imagine the theatre of these times. We are in the 15th century, when France is beginning to feel its way towards national unity. The English King who also aspired to be King of France, is about to renounce his claim. Two major events will have an impact on ways of thinking in the evolution of this period. First, there is the intervention of a young girl from Domrémy in Lorraine who stirs up unprecedented enthusiasm, putting new vigour into the armed forces fighting for the Dauphin, whom she will eventually have crowned King of France in Rheims. The other event which becomes a kind of symbol of a new phase in the Anglo-French conflict is the resistance of a city situated in the heart of France in the Loire valley – Orleans. Paris and Chartres were in the hands of the English, a number of their inhabitants having sided with them. There remained this city which refused to submit and to acknowledge the English sovereign as the King of France. The English attempt to subdue the city, but it heroically endures the siege. Heroism, however, is not enough, and calls for help from the Duke of Burgundy or the Dauphin, the future King of France, elicit little response. It is at this point that Joan appears. She wins over the Dauphin, assumes leadership of the forces that will defend Orleans, and an inspired young girl with bold ideas who is convinced of the mission which her "voices" have entrusted to her, will achieve what the army leaders could not. She forces the English leaders to give up the struggle, and liberates Orleans. The whole of France is shaken by this victory. And at the head of the armies she leads is maréchal Gilles de Rais.

The 15th century also witnesses an extraordinary growth in theatrical performances. Some are modest in nature, designed to bring some relief to the daily grind, or to punctuate the calendar by marking annual festivals. These are the farces, staged by wandering companies of actors, or by young people who wish to enact the misadventures of a few deceived husbands in the public squares. They have a repertoire, they update their performances in accordance with the situations they come across. They flourish especially during carnaval celebrations, when any local transgression of a consensus in sexual morality is dealt with by the people's justice. But theatre also takes the form of spectacles impressive in a different way – the mysteries. Putting on a mystery-play is a large-scale enterprise, requiring months of preparation, drawing on the energies of the town's elite, and depending on the support of the authorities. The plays can last several days, the number of characters is often in excess of a hundred, and spectators sometimes travel long distances to see the mystery-play.

Orleans also takes the lead in this theatrical history in an unparalleled way. The mysteries are, above all, the enactment of religious events. They take as their theme either an episode from the Bible or the life of a saint, and the majority aim to represent the life of Christ, and especially, Christ's passion. Orleans is the only city that exceptionally does not follow this pattern. Amongst all of the mysteries ever performed, the two plays that mark themselves out as treating secular subjects originated from this city. One of these is *The History of the Destruction of Troy* whose theme, therefore, is the taking of Troy by the Greeks. This is the work of a law-student of the University of Orleans, Jacques Milet. The other is *The Mystery of the Siege of Orleans*[1], whose author is unknown to us. But whilst the one echoes great deeds drawn from antiquity, the other attempts to represent a recent event: the resistance of Orleans to the English armies and the decisive intervention of Joan of Arc. We are thus in the presence of a work that is totally unique thematically. We do not know of any other mystery that dares not only to depart from the tradition requiring a religious subject, but to take its subject-matter from the recent history of a city. One might say that Joan of Arc occupies the role of the saints in the mysteries devoted to her. In fact, one must remember that Joan of Arc was not canonised until the 20th century, and actually, the play gives as much space to Orleans as to Joan of Arc whose importance in the play lies only in as much as her fate is linked to that of Orleans.

Gilles de Rais played an active part at Joan's side. Gilles de Rais had a taste for the theatre. Gilles de Rais is a character in *The Mystery of the Siege of Orleans* at Joan of Arc's side.

We know of his taste for the different forms of the theatre of the age, and of the manner in which he liked to spend money on the staging of such spectacles from the complaints of his heirs who judged that he had squandered his wealth in this way: "Item, he put on games, farces, mauresques, mysteries at Whitsuntide and the Ascension, on high stages below which were barrels of hypocras or mulled wine and other fortified wines as in a cellar"[2]. The last detail may appear obscure if one has no conception of the performance of a mystery-play. The stage was an essential element of it. The word, of course, has nothing to do with its modern meaning, but corresponds rather to our modern scaffolding. Plays were performed on platforms built like the old scaffoldings with long poles held together with ropes or with nails. For the mysteries, these scaffoldings were erected in a semi-circle, forming an enclosure for the performance of the play. They were often terraced, and areas were provided in the upper levels which, depending on requirements, were reserved for the actors in the mystery-play when they were not appearing in the performance area down below, or else, these spaces were reserved for spectators whom it was wished to particularly honour. The frame was covered with cloth for protection against the rigours of the sun. This was adorned with flowers and greenery, and embellished with tapestries for the pleasure of those who sat there. In other words, these spaces were a little like luxurious theatre-boxes. As for the provision of wine and hypocras, this can be misleading for the reader who judges this theatre on the basis of our modern customs. Performances were long, often lasting an entire afternoon, and the organiser of such spectacles was anxious to honour those distinguished persons who had come to watch, and frequently took the trouble to prepare a collation to refresh them. Gilles de Rais takes the costs of performances on himself, and behaves like a perfect gentleman who knows how to be as attentive as the most refined of men. Hypocras, which is a sweet wine flavoured with spices, must have been intended for the ladies, and the wine, which was as cool as wine straight from the cellar, for the male dignitaries. Nothing here, then, supports the view of Gilles de Rais as a man of derision and debauchery. In regaling the inhabitants of the city with theatre and feasting, he was playing the role of a patron of the arts, a role that was usually reserved for the aldermen of the city and far less often for the nobility. One can interpret this simply as a gesture of generosity on the part of a great lord who appreciates dramatic entertainment, from comic farces to the more serious theatre of the mysteries, and who likes to share these moments of collective pleasure in which the people of a city come together to affirm the faith that unites them.

But Orleans owed a particular debt to Gilles de Rais – he had come to fight at the side of Joan of Arc, and the city which, every year on 8th May, commemorated the anniversary of the decisive battle which had forced the English to lift the siege, was very grateful to him for the part he had played in this event, a gratitude which was by no means of a vague or purely conventional nature. This can be seen from an article in the Register of Accounts of the city of Orleans for the year 1439. We can in fact read here that, for the sum of seven Tours *livres*, the city acquired "a standard and banner which belonged to Monseigneur de Rais, in order to reenact the manner in which the the fortress of Les Tourelles was taken from the English on the eighth day of May"[3]. This shows how the men of Orleans, especially grateful to Gilles de Rais for the part he had played in this decisive assault, wished to honour him by including his standard in the reenactment which the city devised to commemorate the event.

The Mystery of the Siege of Orleans was doubtless written specifically for this annual commemoration. It clearly can be divided into two main parts. First, the city of Orleans defends itself energetically by itself and without hesitation against the English who wish to subdue this city situated at the heart of France. It endures setback after setback, but stands firm. Upon the arrival of Joan of Arc, the fortunes of the city are reversed: reeling from the ardour universally inspired by the Maid and frustrated by their inability to take the city they are besieging, the English strike camp and leave. This is a huge work of more than 20,000 verses, involving more than one hundred and forty characters, not including extras.

Among the main characters is Gilles de Rais. When the Dauphin agrees to entrust an army to Joan after she has come to see him, he gives her the maréchal de Rais to oversee the conduct of the army:

And to lead your men
You will have the maréchal de Rais,
And a valiant gentleman,
Ambroise de Loré, you shall have;
I expressly command them
To follow you wherever you wish to go;
To any place, near or far,
To ensure the success of your expedition.[4]

This is, indeed, the role that Gilles de Rais will play in the second part of the mystery. He has few lines, but right from the start, those he delivers clearly show the part he plays: he must follow Joan of Arc's orders in leading the army. He apprises himself of her intentions, gathers the troops, plots the route that they should follow, and, if need be, gives advice on the best roads to take. Although speaking little, his role on stage, nevertheless, is not a negligeable one. He is Joan's shadow, and surrounded by a handful of soldiers, he symbolises the army that will accompany her in her battles. When he does speak, it is to reply to Joan who has just harangued the soldiers, exhorting them to confess their sins and to forsake their "mad women" before leaving on campaign:

> *Lady, behold the company,*
> *They are ready, arraigned in battalions,*
> *Happy to serve you,*
> *Wherever they must go.* (v. 11546-11550).

Even though the script seldom gives him the opportunity to speak, Gilles de Rais is thus constantly on stage at Joan's side. The actor who plays his part is certainly recognisable from the standard bearing Gilles de Rais's arms which he carries and which is doubtless the very standard which had led the decisive assault against the English entrenchments, and which the city had been keen to acquire in 1439. It is easy, therefore, to imagine that he shared in Joan's glory. Although the number of lines of the character representing him is tiny in relation to the length of the piece, there is no doubt that, at Joan's side, he was one of the heroes of her battles. He was a glorious object of veneration by the inhabitants of Orleans who were proud to have victoriously resisted the English, thanks to Joan of Arc and the man who led her troops.

Notes

1. *Le Mistère du Siège d'Orléans* published for the first time, and based on the sole manuscript in the possession of the Vatican Library, by F. Guessart and E. de Certain, Paris, Imprimerie Impériale, 1862 (Documents inédits sur l'Histoire de France, VI), Paris, 1862. A new edition has been published by Vicky Lou Hamblin, The Fifteenth Century French "*Mistere du Siege d'Orleans*"; An annotated edition, Ann Arbor (Mich.); University Microfilms International, 1984 (Ph.D. The University of Arizona).
2. Louis Petit de Julleville, *Les Mystères*, Paris, 1880, tome 1, p. 351.
3. J. Quicherat, *Procès de Jeanne d'Arc*, Paris, 1849, tome V, p. 311, (Société de l'Histoire de France).
4. These verses are a transcription from the original (v.11143-11150); we have transposed into modern French those expressions which would be difficult to understand today.

DE RAIS: REALITY AND APPEARANCE

ODILE BLANC

"Majestic in stature, good manners, charming features, quick wit and keen curiosity, well-versed in letters and in religion; in a word, all that is necessary to please men and win their esteem."

Such is the portrait, penned by Abbé Bossard, of the famous and criminal baron who is still identified in some areas with the legendary figure of Bluebeard. This flattering portrait which simultaneously conjures up the image of a learned prince and that of an ideal knight, is a commonplace of historiography. Since the earliest attempts of Gilles de Rais's heirs to win recognition for his prodigality, every author basically tells the story of a fall from grace, of the transformation of an identity. Could it be that in the person of the maréchal, reality and appearance have been cruelly severed? Indeed, one argument that recurs in all proceedings recalls that "he was not content to maintain the rank that accorded with his income but lived the life of a prince and not of a baron". Over and above the necessary observance of custom (living according to one's means), these remarks lead us to reflect on how the outward appearances of a great lord were defined at the end of the Middle Ages: what did it mean "to be someone" at that time? The way one presented oneself was obviously a determining factor in the assertion of one's status in society. The history of Gilles de Rais teaches us that the individual was continually required to prove his legitimacy.

I : PRODIGAL OR MAN OF EXPERIENCE AND INTEGRITY?

The thirteen witnesses who gave evidence at the *Enquiry into*

Dissipation, held at Nantes at the request of René, Gilles's younger brother, are categorical: the deceased "issued from very great dynasties and houses (...) descended from the greatest houses of the kingdom of France"; he "was during his lifetime a very great and powerful lord", the head of an estate with annual revenues estimated at approximately thirty thousand *livres*.

The title of *baron* at this time was not so much an acknowledgement of the political activities incumbent on any lord as a recognition of the status of any nobleman of importance. Outside of his estate to which he is always linked, the lord is more readily referred to as a *knight*. In this case, the term is associated with his military activities, and it was indeed as a reward for fighting in the service of the King of France that Lord de Rais reached the high rank of maréchal. At the age of twenty-five, Gilles was therefore a rich nobleman, head of a vast estate and holder of an office that made him a direct servant of Charles VII, in other words, a person of some importance who had been presented at court.

As a consequence of his elevated rank, he must have acquired an enhanced status as a "very great lord of Brittany", in the words of Enguerrand de Monstrelet who, like his contemporaries, acknowledged the maréchal to be a powerful and even valiant nobleman. The maintenance of a large entourage, and in particular, of a military garrison, as required by the office of an army leader, was not in itself extravagant. As for the entertainments held in Orleans in 1435, in the course of which Gilles was responsible for organising a mystery-play commemorating the siege of the city in 1429, they were at no point brought up by the heirs to demostrate their ancestor's prodigality.[1]

The word itself, moreover, is ambiguous. While the documents in question here use it as a synonym for *squanderer of wealth*, which is the meaning adopted by Du Cange and Littré (who specifies, however, that the prodigal man spends too much, but the spendthrift spends unwisely), the word *prodigal*, which is barely recorded before the second half of the thirteenth century, is not always employed in a negative sense. Indeed, it refers to that form of generosity by virtue of which the nobility manifests its power in the eyes of all, and which in actual fact is accepted as the prerogative of this social class. Nevertheless, there is another side to this need for largesse: the practice of ransom, pillage, and the frequenting of tournaments. Such are the principal activities of the knight, in the course of which he displays as much greed as extravagance. Good self-government, therefore, consists in combining avarice with prodigality, largesse being defined as the socially acceptable happy medium.

II : A KNIGHT IN GOOD FETTLE...

A nobleman's public persona is determined first of all by the *company* he keeps. His retinue of family, friends, servants all make up a strict hierarchy which alone make it possible to assess the rank of a household and the social status of the person at its head.

All of the witnesses who gave evidence at the *Enquiry* recalled that Gilles was always "accompanied by a large retinue of well-born gentlemen, officers, servants, clergymen who were all said to be in his employ". A former equerry in his entourage pointed out that among the permanent residents of his household at Machecoul were eighty people and fifty horses, and that the maréchal left his home escorted by more than eighty horses. According to a cavalry sergeant in the service of the King of France who nevertheless often had occasion to profit from Lord de Rais's generosity, the maréchal's retinue usually comprised between one hundred and one hundred and fifty horses. "And the house of the said late Lord de Rays made greater noise and greater news than the said house of the Kingdom of France."

Indeed, it was the motto of any well-born knight to make a name and win renown. Gilles's entourage is probably similar to that of the jousting knights who are the true heroes of fifteenth-century chronicles, like Jacques de Lalaing, son of a seneschal of Hainault, chamberlain and counsellor to the Duke of Burgundy, who can be seen cleaving his way through Europe in search of adventures. We find him in Gand in 1445 during The Festival of The Golden Fleece. He arrives in the town accompanied by five hundred men at arms on horseback[2], and throws open his house to all-comers. The next day, he is greeted by jubilant crowds as he passes through the town on his way to the joust. In this way, a jousting knight would deploy a whole strategy of display before the games began, in order to win over the public and, if need be, to intimidate his adversary. Let there be no mistake: taking part in a tournament was like setting off on a campaign, or entering a conquered city, and arriving at the games was comparable to putting on a military parade. Moreover, *in good fettle, in great form, elevated in rank* are so many terms that bear testimony to the military power of the knight, *to dress* often retaining in this context its old meaning of to equip. [Translator's note: in the French text, these Old French terms are: 'bien en point', 'en grant estoffe', 'en haut estat', 'habiller'].

The train escorting the maréchal is doubtless a response to the need to put on show the powerfully hierarchical organisation of a household, different groups being easily distinguishable from each other, in spite of their common livery. In a successful procession, which is to the jouster what the jewel-case is to the jewel, quantity is not enough. It is also necessary to order individuals in a manner appropriate to the creation of a visual whole that will seduce the public. The arrangement of materials and colours is of capital importance here.

It is also essential to change dress and other adornments regularly in order to attract attention. Such changes of clothing and the accumulation of the most varied fabrics and colours are first and foremost a way of displaying one's wealth, by parading in public the spectacle of a body constantly reinvented. Although diversity was viewed with some suspicion by traditional Christian morality, it was a permanent feature of the spectacle of the tournament, and the manner in which this diversity was displayed was constantly changed. Witness Antoine, Great Bastard of Burgundy, the natural son of Philippe the Good (le Bon), defender of the *Pas de l'Arbre d'or* organised in Bruges in 1468 on the occasion of the marriage of Charles the Reckless (le Téméraire) and Marguerite of York[3]. For his first joust, he appeared dressed in purple velvet and put on fresh clothes for each new contest: green cloth of gold, tan velvet (tawny brown), white damask dotted with golden tears, crimson silver cloth, blue velvet, black velvet brocade, crimson gold cloth a second time, crimson satin, white armour, yellow damask dotted with silver leopards. All a profusion of colours and materials that comes full circle since, in the last joust in which his opponent is the Duke of Burgundy, Antoine chose to wear the purple velvet he sported when he entered the lists.

Fifteenth-century chronicles abound in descriptions of this kind, exhibiting all the largesse expected of a nobleman. Simultaneously a way of placing pressure on the opponent, a mark of esteem and proof of one's perfect acquaintance with the codes of the society, the ostentation of appearances in the complete spectacle that is tournament is judged as rigorously as the bearer's miltary and sporting prowess. It is not enough for the latter to appear with due pomp and ceremony, adornment is the ideal complement of bearing, although he must display his wealth with discernment so that it appears to be a natural extension of the body. This is how the grace and elegance of the jouster is measured.

III : ...BUT LACKING SELF-CONTROL

Although Gilles de Rais was able to conform skilfully to this model, the *Enquiry* nonetheless emphasises that from the year 1432, following the death of his protector, Jean de Craon, he "maintained a very large and excessive estate". That year also marked the end of his military activities and the beginning of a surprisingly obscure retirement. After the sieges of Orleans and Lagny during which the maréchal won renown fighting at the side of La Hire and Xaintrailles, his name no longer figures in accounts of battles led by these famous army chiefs[4].

The maintenance of an army that was idle for periods of time was indeed a very heavy expense. Could it be that Gilles's army, which the chronicles do not mention, benefitted from especially favourable treatment, representing a potentially heavy drain on the maréchal's fortune? This is what the witnesses at the *Enquiry* give us to understand – including those who, in their functions as sergeant or equerry, directly profited from it. All cast doubt on Lord de Rais's good judgement when he handed out his money with no regard for the recipients' situation. One might as well say that, in the light of the code of chivalry described above, Gilles lacked a keen desire to make money, or even the avarice necessary to keep to the happy medium of generosity. And what about an army whose presence is barely attested to on the battlefields of wars conducted by the King? The maréchal's retirement begins to resemble that of all those heroes who abandon their military career, preferring a more comfortable life at court.Their idle way of life comes dangerously close to that of women: the knight who cannot maintain a balance between residence at court and military action is unmanly.

Le Jouvencel ("The Young Man"), a novel written between 1461 and 1466 under the supervision of Jean de Beuil, a military leader trained by La Hire, warns against taking curative rests because of the "preoccupation with the self" to which they give rise. When his companions beg him to don "some honest robe" now that he is a captain, the Young Man replies: "It is not the cowl that makes the monk. As for myself, I would prefer to use the money to pay for an archer than to buy a robe". This contempt for appearances, as far removed from the spectacle of the tournament as from traditional discourses of morality, reminds us that if, right here and now, one can appear to be what one aspires to be, as Castiglione famously said much later, it is hard at the very least to appear to be something that one never has been. Does it not look as if Gilles de Rais, a maréchal who has retired to his lands, yet maintains an army without taking part in any large-scale military operation, is merely playing at being a warrior? The accusation that the maréchal is living beyond his means perhaps springs from doubts about his bravery, and consequently, about his expenditure, the nature of which is considered less excessive than illegitimate.

IV : THE TRAPPINGS OF RELIGIOUS DEVOTION

The magnificence of a great lord is manifested not only in the wholly secular trappings of his power. In directing itself also to God, it confers a new legitimacy on him who henceforth appears in the role of an intercessor.

The proliferation of private chapels is one of the characteristics of an outward display of piety[5]. Moreover, are not the finest examples of illuminated script at this time for the most part intended for 'chapel books'? Do not objects of devotion figure among the most precious jewels, preserved like relics and exhibited with ostentation?

Among the 'religious treasures' that occupy such an important place in the possessions of princes, textiles doubtless contributed to the splendour of the liturgy in the same way that church ritual would have been unthinkable without an appropriately attired entourage. Like the throne-room, the chapel is the perfect place for the use of cloth, limited exclusively to precious material, for only silks, plain or woven with gold or silver thread, are allowed in this sacred space. The brilliant sheen of deep colours, alternately mat and shiny, gold or silver embroidery reproducing characters and scenes from the Old and New Testaments as in illuminated scripts, and finally, all the vestments and cloths that adorn not only the bodies of the officiating priests and the sacred objects, but even the pieces of furniture, the walls and the floors, make up a whole spectacle comparable to the secular ceremonies that punctuate life at court. Whether at the tournament or in the chapel, the same ostentation is displayed in impressive lengths of cloth.

Moreover, the organisation of the chapel exactly matches that of the entourage. Thus, Gilles de Rais's comprises all the members of a collegiate church, that is, between twenty-five and thirty individuals, salaried, clothed and accompanied by servants and horses according to their rank. All in all, there are about fifty persons who accompany him on all his travels, and care is taken to change their dress on each solemn occasion. In other words, like other nobles of the time, this great lord seeks to demonstrate both his power and his piety through outward appearances.

It seems that the chapel's magnificence made a greater impression on the memory of his contemporaries than those of his military forces, even if the expenses it necessitated are viewed in the same light, from the point of view of prodigality. Whereas not a single person questioned made even the briefest of mentions of the money spent on either Gilles's own clothing or that of his entourage, all retained a mental picture of the vestments and cloths paraded at liturgical services held by the maréchal. A sergeant of the King of Sicily was present at services celebrated in Angers, during the course of which the priests and chaplains and even the choristers and altar-servers "were all clothed in gold vestments". A "chapel of beautiful ornaments covered with gold cloth"[6] was seen by several individuals at Machecoul, and all witnesses recall that the chapel clergy, choristers and altar-boys were usually dressed in the finest cloths and the most precious furs. The last person to give evidence, a chapelain at Angers who had previously been in Gilles's service, gives an interesting and detailed account of the choice of materials: cloths of gold in honour of the apostles, bright red silks in honour of the martyrs, green silks for those hearing confession, white silks for virgins. And having been in a position to compare the chapels of the Duke of Brittany and of the king himself, he maintains that Gilles's is truly extraordinary: "And this chapel was the best served, the most becoming and the most magnificent that he had ever seen..." Assuredly, such ornamentation of the sacred does not appear excessive to this man of the church who is also sensitive to the trappings of religious services and doubtless persuaded that the homage shown to the spiritual by a temporal power is genuine. But could such zeal not be motivated by pride?

The baron de Rais was certainly prodigal; in the manner of a lord secure in his privilege, inadvertantly, if you like. But given the flamboyant practices relating to outward show, his largesse which extended to all members of his numerous staff, the carefully orchestrated pomp of his public appearances, and the magnificence with which he adorned his religious services, all these things mark him out as a model representative of a nobility that is so highly praised by the chroniclers. His expenditure and even his crimes left little stain on the image of an ideal knight that emerges from the documents of the *Enquiry* thirty years after his death. On this point, Gilles de Rais's contemporaries are in no doubt whatsoever: he really was somebody.

References

Archives Nationales, X/1a/4800 and 4801: Registers of the Parliament of Paris containing the records of the legal action between Prégent de Coëtivy and Georges de la Trémouille regarding the sale of Champtocé, 1445.

Archives Nationales, 1AP/586: Petition of Sir René de Retz which demonstrated the facts of Sir Gilles de Rais's prodigality (Enquiry on Squandering), 1462.

Archives Départementales of the Loiret, 3E 10151: Minutes of Jean de Recoin, notary at Orleans between 1434 and 1438 (accessible on microfilm 2mi 10338-10342).

Bossard (abbé Eugène), *Gilles de Rais, maréchal de France dit Barbe Bleue*, Grenoble: Jérôme Millon, 1992 (1886).

Le Jouvencel, éd. Léon Lecestre, 2 vols, Paris, 1887-1889.

Enguerrand de Monstrelet, *Chroniques* éd. Douët d'Arcq, 5 vols, Paris, 1847-1861 (SHF).

Notes

1. *Le mistère du siège d'Orléans* was edited by F. Guessard and E. de Certain in 1862 for the collection of *Documents inédits sur l'Histoire de France*. It seems that it was performed only once. In 1456, René d'Anjou, who was, it is true, the King of Sicily, also spent considerable sums of money on the staging of the *mystère de la résurrection*. In 1493, Guy de Laval, Gilles's cousin, organised a *mystère de Sainte-Barbe* in which there appeared "one hundred players dressed in silk/And fully clothed in velvet" (quoted by Bossard, 81). It is clear that no one frowned upon these urban festivities.

2. Though the figure may well be fictitious, it nonetheless signifies the presence of a large group. On these festivals, see the *Chronique* of Georges Chastellain, éd. Kervyn de Lettenhove, Brussels, 1863-1868, vol. 8, 82 ss.

3. Peculiar to the 15thC, the 'Pas d'arme' is the often complex dramatised festive occasion, in the course of which jousts properly so-called take place. On the subject of dress strategies in this kind of entertainment, see my article in *Communications* 46 (1987) 49-65, and on this event in particular, see *Mémoires d'Olivier de la Marche*, éd. H. Beaune et J. d'Arbaumont, Paris, 1883-1888, vol. 2, 123 ss.

4. Who, among other things, lay waste to the countryside, hence the name, *Ecorcheurs* ('Skinners') attributed to them among others by Monstrelet, vol. 5, 349 ss.

5. The visitor to the château de Pierrefonds can still appreciate the importance of such a building within a prince's residence. Moreover, the very personality of Louis d'Orléans, an inveterate sensualist who alternated between the pleasures of the court and mortification at the Célestins convent in Paris, where he was buried in monk's habit, is not without analogy with that of Gilles de Rais.

6. *Chappelle* denotes all materials connected with the celebration of mass:

vestments of officiating clergy, altar cloths, covers of sacred objects, pieces of furniture (backs of seats, cushions, etc.), and embroideries.

PRINCELY TABLES OF THE 15TH CENTURY

ODILE REDON

On banquet day, the prince displays his grandeur at table. He sits at the top end above the members of his household and guests and, among the various dishes on offer, he is served the richest and most delicate morsels, for not all dishes circulate from the highest to the lowest end of the table. The meal is divided into services – between three and five depending on circumstances – and the different dishes of each service are simultaneously placed on the tables, with the best and finest presented at high table.

The roast meat course sets the tone, served usually as the second service: skewered shoulder of mutton, stuffed piglet, stuffed veal even – its belly full of bacon and a variety of fowl – fine game, goose, quail or capon; or during Lent or on Fridays, roast eel, trout or tench, or any fish that happens to have been caught. It is the roast that is mentioned when "the class" of a banquet is to be summed up.

The roasts are accompanied by sauces, offered to guests for their selection, in a feast of colours and tastes, for their function is less to nourish than to adorn and season. They are as green as the herbs chopped up to flavour them, as pink as the grape-juice or cherry-juice squeezed to moisten them, as blue as an evening sky at the end of August when the blackberries picked in the hedgerows give them their intense colours. With the juice of the grape, the cook is able to conjure all flavours, from the acid of verjuice and vinegar to the bitter-sweet taste of different wines, to the sweetness of must, of dessert wines or raisins. As medieval sauces are often acidic or bitter-sweet, and always free of animal fats, our dieticians would say that they compensated for the over-indulgence in meat. From the point of view of medieval dietetics, dominated by the theory of the humours, they acted in a different way to counter the coolness of verjuice or the moderation of vinegar with the heat and dryness of garlic or spices.

Before the roast came the soups: jugged hare or deer, "Saracen" gruel (capon cooked in fruit), sweet and sour fish, white or green mash, pumpkin soup. Any dish cooked in a pot is called soup (potage) and, as far as vegetables, cereals and all kinds of meat and fish are concerned, the only limitations on variety are climate, the seasons and luck.

The tarts and pies served after the roasts are a great invention of medieval cuisine. The crust may conceal or sculpture a whole trout or rabbit, simple or complex compositions of meat, fish, aromatic bulbs or vegetables, often with an egg or cheese base. The form makes possible a better quality of cooking for the content; it also lends it a spectacular, shiny and golden appearance.

It is tempting to compare the desserts with the pies, even though the desserts can take quite a different culinary form–blancmange, "galantine" (meat in jelly) or "pipefarce" (a sort of crêpe made with wine and cheese), but the list would be too long, as any dish can become a dessert or can offer the delights of sight and sound as a pleasure replacing that of eating. A simple dish may be accompanied by music, juggling or spectacle, and any theatrical presentation of a dish makes for a good dessert. A tree is constructed out of pastry, and cooked and garnished with fruit and birds. For the brief period of time during which the dish is carried from the kitchen to the banquetting-hall , a form of golden brown pastry hides live birds that fly into the air to the delight of guests, as soon as the pastry lid is lifted. The cooked animals or birds are "dressed up again" in their feathers or their skin. The dessert course conjures up that other lordly entertainment, the hunt, but it also introduces a disquieting travesty into the culinary theatre, in which the living animal is confronted with its own death for the pleasure of Man.

While wine flows liberally during meals, the man of standing does well to drink it tempered with water. At the start of the meal, he has already drunk sweet wine ("malvoisie" or Greek wine) or spiced wine ("hypocras") accompanied by sugared almonds and other confectionery, and he will drink these wines again at the end of the meal.

A prince has his chefs and master chefs, all high placed in the hierarchy of servants, as they help to keep their master in good health, to dramatise his pleasure, and also to secure his social standing. Thus, Master Chiquart served Count-Duke Amédée VIII of Savoy, and, in 1420, he wrote *Du fait de cuisine* (About Cooking) to vaunt his experience in the kitchens of princes as a great organiser of culinary feats for the glory of his master. Around the same time in Rome, Jean de Bockenheim, chef to Pope Martin V, and Master Martino, cook to the patriarch of Aquilium, also committed a book of culinary recipes to paper, each in his own way. Half a century later, Taillevent, master chef of the King of France, Charles VI, had written a book of meat cookery which was the written tradition helped to disseminate. We know nothing of the master cooks who served Gilles de Rais.

The tastes of the times made for a huge and varied use of spices, but in the 15th century, pepper was no longer costly enough to be a sign of high cuisine. People preferred ginger, 'long pepper', cardamom – more expensive and more prestigious, – and saffron, cinnamon, clove, mace and nutmeg were also enjoyed. Such products were a sign of the superior status of those who sprinkled them onto dishes offered to their guests. At the same time, the use of these spices was strictly regulated by culinary treatises, for the cook was not trying to mask the putrid odour of spoiled meat (a banal claim often made), his intention being rather to create or to rediscover tastes that would be pleasant for guests. This is why camomile sauce, enjoyed in France, included a mixture of cinnamon with ginger, whereas the Italians preferred to blend cinnamon with clove.

There is no doubt that the cuisine of the high tables of the 15th century follows aesthetic principles of sight and taste, but it is also part of an overall way of explaining the world, dominated by the doctrine of humours mentioned earlier. According to this system of knowledge, the circulation of the human body was composed of blood, which was warm and wet like spring, bile or red choler, warm and dry like summer, black choler or melancholy, cold and dry like autumn, and phlegm, cold and wet like winter. Each individual's relationship with the world bore the mark of the humour that predominated in him. The sanguine individual, for instance, was on best form in springtime. Everything in nature was characterised in the same way. Thus, the meat of a one-year-old lamb was appropriately warm and moist, and so particularly suited to a sanguine man enjoying good health. Spices, on the other hand, were all hot and dry, and so were able to compensate for the coldness of fish, the consumption of which, were it not for this adjustment at the time of cooking, might harm individuals who were already too phlegmatic in character. Historians have indeed noted from their study of oral accounts that expenditure on spices increased during Lent, together with the consumption of fish. The line between these ways of thinking and imagining cooking as a corrective or comforting alchemy is a fine one, and one which it would probably be unwise to cross.

However, I shall quote the author of a culinary treatise of the 14th century, entitled *Tractatus de modo preparandi et condiendi omnia cibaria*, whom some authors have assumed to be from Angers. He says he has travelled the world in his youth, and frequented the prestigious courts "of knights, princes, abbotts and magnates". Drawing on these experiences, he recalls these general principles, linked to the theory of the humours: partridge, pheasant, chicken, capon, hare, venison and rabbit are suitable fare for the rich and the nobility, in other words, for the leisured classes (nobilibus et diuitibus in quiete existentibus); on the other hand, labourers are best fed on beef, salted pork, deer, peas, beans, barley bread and rye bread. Which amounts to saying that social theories mirror medical discourse, making their application in cookery more likely.

Perhaps the cooks of the Breton prince worked to restrain his folies while, at the same time, paying tribute to his prestige.

Bibliography

Du manuscrit à la table. Essais sur la cuisine au Moyen-Age, éd. C. Lambert, Paris-Montréal, 1992.

J.-L. Flandrin, *Chronique de Platine. Pour une gastronomie historique*, Paris, 1992.

A. J. Grieco, *Classes sociales, nourriture et imaginaire alimentaire en Italie* (XIV-XV siècles), thèse de 3° cycle d'Histoire dactylographiée, Ecole des Hautes études en Sciences sociales 1987.

B. Laurioux, *Le Moyen-Age à table*, Paris, éd. Adam Biro 1989.

B. Laurioux, *Les livres de cuisine en Occident à la fin du Moyen-Age*, thèse d'Histoire dactylographiée Université de Paris I 1992.

O. Redon, F. Sabban, S. Serventi, *La gastronomie au Moyen-Age. 150 recettes de France et d'Italie*, Paris, éd. Stock 1991.

La sociabilité à table. Commensalité et convivialité à travers les âges, éd. M. Aurell, O. Dumoulin, F. Themalon, Rouen 1992.

Tractatus de modo preparandi et condiendi omnia cibaria, éd. M. Mulon, "Deux traités inédits d'art culinaire médiéval", Bulletin Philologique et historique 1968 (1971) I, p. 380-395.

PART III

THE CONFESSIONS OF GILLES DE RAIS

Saturday, October 22, 1440.

Saturday, October 22nd, arraigned before the said Lord Bishop of Nantes and Friar Jean Blouyn, Vicar of the Inquisitor, sitting on the bench to administer the law in the place designated above, at the hour of Vespers, the said Master Guillaume Chapeillon, prosecutor and plaintiff, on the one hand, and the said Gilles de Rais, the accused, on the other, appeared in person.

In conformity with the appointed term, the prosecutor asking that the said Lords Bishop of Nantes and Friar Jean Blouyn, Vicar of the Inquisitor, interrogate the said accused to know whether he intended to say anything else against or object to what had been said in the case, the accused said and responded that he did not intend to say anything, but voluntarily and freely, with great contrition of heart and great grief, according as it appeared at first sight, and with a great effusion of tears, confessed what he had confessed out of court in his room in the presence of the Reverend Father, Lord Bishop of Saint-Brieuc, Master Pierre de L'Hôpital, President of Brittany, Jean de Touscheronde, and Jean Petit. And he acknowledged that each and every one of the things contained and published in the said articles were and are true. And the accused himself adding to his other out-of-court confession without straying, 'wanted to repeat and recite it here, and to remedy its faults in the event that he had omitted anything, and to make more thorough declarations of the points developed summarily in the aforesaid articles; he voluntarily confessed and declared that he had committed and perpetrated iniquitously other high and enormous crimes, since the beginning of his youth, against God and His commandments, and that he had offended our Savior on account of the bad management he had received in his childhood when, unbridled, he applied himself to whatever pleased him, and pleased himself with every illicit act, and he urged those present who had children to instruct them in good doctrines and instill in them the habit of virtue during their youth and childhood.

After this confession made in arraignment by the said Gilles de Rais, the accused, as has been recorded, on the subject of the content of the aforesaid articles, and once the out-of-court confession had been repeated and recited – seeing as he affirmed that, among the crimes and .offenses, there figured enormous crimes, *e.g.*, the sin against nature not as fully stated in the articles, already voluntarily acknowledged as true by him and whose secret confession he had made before the Reverend Father in God, Lord Jean Prégent, Bishop of Saint-Brieuc, and noblemen Pierre de L'Hôpital, President of Brittany, and Jean Labbé, squire, and me, Jean Petit, notary public, general examiner of witnesses for the ecclesiastical court of Nantes, and Jean de Touscheronde, scribe also to the secular court of the same place – so that the said secret confession would be committed the best way possible to the memory of men, it pleased the same Gilles, the accused, not to diminish but rather to fortify and reinforce it; and he asked that the aforesaid confession be published in the vernacular language for any and all of the people present, the better part of whom did not know Latin, and that the publication and confession of perpetrated offenses be set forth for his shame, in order for him to attain more easily the forgiveness of his sins and God's grace in absolving them; he said that in his youth he had always been of a delicate nature and for his pleasure and according to his will had done whatever evil he could, and that he had put his hope and intention in the illicit and dishonest acts and things that he did; he most tenderly besought and exhorted the fathers, mothers, friends, and neighbors of every young boy and every child to raise them with good manners, by good examples and doctrines; and to instruct them in these things and chastise them lest they fall in the trap wherein he himself had fallen. By which secret confession that in the said Gilles' presence was read in trial and published, and approved by him, the said Gilles de Rais, the accused, voluntarily and publicly, before everyone, confessed that, because of his passion and sensual delight, he took and had others take so many children that he could not determine with certitude the number whom he'd killed and caused to be killed, with whom he committed the vice and sin of sodomy; and he said and confessed that he had ejaculated spermatic seed in the most culpable fashion on the bellies of the said children, as much after their deaths as during it; on which children sometimes he and sometimes some of his accomplices, notably the aforesaid Gilles de Sue, Milord Roger de Briqueville, knight, Henriet and Poitou, Rossignol and Petit Robin, inflicted various types and manners of torment; sometimes they severed the head from the body with dirks, daggers, and knives, sometimes they struck them violently on the head with a cudgel or other blunt instruments, sometimes they suspended them with cords from a peg or small hook in his room and strangled them; and when they were languishing, he committed the sodomitic vice on them in the aforesaid manner. Which children dead, he embraced them, and he gave way to contemplating those who had the most beautiful heads and members, and he had their bodies cruelly opened up and delighted at the sight of their internal organs; and very often, when the said children were dying, he sat on their bellies and delighted in watching them die thus, and with the aforesaid Corrillaut and Henriet he laughed at them, after which he had the children burned and their cadavers turned to ashes by the said Corrillaut and Henriet.

Interrogated as to where he perpetrated the said crimes, and when he began, and the number of deaths, he stated and responded: in the first place, at the Champtocé castle, in the year when Lord de La Sure, his grandfather, died, at which place he killed children and had them killed in large numbers – how many he is uncertain; and he committed with them the said sodomitic and unnatural sin; and at this time Gilles de Sillé alone knew, but then Roger de Briqueville, then Henriet, Etienne Corrillaut, also known as Poitou, Rossignol, and Robin successively became his accomplices; and he said that he had the bones of the children killed at Champtocé removed, heads as well as bodies, which had been thrown into the base of the tower; and he had them put in a coffer and transported to the castle of Machecoul, where they were burned and reduced to ashes; and that in the said place of Machecoul he had taken and killed other children, and caused them to be taken and killed – a large number of them, how many he did not know – and in the house named La Sure, in Nantes, which he possessed at that time, he killed, caused to be killed, burned, and turned to ashes many children, whose number he could not remember, whom he abused and defiled, committing with them the unnatural vice of sodomy, as above. Which crimes and offenses he committed solely for his evil pleasure and evil delight, to no other end or with no other intention, without anyone's counsel and only in accordance with his imagination.

Moreover, the said Gilles said and confessed that a year and a half ago the said Milord Eustache Blanchet brought to the said Gilles, the accused, from Florence, in Lombardy, the said Master François Prelati, with the intention of practicing the invocation of demons; and that the said François told him that in the country he came from he had found the means by which to conjure a spirit who promised this same François that he himself could conjure a certain demon who called himself Barron as many times as the same François wanted.

Item, the said Gilles said and confessed that the said François performed many invocations by his order, as much in his absence as in his presence, and that he, the accused, had assisted François at three invocations performed by the latter: once at Tiffauges castle; again at Bourgneuf-en-Rais; he does not remember where the third one took place; he adds that the said Eustache Blanchet knew well that the said François was performing the aforesaid invocations, but that he was not present at them, because neither he, the accused, nor François would have tolerated it, seeing as the said Eustache was a vicious gossip, fertile with idle remarks.

Item, the said Gilles, the accused, stated and confessed that in order to perform the said invocations they traced signs in the form of a circle or of a cross, and of characters in the earth; and that the said François possessed a book that he had brought from Italy, so he said, in which there were the names of many demons and words to conjure and invoke them by, which names and which words he does not remember; which book the said François held and read for nearly two hours during the said conjurations and invocations; and that he, the accused, during none of these invocations saw or perceived any devil to speak to, which greatly irritated and disappointed him.

Item, the said accused stated and confessed that he was told on his return that at one invocation of the said François' in his absence, François had seen the demon named Barron and spoken with him, who said that he would not approach the accused because of his having fallen short of his promise and because he didn't fulfill it; and he, the accused, upon learning this, charged the said François to ask that same devil what he wanted of him and to assure him that whatever the devil wanted he would give, with the exception of his life and soul, provided that in this way, the devil conceded and gave to him what he asked for; the said accused adding that he intended to ask for knowledge, power, and riches, in order to recover the original state of his lordship and power; and that not long after this, the said François said that he had spoken with this same devil who, among other things, demanded that Gilles de Rais give him some members of a child; whereupon the said Gilles gave the said François the hand, heart, and eyes of a young boy to offer to the devil on behalf of Gilles, the accused.

Item, the said Gilles, the accused, said and confessed that before going to one of three invocations that he attended, he wrote a note in his own hand, which he signed with his own name in French: "Gilles"; but he does not remember the content of the said note, which he wrote intending to give it to the devil should he appear at the invocation performed by the said François; which he had done on the advice of the said François, who had told him that it was important to deliver the said note to the devil as soon as he appeared; and during the invocation he held the note constantly in his hand, awaiting the pacts or promises that the said François and the devil would formulate and their agreement as to what the said Gilles, the accused, would promise to accomplish for the devil; but the devil did not appear and did not speak with them.

Item, the accused stated and confessed that one night he sent the said Etienne Corrillaut, also known as Poitou, with the said François to perform an invocation; both of whom returned completely drenched and soaked, telling him that nothing had come of the aforesaid invocation.

Item, the said accused stated and confessed that he wanted to be present at an invocation that the same François was to perform, but that the latter did not want his presence; and that on his return from the said invocation, he assured the said Gilles that if he had been present at that invocation, he would have been in great danger, because a serpent appeared that François was greatly afraid of on hearing this, the said Gilles took hold of a splinter of the Holy Rood, which he possessed, and thought of going to the said place of invocation where the said François said he had seen the snake; which he did not do, because the same François dissuaded him.

Item, the same Gilles de Rais, the accused, stated and confessed that at one of the three invocations he attended, the said François related to the said accused how he himself had seen the demon named Barron, who had shown him a large quantity of gold, and among other things a gold ingot but the said accused declared that he did not see the devil or the ingot but only a sort of foil in the form of a sheet or sheets of gold, which he did not touch.

Item, the accused stated and confessed that the last time he was at Josselin, in the Saint-Malo diocese, close to the illustrious Prince and Lord Duke of Brittany, the same accused had several children killed who had been procured for him by the aforesaid Henriet; and that he committed and exercised on them the vice and sin of sodomy in the aforesaid manner.

Item, the same accused stated and confessed that the said François, by his order and in his absence, performed many invocations of the devil at Josselin, which nothing came of or appeared at.

Item, he said that before leaving for Bourges he sent the said François to 'Tiffauges, entreating him to conjure in his absence and to notify him of what he did and knew, and to write to him in guarded terms that his work was going well; which François wrote to him and sent a sort of unguent in a silver tube, placed in a purse and a box made of silver also, writing to him that this here was a precious thing and that he ought to guard it carefully; and he, trusting the said François' affirmation, hung the said purse about his neck for several days; but shortly thereafter he threw it away, discovering that it was not doing him any good.

Item, the same accused stated and confessed that the said François once told him that the said Barron had ordered him to give a dinner to three poor people in his name on three important feasts of the year; which he, the accused, did only once, on All Saints' Day.

Interrogated as to the motive that made him keep the said François close to him and among his family, he responded that the said François was exceptionally gifted and agreeable to converse with, speaking Latin eloquently and learnedly, and that he applied himself zealously to the affairs of the said Gilles, the accused.

Item, the same accused stated and confessed that after last Saint John the Baptist's Day a beautiful young man who was living with a certain Rodigo, at Bourgneuf-en-Rais, where the accused himself was then staying, was brought to him one certain evening by the said Hem-jet and Corrillaut, and during the night he practiced the said unnatural and sodomitic vice with him in the aforesaid manner, then killed him and had him transported to Machecoul to be burned.

Item, he stated and confessed that having been alerted that the men of the castle at Palluau were planning to lay hands on the captain of the castle at Saint-Etienne-de-Mermorte, and for this reason indignant with them, one morning, what day he cannot remember, he left on horseback with his men-at-arms intending to surprise the men of the castle at Palluau, make them prisoners, and punish them; and at the outset of the expedition, the said François, being among his company, told him that he would not find them; and in fact, the said accused did not find them and his project was frustrated.

Item, the said Gilles de Rais, the accused, stated and confessed that he had killed two young pages, one of Guillaume Daussy's, and another of Pierre Jacquet's, called Prince, on whom he committed and exercised the said unnatural lust.

Item, the same accused stated and confessed that when he last went to Vannes, last July, André Buchet delivered a young boy to him, at his lodgings in the house of a man named Lemoine, with whom he committed the unnatural vice, as above-noted. And having killed him, Gilles had him thrown by the said Poitou into the latrines of an inn owned by a man named Boetden, near the aforesaid Lemoine's house; the said friends of the accused lodging in Boetden's inn or house, near the marketplace of Vannes; which Poitou descended into the latrines, in order to sink the cadaver and cover it, so that no one might discover it.

Item, the aforesaid Gilles de Rais, the accused, stated and confessed likewise that before the said François' arrival, he had employed other conjurors, namely a trumpeter named Dumesnil, Master Jean de La Rivière, a man named Louis, Master Antoine de Palerne, and another whose name he does not remember. Which conjurors by his command performed many invocations, some of which he attended, as much at Machecoul as at other places; and, in particular, to see drawn in the soil a circle or figure in the form of a circle, which is necessary in that sort of invocation where the intention is to see the devil and to speak and make a pact with him. But the said accused said that he was never able to see the devil or speak with him, although he did everything he could, to the point that it was not his fault if he could not see the devil or speak with him.

Item, the same Gilles de Rais, oft-named, stated and confessed that the aforesaid Dumesnil, conjuror, told him once that the devil, in order to do and accomplish what the said accused intended to solicit and obtain from this same devil, expected to see done and to receive from him a note signed in the hand of the accused himself with blood from his finger, by which the latter promised to give the said devil, when he appeared at his invocation, certain things which he did not remember; and for that reason and to that end he signed his name, *Gilles*, to the said note with blood from his little finger. As to what was written in the said note he did not remember, except that he promised the devil what was mentioned there, on condition that the devil give to him and procure knowledge, power, and riches. But he is absolutely certain that as he has affirmed, whatever he might have promised the devil he had always retained his soul and life, and he said that the aforesaid note was not delivered, the devil not appearing to him and not having responded to that same invocation.

Item, the said accused confessed that at an invocation by the aforesaid Master de La Rivière, in a wood not far from the garrison or the city of Pouzauges, the said La Rivière armed himself beforehand with weapons and gear, and then entered the aforesaid wood to perform the said invocation; and that he, the accused, with his servants and especially Eustache Blanche; Henri, and Etienne Corrillaut, also known as Poitou, upon entering the wood, discovered the said La Rivière returning, who told him that he had seen the Devil in the guise of a leopard coming toward him, which passed by him without saying a word; and he, the accused, was frightened and terrified by what he said. And the accused added to his narration that the said La Rivière, to whom he had paid the sum of twenty gold royals, promised to return, which he did not do.

Item, the same accused stated and confessed that at another invocation of demons practiced by him and a conjuror whose name he does not remember, with Gilles de Sillé as well, in a room of the aforesaid Tiffauges castle, while he was in the said room, the said Sillé did not dare to enter the circle to perform the invocation, but retired to a window with the intention of throwing himself out of it if he perceived something fearful approaching, and he held in his arms an image of the Blessed Virgin Mary; the said accused himself was afraid in the circle, because the invoker had forbidden him to cross himself, because if he did, they would all be in great danger; but he remembered a prayer to Our Lady that begins with *Alma*, and at once the conjuror ordered him to leave the circle, which he immediately did while crossing himself; and he left the room promptly, leaving the invoker and locking the door behind him; then he discovered the said Gilles de Sillé, who told him that someone was beating and striking the invoker left alone in the room, which sounded as if someone were beating a featherbed; which he, the accused, did not hear, and he had the door of the room opened and at its entrance he saw the conjuror wounded in the face and in other parts of his body, and among other things, having a bump on his forehead so large he could barely stand up; and for fear that he might die in consequence of the said wounds, Gilles wanted him to be confessed and have the sacraments administered; but the conjuror did not die, and recovered from his wounds.

Item, the said Gilles de Rais, the accused, stated and confessed that he sent the said Gilles de Sillé into a region farther north, to find conjurors of demons or evil spirits. Which Gilles de Sillé, having returned, told him that he had found a woman who busied herself with like invocations: which woman had said to Sillé that if Gilles de Rais did not turn his soul away from the Church and his chapel, he would never accomplish what he desired; and that Sillé had met in the same region another woman who told him that if the said accused did not abandon a work begun by him or that he intended to pursue, or have it stopped, nothing good would ever come to him.

Item, that the said Gilles de Sillé had found in the same region an invoker whom he proposed sending to the said accused, which conjuror, who was preparing to join the said accused, drowned while crossing a river or stream.

Item, the said Gilles, the accused, stated and confessed that the said Sillé brought him another conjuror who also died immediately. And because of these unlucky deaths and the difficulties counterpoised to his guilty intentions in the aforesaid invocations or the like he said he believed that divine clemency and the intercession of the Church, from which his heart and his belief have never strayed, had mercifully arrived and prevented him from succumbing to so many tests and perils; and for this reason he intended to renounce his evil life, and make a pilgrimage to Jerusalem and the sepulcher of Our Lord and other places included in the Passion of his Redeemer and to do all that he could to obtain forgiveness for his sins, through the mercy of his Redeemer.

And then, after the said confession in arraignment, given

freely and voluntarily, he exhorted the people there, and principally the ecclesiastics, there in considerably larger numbers, to always venerate our Holy Mother Church, and to honor her greatly and never to separate from her, adding expressly that if he himself, the accused, had not directed his heart and his affection toward that same Church, he never would have escaped the devil's malice and intention; moreover, he believed that had he not, because of the enormity of his villainies and crimes the devil would have long since destroyed his body and carried off his soul; exhorting, moreover, the fathers of families to watch that their children be not too finely dressed, and to tolerate no laziness, noting and asserting that many ills are born of laziness and of the excesses of eating and drinking, and declaring more expressly still that with him laziness, an insatiable desire for delicacies, and the frequent consumption of mulled wine, more than anything else, kept him in a state of excitement that led to the perpetration of so many sins and crimes.

On the subject of which crimes and offenses perpetrated by him, Glues de Rais, the accused, humbly and tearfully implored the mercy and pardon of His Creator and most blessed Redeemer, as well as that of the parents and friends of the children so cruelly massacred, as well as that of everyone whom he could have injured in regard to whom he was effectively guilty, whether they were present there or elsewhere, and he asked all Christ's faithful and worshippers for the assistance of their devout prayers.

And this is why the aforesaid Master Guillaume Chapeillon, prosecutor, in the presence of the aforesaid Gilles de Rais, the accused, considering the voluntary confession of the said accused, and other proofs lawfully brought against him, requested instantly that a timely day and term be appointed to the accused in order to conclude – and at the same time, on the other hand, to see concluded – the sentence and definitive sentences by the said Reverend Father in God, Lord Bishop of Nantes, and Friar Jean Blouyn, Vicar of the said Inquisitor, and by each of them, or by those whom they would charge with this responsibility, sentences to be written and promulgated in the case and the cases of this order, unless the aforesaid Gilles de Rais, the accused, could give any valid reason this should not be done. Thereupon the said Lords Bishop of Nantes and Vicar of the Inquisitor assigned the following Tuesday to the prosecutor and Gilles de Rais, the accused, who did not object, in order to proceed as by law, as was necessary in the case and the cases of this order.

Of which things the aforesaid prosecutor asked us, the undersigned notaries public and scribes, to make one and several public instruments.

In the aforesaid place in the presence of the Reverend Father in God, Milord Jean Prégent, Bishop of Saint-Brieuc, Masters Pierre de L'Hôpital, President of Britanny, Robert de La Rivière and Milord Robert d'Epinay, aforesaid knight, and nobleman Yvon de Rocerf, including the honorable Masters Yvon Coyer, dean, Jean Morelli, chorister, Gatien Ruytz, Guillaume Groyguet, licensed in both courts of law, Jean de Chateaugiron, Pierre Avril, Robert Viger, Geoffroy de Chevigny, licensed in law, the mayors of Nantes, Geoffroi Piperier, treasurer, Pierre Hamon, Jean Guérin, Jean Vaedi and Jean Symon, canons from Notre-Dame-de-Nantes and Saint-Brieuc, Hervé Levy, seneschal of Quimper, and Master Guillaume de La Lohérie, licensed in law, attorney to the secular court of Nantes, with many other witnesses assembled in the same place in large numbers, specifically called and requested.

[Signed:] *Delaunay, J. Petit, G. Lesné*

A CHRONOLOGY OF GILLES DE RAIS

1404
Birth, in September or October, in the black tower of the château de Champtocé (or in the château de Machecoul, depending on the source), of Gilles de Laval, son of Guy II, knight, lord of Blaison and Chemillé, and of Marie de Craon, grandson of Brumor de Laval, and great-nephew of Bertrand du Guesclin.

1407
Birth of his brother, René de la Suze. Birth of Joan of Arc.

1415
Death of Gilles's parents, his mother's at the beginning of the year and his father's on 28th September. Gilles's education is entrusted to Jean de Craon, his maternal grandfather, a violent and greedy man, devoid of scruples. On 25th October, Amaury, son of Jean de Craon, dies at the defeat of Agincourt. At the age of eleven, Gilles becomes one of the richest heirs in the kingdom.

1420
Having been betrothed twice by Jean de Craon, Gilles abducts Catherine de Thouars, his cousin four times removed, and marries her in secret. She brings him the châteaux of Tiffauges and Machecoul in her dowry. Jean de Craon and Gilles side with Jean V de Montfort against the Penthièvres. Gilles experiences his first campaign.

1422
On 22nd April, the union of Gilles and Catherine is blessed by the bishop of Angers in his château at Chalonnes.

1427
Gilles sides with Charles VII to whom Brittany has rallied two years earlier. He fights the English under the banner of Ambroise de Loré and performs a spectacular military deed in le Lude: during his assault on the fortress held by the English, Gilles cuts Captain Blackburn in two with a single blow of his sword. Jean V again abandons the French cause and has the parliament of Brittany approve the treaty of Troyes.

1428
The English besiege Orleans. Gilles is presented at court by his cousin, Georges de la Trémouille, who has been Grand Chamberlain of Charles

VII since the previous year.

1429

On 25th February, Joan of Arc, aged sixteen years, appears at the château de Chinon where the Dauphin has agreed to receive her. Gilles de Rais is probably present in the throne-room where the meeting takes place (although his presence has not been established beyond doubt). Joan, who "recognises" the Dauphin hiding among his courtiers without ever having seen him before, is then accommodated in a tower of the château de Couldray; it seems likely that Gilles and Joan meet on a regular basis.

In April, Charles VII decides to send an expedition to Orleans and entrusts part of the responsibility for the Maid and her safety to his liege subject, Gilles de Rais – at the request of Joan herself, according to one chronicler.

On 29th April, Joan enters Orleans, and is received by cheering crowds. Gilles de Rais is among those accompanying her.

On 8th May, the siege of Orleans is lifted.

On 11th May, Gilles and Joan arrive at Loches to inform the Dauphin officially that Orleans has been liberated.

On 17th June, the royal army takes Beaugency. Gilles de Rais again proves himself "a most valiant knight at arms"; he repeats his prowess the following day at Patay where the English are again defeated and their leader, John de Talbot, is taken prisoner.

On 17th July, Charles VII is crowned in Rheims. Joan stands on his right hand and Gilles on his left, holding the holy chrism. On that same day, he receives the baton of maréchal. From this moment on, he will maintain a splendid military force.

8th September: twelve thousand Armagnacs, commanded by Joan and La Trémouille, to whom Gilles is subject, attack the gates of Paris. Joan is wounded at the gate of Saint-Honoré. She has to be laid on a camp-bed in her tent.

On 13th, the order to retreat from Paris is given by Charles VII, who leaves the high ground of Montmartre for Saint-Denis, then for the banks of the Loire.

Towards the end of the year – during the siege of Paris according to some chroniclers – Marie, daughter of Gilles and Catherine, is born, probably at Champtocé.

1430

Having taken Compiègne, Joan is brushed aside by La Trémouille and abandoned by Charles VII, and she is taken prisoner on 23rd May by the Burgundians who sell her to the English.

Some chroniclers report that in December, Gilles vainly attempts to cross the Seine at Louviers to reach Rouen with the intention of rescuing Joan. Nothing of the kind. Rather, Gilles spends most of his time conducting questionable operations: the occupation of Sablé in the conflict between La Trémouille and Yolande of Aragon, an armed assault against the same Yolande, pillage, etc.

Having been condemned as a heretic and witch by an ecclesiastical tribunal presided by the bishop of Beauvais, Pierre Cauchon, Joan of Arc is burnt at the stake at Rouen on 30th May. Gilles watches in despair.

1431

Henry VI of England is crowned King of France on 16th December at Notre-Dame-de-Paris.

1432

Gilles de Rais's second great military feat after the Tourelles (Orleans): on 10th August, the royal army forces the English regent to lift the siege of Lagny. Gilles then leaves the court to retire to his lands, particularly to Tiffauges.

Death of Jean de Craon on 15th November; frightened by Gilles's excesses and prodigality, he has bequeathed his sword and breastplate to his younger grandson, René. Jean de Craon's death nevertheless places Gilles at the head of an immense fortune. His escort assumes a princely importance. The first child-murders committed by Gilles date from this year. These acts are kept secret from all except Gilles de Sillé, his cousin and accomplice. Gilles de Rais develops a passion for church plainchant.

1434

Gilles is made canon of Saint-Hilare at Poitiers. He pays several visits to Orleans during the course of this and the following year.

1435

On 26th March, Gilles founds the Chapelle des Saints-Innocents at Machecoul, which is the equal of any collegiate church or even cathedral in wealth and importance. He himself writes the rules of the chapel.

Gilles spends extravagant sums of money to organise festivities commemorating the lifting of the siege of Orleans, which has been celebrated since its liberation in 1429. He is in charge of the performances of *The Mystery of the Siege of Orleans* which cost him 80,000 ecus, or 20 billion modern centimes.

On 2nd July, at the request of his brother and his cousin André de Laval-Lohéac, Charles VII signs letters of prohibition stripping Gilles of the right to sell his property. He then begins to pawn precious objects, books and his own horse, Cassenoix.

1436

In Angers, in May, Gilles abducts Michel de Fontenay, a distinguished figure and man of the church who was his tutor, because he had overseen the publication of the royal letters in Champtocé which had limited his rights. Following numerous official protests, he will be forced to set him free after locking him up at Champtocé and then at Machecoul.

1437

To wreck the negotiations between Gilles and Jean V, Gilles's brother and cousin seize the château de Champtocé, then the château de Machecoul where they discover the bones of forty children. In Gilles de Rais's entourage, the disappearances of children increase.

1438

At the beginning of May, after a period at Saint-Florent-le-Vieil, Father Eustache Blanchet, Gilles's moral preceptor, returns from Florence with the conjurer of demons and alchemist, François Prelati. The first conjurings of demons begin at Tiffauges. Murders of children occur one after another (but a number of disappearances attributed to him seem unlikely or even impossible). Gilles gets into debt.

1439

Gilles receives a Joan of Arc who has been attempting to make people believe since 1436 that she had herself replaced by a double at the stake in Rouen. A credulous Gilles entrusts part of his garrison to her before the deceit is exposed by Charles VII who had expressed a desire to meet this "maid".

The conjurings start at the beginning of summer in the great lower hall of the château de Tiffauges, then in a meadow. Later, Prelati will pretend that he has been beaten black and blue by the devil, that he has seen apparitions of "Barron" and of a large, green-coloured serpent, as big as a dog, that he has received a large quantity of gold from it... all play-acting which Gilles will believe to be real.

Ruined, abandoned and subject to attacks of remorse, Gilles makes known his intention to change his ways and to go on a pilgrimage to the Holy Sepulchre. Rumours grow that Gilles is a child-murderer.

In December, the Dauphin de Viennois (son of Charles VII and the future Louis XI), who has been sent to Poitou to "put an end to the pillage and expel the warmongers", pays a visit to the lord of Tiffauges. Gilles feels under suspicion and hurries to destroy his laboratory and his alchemical ovens.

1440

Year of rebellion of the nobility against Charles VII's military reforms; now in disgrace, La Trémouille is one of the leaders of this "Praguerie".

On 27th March, Easter Sunday, Gilles de Rais confesses his sins and takes communion, humbly among the crowd in the Church of the Holy Trinity in Machecoul.

On 15th May, jour de la Pentecote, Gilles invades the Church of Saint-Etienne-de-Mer-Morte and insults the officiating priest, Jean Le Ferron, who had acquired one of his properties at low cost. He takes him prisoner. This is the beginning of Gilles's journey to the gallows. He has violated ecclesiastical privilege and at the same time, has encroached on the rights of his own suzerain, the Duke of Brittany. A secret enquiry is launched against him by Jean de Malestroit, Bishop of Nantes and Chancellor of Brittany. The Duke of Brittany imposes a very large fine on him of 50,000 gold ecus.

In July, Gilles travels to Josselin to negotiate with Jean V.

On 24th August, Jean Le Ferron is set free, and the High Constable, Arthur de Richemont, seizes Tiffauges. Decisions concerning the sharing out of Gilles's property to Richemont's advantage are taken by the son of Jean V...

On 15th September, Gilles, Prelati, Blanchet, Henriet and Poitou (his two personal servants) are arrested by the captain at arms, Jean Labbé, in the name of Jean de Malestroit, and taken to Nantes. Gilles is imprisoned in the New-Tower of the château...

On the 19th, the trial opens in the large upper chamber of the New-Tower. Gilles appears before Jean de Malestroit.

On 8th October, the prosecution cites all the crimes and offences with which Gilles is charged. Gilles responds by appealing to his judges. When the appeal is rejected, Gilles violently denies all charges.

On the 13th, a list of charges comprising 49 articles is read out in the presence of the Vice-Inquisitor, Bishop Jean Blouyn, and numerous distinguished Nantes citizens. It covers three main areas: crimes against children (140 girls and boys), heresy (conjuring of demons, practice of the magical arts...) and violation of ecclesiastical immunity. Gilles refuses to recognise the authority of the judges and insults them. His excommunication is pronounced by the ecclesiastical tribunal. Gilles appeals against it in vain.

On 15th, Gilles recognises the Bishop and the Assistant Inquisitor as his judges. He confesses his crimes and "devoutly" asks for pardon. He nevertheless denies having conjured demons and offers to undergo "trial by fire" to prove it.

On 16th and 17th, Prelati, Blanchet, Henriet and Poitou give overwhelming evidence against Gilles.

On 20th, Gilles maintains that he has no objections to make against the list of charges. The judges contemplate "putting him to the question and to torture".

On 21st, Gilles requests that the tortures be delayed until the following day. He confesses "hors jugement", in other words, outside of ecclesiastical and secular processes. He indicates that his earliest crimes date back to 1432. Some eight hundred murders are now taken into consideration.

On 22nd, Gilles repeats the confession he made the previous day, this time before his judges. He emphasises the disorderliness of his childhood which had encouraged his parents to be strict, and gives details concerning the way in which he tortured his victims and the conjuring of demons. He blames alcoholism and idleness, exhorts the people to be pious and begs God's forgiveness. Gilles again confesses his crimes "in vulgar tongue" to the crowds surrounding him.

On 23rd, the secular court sentences Henriet and Poitou to death.

On 25th, the ecclesiastical court excommunicates Gilles who comes within the provisions of other legal sanctions. This sentence is automatically repeated in the secular court which follows the same day. Once this sentence has been promulgated, the judges offer to receive the condemned man back into the Church. Gilles confesses his sins in secret to a monk of the Carmelite Order. At the fortress of Le Bouffay, Gilles is then prosecuted in the secular court. He is sentenced to be hanged and burnt, the sentence to be carried out the next day at eleven o'clock.

On 26th October, Gilles, Henriet and Poitou are led in "general procession" from the New-Tower to the Prairie de Biesse where three funeral-pyres have been erected surmounted by three gibbets, the middle one higher than the others. Gilles kneels and begs the crowd's forgiveness. He is hanged and burnt, but his body is quickly pulled out of the fire. Henriet and Poitou are executed in turn, their bodies burnt to a cinder, whilst Gilles's remains are borne to the Church of Notre-Dame-du-Carmel in Nantes.

1450

Charles VII sets up an enquiry on Joan of Arc which will lead to a legal process of rehabilitation.

1456

Joan of Arc is rehabilitated. Charles VII dies.

1793

Numerous tombs in the Church of Le Moutier de Notre-Dame des Carmes in Nantes, including Gilles's, are desecrated by revolutionaries. His coffin was probably one of many thrown into the Loire.

DIRECTORY OF KEY FIGURES

Marie d'Anjou Daughter of Yolande of Aragon, wife of Charles VII and mother of Louis XI.

Arthur III, comte de Richemont Brother of Jean V, Duke of Brittany (1457-1458). Taken prisoner by the English at Agincourt (1415), he was appointed High Constable of France (1424) by Queen Yolande of Aragon – against the wishes of Georges de la Trémouille who removed him later – , became companion to Joan of Arc and one of Charles VII's most faithful servants. In 1428, he was removed from his post and retired to his small seignory at Parthenay. After his rival, La Trémouille fell into disfavour (1433), he was able to consolidate Joan's victories, allowing France to deliver itself definitively from English hands. On August 24th 1440, at his brother's request but acting ostensibly in the name of the King, he seized Tiffauges. Chroniclers represent him as energetic, austere and upright.

Barron The demon most regularly summoned by Prelati and Gilles.

Bedford (John of Lancaster, Duke of) Third son of Henry IV, Henry V named him regent of the kingdom of France (1422), where he then resided most of the time. Gilles, Dunois and Xaintrailles defeated the Englishman at Lagny (1432). The Duke of Bedford's task was rendered impossible by the treaty of Arras of 1435, signed by Charles VII and Philippe III le Bon who was forced to abandon his alliance with the English.

Beelzebub Prince of demons, according to Prelati, often invoked at Tiffauges.

Blackburn English captain killed (cleaved in two!) by Gilles during the battle of Le Lude (1427).

Eustache Blanchet Priest in Gilles's service with the function of moral tutor. He returned from a journey to Florence in the company of Prelati (May 1439). With rumours of child-murders on the increase, he fled (December 1439) and took refuge at Mortagne, where Jean Petit was dispatched by Gilles to bring him back, but in vain – this errand supposedly led to the goldsmith emissary's being imprisoned in the dungeons of Saint-Etienne-de-Mer-Morte. A few days later, Gilles de Sillé, Poitou and Henriet brought him back, via Rocheservière, to Machecoul where he lived at liberty until the arrest of all parties (15 September 1440). His testimony was heard on October 17th.

Jean Blouyn Vice inquisitor of Nantes and of his diocese, brother of the order of the Preaching Friars. At the ecclesiastical trial, Gilles appeared before him and Jean de Malestroit.

Tiphaine Branchu Widow of Robin Branchu; procured children at Gilles's behest. She was heard as a witness at Gilles's ecclesiastical trial, but her testimony was not preserved.

Roger de Briqueville Norman gentleman, relative, counsellor, equerry, general dogsbody and accomplice of Gilles's, acting as one of the procurers of children, and playing a part in some murders. He managed to escape the arrest of all parties at Machecoul (15th September 1440). A few years later, he entered the service of Prigent de Coëtivy, so that Marie de Rais's husband might be fully informed of all matters concerning his father-in-law's affairs.

André Buchet Choir-boy in the chapel of Tiffauges, native of Vannes. A favourite of Gilles's, on at least two occasions, he procured young victims for him. He enjoyed a prebend (or ecclesiastical sinecure) granted him by his master.

Jean de Bueil Captain in the service of Yolande of Aragon.

Jean Bureau Grand master of artillery under Charles VII, and companion of Joan of Arc. He took part in the battle of Castillon (1453) and was appointed mayor of Bordeaux.

Adam de Cambray President of the Parliament of Brittany. He was attacked by Gilles de Rais and Jean de Craon at Pouzauges.

Antoine de Chabannes Warrior and companion of Joan of Arc. He became chief of a band of *Ecorcheurs* (brigands who held peasants for ransom during the Hundred Years War), and later entered the service of Charles VII (1430). From 1468 on, he served Louis XI and then his son, Charles VIII who appointed him governor of Paris.

Guillaume Chapeillon Parish priest of Saint-Nicolas (Nantes), acting as plaintiff at Gilles's trial before the ecclesiastical tribunal. He accused him of having accepted "heretical doctrines" and read out the 49 articles of the list of charges. He asked the judges for permission to put him to torture, but Gilles avoided this by offering to respond directly to Pierre de L'Hospital and Jean Prégent.

Odette de Champdivers Mistress of Charles VI. She took care of the King after he had gone insane (1392) and had been abandoned by his family.

Charles VI the Well-Beloved or the Insane King of France (1380-1422). Elder son of Charles V and of Jeanne de Bourbon. After the wise government of the Marmousets (1388), the King having gone mad (1392), France was ravaged by civil war. The King of England, Henry V, took advantage of the situation in alliance with the Burgundians and won the battle of Agincourt (1415). At the end of his reign, the treaty of Troyes (1420) was signed. With the support of Queen Isabeau of Bavaria, this treaty disinherited the future Charles VII, recognised Henry V of England as heir to the throne of France and entrusted the regency to him.

Charles VII the Victorious King of France (1422-1461). Son of Charles VI and Isabeau of Bavaria, father of Louis XI, son-in-law of Jean de Craon and Yolande of Aragon. He offered Joan of Arc the chance to fight the English and she had him crowned in Rheims (1429), having delivered Orleans with the help of Gilles. Charles VII then granted the maréchal de Rais an additional coat-of-arms of a surround of fleurs de lis on a blue background. After the reconquest of part of Northern France, he was reconciled with Philippe III le Bon, Duke of Burgundy, who was allied with the English by the treaty of Arras of 1435. Once Paris had been retaken (1436), Charles VII reorganised the army and the kingdom. With the support of Dunois, La Hire, Xaintrailles and other war leaders, he pursued the reconquest of France. In 1435, Charles VII signed letters of prohibition, stripping Gilles of the right to sell his property.

Olivier de Clisson Warrior, appointed High Constable of France on the death of Du Guesclin. He organised the army and contributed to Rozebeke's victory over the Flemish (1382). He fell out of favour, together with the other Marmousets, after Charles VI went mad, and died in 1407.

Prigent de Coëtivy Important Breton nobleman and admiral of France. He seized Georges de la Trémouille in the château de Chinon (1433) on the orders of Charles of Anjou, son of Yolande of Aragon. He was married by the de Rais family to Marie de Rais less than a year after Gilles's execution, and died from shot from an English arquebus outside Cherbourg in 1450. Georges Bataille represents him as a major predator, a businessman devoid of scrupules or any sense of honour.

Jean Coppegorge Witness responsible for the eccesiastical procedures at Gilles's trial.

Amaury de Craon Son of Jean de Craon, killed at the battle of Agincourt (1415).

Jean de Craon Gilles's maternal grandfather and guardian, powerful vassal of the Dukes of Anjou and Brittany, lieutenant general of Anjou. He takes charge of Gilles's upbringing after the death of his parents (1415) and exercises a very strong influence upon him. His situation on the Loire at Champtocé, his lands and farms assured him an extensive income. He died in 1432. Most accounts portray him as violent, grasping, contemptuous and cynical.

Marie de Craon Only daughter of Jean de Craon and mother of Gilles.

Bertrand Du Guesclin Famous warrior, model of the perfect knight, he fought the English in Poitou, Normandy, Guienne and Saintonge, and died in 1380. He was the uncle of Guy II of Laval.

Jean Dunois, comte de Longueville, known as the Bastard of Orleans Warrior, born in 1403 and died in 1468. Companion of Joan of Arc, he took part in the defence of Orleans and the victory of Patay (1429). With Gilles and Xaintrailles, he fought against the English at Lagny (1432). He helped to reconquer Normandy and Guienne, and participated in the League of Public Good against Louis XI (1465). He was the illegitimate son of Louis, Duke of Orleans.

Charles d'Estouville Second husband of Marie de Craon.

Eugène IV (Gabriele Condulmer) 205th pope (1431-1447), he tried to dissolve the Council of Bâle which had declared itself superior to the Pope. To humour the Byzantines who had come to seek reconciliation, he moved the assembly to Ferrare and then to Florence. A faction who had remained in Bâle sought to depose him and replace him with Felix V, but he prevailed. He gave work to Ghiberti, Pisanello, Donatello, Fra Angelico.

Olivier des Ferrières Priest who heard Gilles's spontaneous confession in the Church of the Holy Trinity (église de la Sainte Trinité) in Machecoul on Easter Sunday 1440. Gilles took communion afterwards, humbly among the humble.

Nicolas Flamel Sworn writer of the University of Paris. Works of hermeticism and alchemical practices were attributed to him. He had the Church of Saint-Jacques-de-La-Boucherie built in Paris (with alchemical gold, according to the legend). Upon his death (1418), he made donations of considerable size to chapels and hospitals.

Michel de Fontenay Leading citizen and churchman, and Gilles's tutor. Gilles became angry with him because he had arranged in Champtocé for royal letters of prohibition to be issued against him, and arrested him in Angers and imprisoned him (1436) in Champtocé, then in Machecoul. He was forced to free him after many official protests.

Henriet Griart Personal servant and accomplice of Gilles's, and a native of

Paris, he entered his service around 1434. Poitou, the other personal servant, apprised him of their master's secrets about three years after his arrival. He was arrested with Gilles, Prelati, Blanchet and Poitou at Machecoul (15th September 1440), and contemplated slitting his own throat on his way to prison in Nantes. His testimony agreed with Poitou's at the ecclesiastical trial. He was executed with his master and Poitou.

Robin Guillaumet Notary who, with four colleagues as clerks, performed the office of usher at Gilles's trial.

Pierre de Guingamp Son of Jean V and brother of François de Montfort.

Guy II de Laval-Montmorency Knight, lord of Blaison and Chemillé, husband of Marie de Craon and father of Gilles. He died in 1415, gored by a wild boar.

Henry V King of England (1413-1422), son of Henry IV, he fought against the Lollards in England. Taking advantage of the troubles in France, he resumed battle and vanquished the French at Agincourt (1415). After conquering Normandy, he appointed himself regent and declared himself heir to the throne of France according to the provisions of the treaty of Troyes (1420), and by virtue of his marriage to Catherine de Valois. Father of Henry VI.

Henry VI King of England, son of Henry V, he reigned at first under the guardianship of his uncles Humphrey, Duke of Gloucester, and Lancaster, Duke of Bedford for France. At ten years of age, he was crowned King of France at Notre-Dame-de-Paris (1431). The end of the Hundred Years War (1337-1453), the government of Suffolk and the excessive influence of his wife, Marguerite d'Anjou, caused the War of the Roses (1455) to break out. He was dethroned by Edward IV in 1461, then restored to the throne in 1470, but Edward IV seized power again and murdered him (1471).

Isabeau de Bavière (Isabeau of Bavaria) Queen of France, daughter of the Duke of Bavaria, Etienne II, she married Charles VI. After the King went mad (1392), she led the Council of Regency, favouring Louis of Orleans over John the Fearless (Jean sans Peur), leading to the quarrel between the Armagnacs and the Burgundians. Abandoning the alliance with the Armagnacs, she allied herself to the Burgundians and the English, and was complicit in the treaty of Troyes (1420) which disinherited the future Charles VII.

Jean V de Montfort Duke of Brittany (1399-1442). In 1420, he fell into a trap laid by his enemies the Penthièvres and was imprisoned again at Champtocé. Jean de Craon then sided with the Montforts, the Penthièvres faction was defeated and Jean V was set free. Then he left the French side. In 1425, thanks to Yolande of Aragon, he drew closer again to France. In 1427, he left the French side once again and had the parliament of Brittany approve the treaty of Troyes. In 1436, he made sure of the loyalty of the captains holding Gilles's châteaux. In 1440, he took part in the revolt of the great lords against Charles VII (the Praguerie). Following the secret enquiry held by Jean de Malestroit concerning the disappearances of children in Gilles's entourage, he imposed a fine on him of considerable size: 50, 000 gold ecus. Gilles tried in vain to negotiate by visiting him at Josselin. Some testimonies represent the Duke of Brittany as sly, craven and rapacious, whilst others claim him to have been affable, level-headed and peace-loving.

Jean the Fearless (Jean sans peur) Duke of Burgundy (1404-1419), son of Philippe II le Hardi (the Bold) and father of Philippe III le Bon. As soon as Charles VI went mad, he disputed Louis of Orleans's claim to the throne and had him assassinated (1407), sparking off the quarrel between the Armagnacs and the Burgundians. Unable to control events, he was driven out of Paris (1413) and allied himself with the English before attempting a reconciliation with the Dauphin (the future Charles VII). He was assassinated by a follower of the latter.

Joan of Arc (Jeanne d'Arc) At the age of 16, this young girl of modest origins was urged to leave Domremy by the divine voices that had spoken to her, to travel, via Vaucouleurs, to Chinon where she persuaded Charles VII, whom she recognised among his courtiers, to entrust her with an army to kick the English out of France. She delivered Orleans with the help of Gilles, Jean Dunois and La Hire. After the victory of Patay (1429), she took Auxerre, Troyes and Châlons, thus clearing the way to Rheims where she had Charles VII crowned, legitimating his claim against his own mother Isabeau de Bavière. Joan was wounded while attempting to take Paris, retreated, took Compiègne, then was captured by the Burgundians who sold her to the English. She was sentenced and burned alive at Rouen (1431). Charles VII, who had made no attempts to save her, set up an enquiry in 1450 which led to her rehabilitation (1456). She was beatified in 1909 and canonised in 1920.

Joan of the Artemisias (Jeanne des Armoises) Double of Joan of Arc's who, in 1439, visited Gilles and convinced him that she was the real Joan who had, by subtle machinations, escaped the stake in Rouen. Gilles entrusted a number of his men-at-arms to her for an expedition to Le Mans, but Charles VII asked to meet her and exposed the fraud.

Jeanne Chabot, the Wise (la Sage) Adoptive mother of Guy II of Laval.

Last baroness de Rais, who died in 1406.

Jean Jouvenel Brother of the Carmelite order of Ploërmel, and confessor of Gilles's, appointed by the tribunal.

Jean Labbé Breton captain-at-arms. In the name of Jean de Malestroit, he arrested Gilles, Prelati, Henriet and Poitou at Machecoul (15th September 1440). With Jean Petit and Jean de Touscheronde, he assisted Pierre de L'Hospital and Jean Prégent when Gilles made his first "extra-judicial" confession.

La Hire (known as Etienne Vignolles) Warrior in the service of Charles VII, companion of Joan of Arc's, he took part with Gilles in the defence of Orleans and the victory of Patay (1429). He was taken prisoner attempting to rescue Joan at Rouen, escaped, and later achieved many successes against the English in Northern France.

Guillaume de La Jumelière Sire (Lord) de Martigné, fencing master and counsellor of Gilles's. He was in his service from childhood and accompanied him to Orleans for the performances of the *Mystery of the Siege of Orleans* (1435) where he left his service.

Denis de La Lohérie Bishop *in partibus* of Laodicée, assessor of the ecclesiastical tribunal which sentenced Gilles.

Jean de La Noë Captain of the locality to which Tiffauges belonged.

Jean de La Rivière Physician and conjuror of demons employed by Gilles.

René de La Suze Younger brother of Gilles's, born in the same year as Joan of Arc (1407). On his death, Jean de Craon left him his sword and his breast-plate. On Gilles's death, to justify his claims to Champtocé which he took up again, he set about demonstrating his brother's prodigality, the result of which was the *Memoir of the Heirs of Gilles de Rays to Prove his Prodigality*.

Georges de la Trémouille Baron of the Haut Poitou, lord of Talmont, Mareuil and other seignories, cousin of Gilles's (older than him by 22 years) on the Craons' side, confident of Arthur de Richemont, then favourite and grand chamberlain of Charles VII. He was taken prisoner at Agincourt in 1415. In 1429, after presenting Gilles at court, he signed a pact with him "unto death and life, towards all and against all lords and all others, without exception..., in the good grace and love of the King", making his protégé promise to report to him all the Maid's actions and movements so that her deeds should not overshadow his own. He had him appointed maréchal de France (1429) and always managed to take advantage of his credulity and his prodigality. From 1430, he sought to remove Joan of Arc before falling into disfavour (1433) and taking part in the Praguerie (1440).

Geoffroy Le Ferron Treasurer and principal tax-collector of Brittany, brother of Jean (see below). Gilles sold him his château de Saint-Etienne-de-Mer-Morte but later challenged this purchase.

Jean Le Ferron Tonsured cleric, brother of the above. He was attacked by Gilles, accompanied by sixty armed men, on 15th May 1440, Whit-Sunday, whilst holding a service in the Church of Saint-Etienne-de-Mer-Morte, and imprisoned for four months at Saint-Etienne-de-Mer-Morte, then at Tiffauges. Gilles had a grudge against him for guarding the fortress of Saint-Etienne-de-Mer-Morte which Geoffroy had acquired at too low a price. This act of force was considered a violation of ecclesiastical immunity and proved fatal to Gilles.

Pierre de L'Hospital President (Supreme Judge) of Brittany, he presided at the secular court of Nantes which sentenced Gilles. With Jean Prégent, he heard Gilles's first "extra-judicial" confession, made outside of secular and ecclesiastical processes, "voluntarily, freely and painfully". He granted Gilles the triple grace of being executed after Henriet and Poitou, of having his corpse withdrawn from the flames before it was reduced to cinders so that it might be interred in the Church of Notre-Dame-du-Carmel, and of requesting that the bishop order "an official procession to ask God to preserve in him and his servants the firm hope of salvation".

Ambroise de Loré Warrior upon whose command Gilles began fighting the English.

Louis XI King of France (1461-1483). Son of Charles VII, he rebelled against his father by taking part in the Praguerie (1440). Having been pardoned, he was sent to govern the Dauphiné, but revolted again and took refuge with the Duke of Burgundy, Philippe III le Bon. Once on the throne, he initiated the struggle against the nobility who formed the League of Public Good against him. In December 1439, the Dauphin of Viennois, aged 16, had been sent to Poitou to "put an end to the pillaging and expel the warriors". His visit to Tiffauges forced Gilles to destroy his alchemical equipment in a hurry.

Guillaume de Malestroit Bishop of Le Mans, assessor of the ecclesiastical tribunal which sentenced Gilles.

Jean de Malestroit Sixth son of a family of the gentry of western Brittany, bishop of Saint-Brieuc (1405-1419), then of Nantes (1419-1443), president of the Chamber of Accounts and Chancellor of Brittany (1409-1443). In 1426, he was taken prisoner by Arthur de Richemont who was jealous of him. In 1440, he launched a secret enquiry against Gilles following rumours concerning the disappearances of children. The results of the enquiry offered overwhelming proof, and were published on 29th July in the form of letters patent. He presided over the ecclesiastical tribunal which sentenced Gilles. Jean de Malestroit is most often portrayed as a grasping anglophile.

Perrine Martin alias La Pellisonne or La Meffraye Supplier of children for Gilles's service. She gave evidence as a witness at Gilles's ecclesiastical trial, but her testimony has not been preserved.

Martin V (Oddone Colonna) 204th pope. After two years' negotiations, he granted a pardon to Gilles and his cousin, Catherine de Thouars for their marriage.

Jean Mauléon Treasurer of l'Epargne (the Treasury).

Guillaume Mérici Brother of the Order of the Preaching Friars, professor of theology, grand inquisitor of heresy in the kingdom of France, delegate with apostolic authority. He granted letters of authority to Jean Blouyn in 1426, which were read out at Gilles's ecclesiastical trial.

Jacques Meschin de La Roche-Aireault Former chamberlain at the court of the Dauphin, penniless knight and second husband of Béatrice de Montjean.

François de Montfort Son of Jean V and brother of Pierre de Guingamp.

Béatrice de Montjean Mother of Catherine de Thouars. In 1423, she was arrested with her younger sister by Jean de La Noë and confined in Le Loroux-Bottereau, then at Champtocé, on the orders of Jean de Craon who demanded that she renounce her marriage settlement claims to Tiffauges and Pouzauges. The affair was brought before the royal parliament of Charles VII at Poitiers, and was resolved by an agreement according to which the freed captive obtained two seignories from her deceased husband on the borders of the Poitou and the Limousin as part of a new marriage settlement, while Gilles kept the two localities in the Vendée.

Antoine de Palerme Conjuror of demons and alchemist from Lombardy employed by Gilles de Rais.

Jacques de Pentcoëtdic Official of the church of Nantes, and assessor of the ecclesiastical tribunal which sentenced Gilles.

Jean Petit Goldsmith from Paris employed by Gilles at Tiffauges as alchemist; also, the name of a notary of the ecclesiastical court who assisted Pierre de L'Hospital and Jean Prégent with Gilles's first "extra-judicial" confession.

Jeanne Peynel Daughter of Foulques, lord of Hambye and Briquebec, Gilles's first fiancée (1417). The parliament of Paris forbade the marriage to Jeanne, who was an orphan and a very rich Norman heiress, until she reached the age of majority.

Poitou (alias Etienne Corrillaut) Native of Pouzauges, he entered Gilles's service as a page at the age of ten years (around 1427), and became his personal servant, then, when he was about twenty, his lover and accomplice, acting as a supplier of children whose throats he often slit himself. He was arrested with Gilles, Prelati, Blanchet and Henriet at Machecoul (15th September 1440). He gave evidence at the ecclesiastical trial, and was executed with his master and Henriet.

Alain de Porhoët Father of Béatrice de Rohan.

Jean Prégent Bishop of Saint-Brieuc, assessor of the ecclesiastical tribunal which sentenced Gilles. He took part in the examination of the "unofficial confession" of 21st October with Pierre de L'Hospital.

François (Francesco) Prelati Priest, conjuror of demons and alchemist from Tuscany who entered Gilles's service in 1439. At Tiffauges, he shared a room with Eustache Blanchet, Jean Petit and an old woman named Perrote. He was arrested with Gilles, Blanchet, Henriet and Poitou at Machecoul (15th September 1440). His testimony was heard on October 16th, and the inquisitor sentenced him to life imprisonment. However, he escaped and found refuge with René 1st le Bon who thought him still capable of making gold, and appointed him captain at La Roche-sur-Yon. Here, he again encountered Geoffroy Le Ferron and arrested him, but once the latter was released, he had the Italian hanged (1445).

Marie de Rais Daughter of Gilles and Catherine de Thouars, born in 1429. On Gilles's death, the ten-year-old Marie's estate was so considerable that her mother soon proved too weak to maintain her trusteeship over it. Jean V ordered the confiscation of her properties, and in 1442, Gilles's family arranged for her to marry one of Charles VII's counsellors, Prigent de Coëtivy, (the marriage was agreed but never celebrated). A year after the death of her first husband, Charles VII arranged a second marriage for her to a de Rais cousin, André Laval-Lohéac (1451). Marie died childless in 1457. She was interred in the chancel of Notre-Dame de Vitré, where mothers later pointed out the tomb of "Bluebeard's daughter" to their children.

René 1st le Bon Duke of Bar and Duke of Lorraine by his marriage to Isabelle of Lorraine, Duke of Anjou and comte de Provence, titular King of Naples. Son of Louis II of Anjou and of Yolande of Anjou, he inherited the kingdom of Naples on the death of Jeanne II in 1435, but was unable to take it from Alphonse V of Aragon. He supported Charles VII against the English. In 1456, he spent considerable sums on performances of the *Mystery of the Resurrection*. Patron of the arts, poet, and patron of the painter, Nicolas Froment, he took in François Prelati after his escape.

Béatrice de Rohan Daughter of Alain de Porhoët, niece of the Duke of Rohan and of Duke Jean V. She was Gilles's second fiancée, having been "promised" to him in November 1419, however, this intended marriage never took place, despite the signing of a dated marriage contract at Vannes.

Jean Rossignol Choir-boy in the chapel of Tiffauges, native of La Rochelle, and favourite of Gilles's. He enjoyed a prebend or sinecure granted to him by his master, and obtained from him the lands of La Rivière near Machecoul, while his parents received the gift of two hundred ecus.

Anne de Sillé Jean de Craon's second wife (around 1420), Catherine de Thouars's grandmother and Gilles de Sillé's cousin.

Gilles de Sillé Gilles's cousin, counsellor and first accomplice, he was one of those who provided Gilles with children whom he sometimes killed himself. He managed to escape the arrests at Machecoul (15th September 1440).

Jean de Siquenville One of Gilles's captains. When the Dauphin of Viennois visited Tiffauges (1439) with a view to putting an end to the pillaging, he was arrested and thrown into prison at the château de Montaigu where the future Louis XI had established his residence. He escaped.

Agnès Sorel Mistress of Charles VII (1444), she was the first official favourite in the history of France and died in 1450.

John Talbot, Earl of Shrewsbury English warrior, he fought in France, could not prevent Joan of Arc from delivering Orleans and was taken prisoner at Patay (1429). He conquered Guienne (1452) but was defeated and killed at the battle of Castillon (1453).

Catherine de Thouars Only daughter of Milet de Thouars and Béatrice de Montjean, and Gilles's cousin four times removed. Gilles abducted her against her will and married her in secret, without the publication of bans (1420), then officially (1422). One of the richest heiresses in the west, Catherine brought with her a dowry that included the châteaux of Tiffauges and Machecoul, enabling the Craons (the most powerful feudal lords of Anjou) to form a bulwark running from the ocean as far as Anjou, spanning and containing the entire Lower Loire (basse Loire) area. From

1434, she led a separate life from Gilles as a recluse in Pouzauges. Having retained Pouzauges, Tiffauges and the properties she had brought with her in her dowry, Catherine married Jean de Vendôme, vidame of Chartres, in 1441 (vidame = an officer who replaced bishops and other ecclesiastical leaders in juridical or military functions). The latter became chamberlain to the Duke of Brittany (1441).

Jean de Touscheronde Clerk responsible for the civil enquiry at Gilles's trial. Commissary of the Duke of Brittany, he assembled the tearful testimonies of the families whose children had disappeared, and recorded the debates of the secular court. With Jean Petit and Jean Labbé, he assisted Pierre de L'Hospital and Jean Prégent with Gilles's first "extra-judicial" confession.

Catherine de Valois Daughter of Charles VI and wife of Henry V.

Xaintrailles (Jean Poton, lord of) Warrior in the service of Charles VII, companion of Joan of Arc, he played a part with Gilles in the victory of Patay (1429) where he took John Talbot prisoner. He fought the English again at Lagny (1432) with Gilles and Dunois. He conquered Guienne (1453) and, like Gilles, was appointed maréchal de France.

Yolande of Aragon Queen of Sicily, wife of Louis II of Sicily, mother of Louis III, of Charles of Anjou, of René 1st and of Marie of Anjou who married Charles VII. Her influence over the latter was decisive at the beginning of his reign. In 1431, she married François of Brittany, son of Jean, at Nantes. An enemy of La Trémouille's, she was attacked and arrested by Gilles – and doubtless by Jean de Craon – at Ancenis (around 1432).

DIRECTORY OF KEY SITES

*Amboise*See *Angers*.

Ambrières Seigniory comprising a château belonging to Gilles, situated 60 kilometers west of Alencon; it is linked to the seigniory of Saint-Aubin-Fosse-Louvain and their province extends over ten or so parishes. In 1423, the two seigniories are annexed by the English to the benefit of John de Montgomery.

Ancenis Around 1430, near this small town situated on the right bank of the Loire, halfway between Angers and Nantes, Gilles and Jean de Craon's men, on their way from Champtocé, rob and arrest Yolande of Anjou who was riding peacefully through her estate. On 13th September 1436, Charles of Anjou, count of Le Maine, has a meeting with Jean V and the High Constable de Richemont at Ancenis; the Duke wants to acquire Champtocé and Ingrandes, gateway to Brittany on the Loire. The business is settled by letters of alliance with Yolande of Aragon – that no one intends to observe...

Angers Gilles confesses that, whilst he was fighting for Yolande of Aragon, he met a knight in the city of the good king René (who will give refuge to Prelati after the trial); imprisoned for the crime of heresy, this knight offered him "a certain book on the art of alchemy and the conjuring of demons...". In the city's cathedral, he attends religious ceremonies, the luxury of which fascinates him. In May 1436, as he passes through the city, Gilles abducts Michel de Fontenay, a distinguished citizen and man of the church with a high profile at the University. This man, who had been Gilles's tutor, had overseen at Champtocé the publication of royal letters (dated Amboise the 2nd July 1435) which imposed restrictions upon him.

Auzance Seigniory of Gilles's, situated 5 kilometers to the north of Poitiers.

Agincourt (Azincourt) Village situated 80 kilometers to the north of Amiens. Henry V of England defeats the Armagnacs there on 25th October 1415. Amaury de Craon, Jean's son, and several of his cousins are killed; Georges de La Trémouille and Arthur de Richemont are taken prisoner.

Beaugency On 17th June 1429, this stronghold situated on the Loire 25 kilometers sout-west of Orleans, which had fallen into the hands of the English, is retaken by Joan of Arc under the command of the Duke d'Alençon. She is accompanied by Gilles and de Richemont.

Bénate (la) Seignory comprising a château belonging to Gilles, and extending over 26 parishes in 13 Marches in Brittany and 13 Marches in Le Poitou. The seat is located in the parish of Saint-Jean-de-Corcoué, situated 20 kilometers east of Machecoul. Anne de Sillé, Jean de Craon's second wife, holds the life interest. Jean V buys La Bénate at the beginning of 1437 in the name of his son, Pierre, but meets opposition from Anne de Sillé.

Blaison Seignory comprising a château belonging to Gilles, situated 20 kilometers south-west of Angers, and linked with the seignory of Chemellier since the 13th century. This is the first property sold by Gilles in 1429, thus beginning the liquidation of his patrimonial fortune.

Boucardière (La) Hamlet neighbouring Machecoul, and linked to the parish of Sainte-Croix in Machecoul; it is in a house in this hamlet that the young son of the Sergent couple disappears around May 1439.

Bouin Half-seignory of Gilles's, situated 10 kilometers south of Bourgneuf (see *Rais* and *Tiffauges*).

Bourges In 1439, having left Tiffauges, Gilles stays in this city where Charles VII has taken up residence the previous year. The exact dates and motives for this trip which occurs while Gilles is in disgrace at court are not known with any certainty.

Bourgneuf-en-Retz Village and "châtellenie" (jurisdiction of a chatelain or chateau-owner) of Gilles's, situated 15 kilometers to the north-west of Machecoul, where, on the occasion of a meeting with Jean V who is passing through the area towards the end of August 1439, a hard-pressed Gilles is reduced to asking the devil Barron (who remains silent) to win over the Duke's good graces. On the eve of St Bartholomew's Day, his men take the young Bernard Le Camus, a native of Brest who is staying with Guillaume Rodigo, a native of Guérande, into the room in the convent where he is lodging to teach him French. The confessions of Gilles, Henriet and Poitou confirm that the child died and that his body was burnt in Machecoul. The convent (of the *Frères Mineurs*) is considered at the trial to be one of the six scenes of Gilles's crimes. Arthur de Richemont obtains the fief of Bourgneuf from his brother Jean V in exchange for the liberation of Jean Le Ferron and the taking of Tiffauges (24th August 1440).

Breuil Mingot Lands of Gilles's situated 5 kilometers east of Poitiers.

Briollay Barony comprising a château belonging to Gilles, situated 20 kilometers north of Angers. This is the first of the four baronies belonging to the bishopric of Angers. Gilles is forced to surrender it to his brother in 1434.

Brissac Dependence of Gilles's situated 25 kilometers to the sout-east of Angers.

Brocéliande (or Paimpont) Dependence of Gilles's situated in forest land 40 kilometers west of Rennes.

Chabanais Seignory comprising a château belonging to Gilles, situated 40 kilometers to the north-east of Angoulême.

Chalonnes In St. Maurille's, the church of this château situated 25 kilometers south-west of Angers, the Bishop of Angers marries Gilles to his cousin, Catherine de Thouars in a public service in 1422, after permission has been given by Pope Martin V, seized two years earlier.

Champtocé (or Chantocé) By virtue of its location, the seignory of Champtocé and of Ingrandes is of capital importance. It extends from Epiré, near Bouchemaine, to Ingrandes, and belongs to the duchy of Anjou. The Black-Tower of the château of Champtocé, an old property of the Craon family where his grand-father Jean lived, is Gilles's most likely birth-place. The mighty fortress and the village are situated on the right banks of the Loire, 25 kilometers west of Angers, barring the way to Nantes. Jean de Craon draws confortable revenues from the river-tolls he collects, tolls that are contested, though they are more or less legitimate. In 1420, Jean V de Montfort falls into a trap laid by the Penthièvres and is imprisoned at Champtocé; Jean de Craon sides with the de Montforts; the Penthièvres are defeated and the Duke of Brittany is freed. In 1422, Béatrice de Montjean, Gilles's stepmother, is abducted with his younger sister, on the orders of Jean de Craon who demands that she give up her marriage settlement comprising Tiffauges and Pouzauges. They are imprisoned here, where they are later joined by Gilles Meschin de la Roche-Aireault and his companions, one of whom dies as a consequence of ill-treatment. Gilles and Jean de Craon act as intermediaries between La Trémouille, Jean V and Yolande of Aragon, organising several meetings at Champtocé aimed at forging an alliance between the houses of Anjou and Brittany. Towards the end of 1429, Marie, daughter of Gilles and Catherine, is born, most probably in the château. Some time later, the garrison of Champtocé attacks Yolande of Anjou as she is riding through her lands around Angers, near Ancenis. Gilles confesses to committing his first crimes "at the fortress of Champtocé, in the year that the lord of La

Suze, his grandfather, died", that is, in Anjou and not in Brittany, and therefore beyond the limits of the jurisdiction of the judges of Nantes. Michel de Fontenay, Gilles's tutor in his youth, is a new prisoner of his in this château in 1436 (see *Angers*). In 1435, Gilles had promised that Champtocé would revert to La Trémouille, should he die without an heir. At the beginning of 1437, after his liberation, René d'Anjou, under pressure from René de la Suze and André de Lohéac, declares Champtocé confiscated by him and obtains from Jean V a promise not to acquire the seignory. The latter, who is forbidden by Breton custom to buy his vassals' lands, nevertheless pursues his negotiations with Gilles. In October of the same year, René and André seize the fortress. Gilles takes fright and removes "the bones of forty children or thereabouts" from a tower near the lower chamber and has them transported in a chest upstream to Machecoul where they are burnt. In spite of this "clean-up", two skeletons will be discovered. As a result of the deal concluded with Jean V at Vannes on Christmas Day, 1437, Gilles recovers Champtocé from his brother in return for seven thousand gold écus and the fortress of la Mothe-Achard. Before he has to hand the fortress over to the Duke, he has a further three chests of child skeletons removed to be burnt at Machecoul.

Château-l'Hermitage Village situated 45 kilometers west of Sablé. In the conflict between La Trémouille and Yolande of Aragon, Gilles, then captain of the fortress of Sablé, vainly tries to take the château occupied by Captain Jean de Bueil in the service of the regent of the duchy of Anjou. This occurs towards the end of 1429 or the beginning of 1430. This great nobleman and writer is nevertheless taken prisoner, and the fortress will be taken by Gilles a little later.

Château Morant Seignory in Anjou belonging to Gilles.

Chemellier Seignory of Gilles's situated 25 kilometers south-east of Angers (see *Blaison*).

Chéméré Jean de Lanté, prior of this village situated 8 kilometers north of Bourgneuf, entrusts a nephew to a certain Tabard who teaches him to read and write. At about fifteen years of age, the child is put to death at Machecoul towards the beginning of 1440.

Chenechë Seignory comprising a château belonging to Gilles, situated 20 kilometers north of Poitiers.

Chênes (Les) Seignory of Gilles's situated 90 kilometers south of Nantes and belonging to Catherine de Thouars's marriage settlement according to the agreement concluded with René de Rais in 1448.

Chinon At the beginning of 1429, in the throne-room of the château du Milieu on the banks of the Loire, Joan of Arc recognises the Dauphin hiding among his courtiers, and wins his confidence. She is then accommodated in a tower of the neigbouring château du Coudray where it is likely that she often comes across Gilles. A month later, it is here that Gilles and his cousin La Trémouille sign their *life and death* pact. The future maréchal becomes a royal counsellor and one of Joan's companions. After the failed attack on Paris, Charles VII retreats again to Chinon. During a night in July in 1433, conspirators supporting the son of Yolande of Anjou, Charles of Anjou, including Prigent de Coëtivy, Jean de Bueil and Pierre de Brézé, enter the château and take La Trémouille captive. The latter is obliged to buy his freedom, the price of which is a large ransom, his absence from court and the promise (which he kept) to have the King free Louis of Amboise. This disgrace puts an end to Gilles's career.

Clisson Barony comprising a mighty fortress situated 25 kilometers south-east of Nantes, on the frontier of the Frankish marches of Poitou and Brittany, at the confluence of the Moine and the Nantes section of the Sèvre. Thus, Clisson controls a waterway that is not without importance, and the part of the Poitou frontier which escapes Rais's barony. Pierre de Craon had attempted to kill Olivier de Clisson, High Constable of France and a relative of Gilles's by marriage on his father's side.

Cloué Seignory of Gilles's, situated 25 kilometers south of Poitiers.

Compiègne Key city in Champagne which Bedford has just promised Philippe le Bon when Joan of Arc intervenes, acting on her own authority and without Charles VII's support. The fortress was resisting the Anglo-Burgundians thanks to Italian mercenaries. The Maid is captured there on 23rd May 1430 and sold by the Burgundians to the English who organise the trial of Rouen in November.

Confolens Seignory comprising a château belonging to Gilles, situated 50 kilometers north-east of Angoulême.

Coustumier (Le) Fiefdom of Gilles's situated 10 kilometers south-west of Machecoul (see *Rais*).

Falleron Seignory of Gilles's situated 45 kilometers south of Nantes and belonging to Catherine de Thouars's marriage settlement according to the agreement concluded with René de Rais in 1448.

Fief Macqueau Seignory of Gilles's, situated 85 kilometers south of Nantes and belonging to Catherine de Thouars's marriage settlement according to the agreement concluded with René de Rais in 1448.

Florence On a "business trip" to the Tuscan city of art in 1439, Eustache Blanchet makes the acquaintance of the young priest, conjuror of spirits and alchemist, Prelati, whom he convinces to go to Tiffauges and enter Gilles's service.

Fontaine Milon Seignory comprising a château, situated 20 kilometers north-east of Angers, and sold by Gilles to the family from Marseilles in 1432.

Fosse-Louvain Seignory of Gilles's, situated 70 kilometers west of Alençon (see *Ambrières*).

Fresnay-en-Rais Two of the children of Ysabeau Hamelin's, an inhabitant of this village situated 5 kilometers north-west of Machecoul, disappear around Christmas 1439 after going off to buy bread. The following day, she receives a worrying visit from Prelati and the Marquis de Ceva, a captain in Gilles's service.

Goyau Fief of Gilles's not belonging to the Rais barony and situated eight kilometers north-west of Machecoul.

Grancey Town situated 45 kilometers north of Dijon, belonging to the Duke of Bourbon and besieged in Spring 1434 by the troups of the Duke of Burgundy. Gilles, to whom La Trémouille has lent money to lift the siege, halts on his way there and hands his troups over to his young brother, preferring to be made a canon at Poitiers. Grancey surrenders to Philippe le Bon's army on August 15th.

Grattecuisse Small seignory, situated 40 kilometers north of Angers, and sold by Gilles to the bishop of Angers in 1433.

Grez Seignory comprising a château belonging to Gilles, situated 20 kilometers north-west of Angers.

Hugetières Vassal château and lands of Gilles, situated 15 kilometers south of Nantes.

Ingrandes Seignory of Jean de Craon's, and later of Gilles's, situated 40 kilometers west of Angers (and 5 kilometers from Champtocé), on the right bank of the Loire, and apanage of the royal family, and so subject to the salt-tax which brought sizeable profits to Jean de Craon, acting in collusion with dealers in contraband salt. In the last years of Gilles's life, Jean V shows interest in this area near Angers which falls into the hands of the house of Anjou.

Jammonières (Les) Small seignory of Gilles's, situated in the parish of Saint-Philbert-de-Grandlieu, 15 kilometers north-east of Machecoul.

Jargeau Situated 17 kilometers east of Orleans on the left bank of the

Loire, this town falls into English hands before being recaptured on 12th June 1429 by Joan of Arc, accompanied by Gilles (who, according to the eighth set of accounts of G. Charrier cited by the abbé Bossard, was rewarded for it by Charles VII).

Josselin In July 1440, Gilles, who is becoming increasingly worried, attempts to negotiate with Jean V who is at his country residence in this small town overlooking the Oust and situated 120 kilometers north-west of Nantes. His journey there and back again which takes him through Vannes in both directions and is made in the company of Prelati and Henriet, is punctuated with crimes and devil-conjurings. Gilles's personal valet will later confess to the murders of three children in a meadow.

Lagny On August 10th 1432, Gilles, Dunois, Xaintrailles, de Gaucourt and the bastard of Orleans beat the English in this village situated 35 kilometers north of Compiegne, in spite of the presence of the Regent Bedford, thus ensuring control of the lower Marne near Paris.

Langres After the peace treaty of Nevers (February, 1435), La Trémouille and Gilles are in le Forez and decide to go to Langres (100 kilometers north of Dijon) then to Laon (300 kilometers to the north) where the war is continuing. But Gilles needs money and goes off on his own to Lyon (300 kilometers to the south) to borrow from bankers. He returns to Langres with insufficient funds to pay the wages due to the troops and gives up, joining up again with Orleans after signing a declaration according to which, in the event of his brother's and his own death, Champtocé will revert to La Trémouille.

Laon See *Langres*

La Suze Seignory comprising a château belonging to Gilles, situated 25 kilometers south of Le Mans.

Laval This town falls into the hands of the English in 1428. Gilles must stand surety for the ransoms of his companions and pay a thousand ecus to obtain the freedom of his young cousin, André de Lohéac. The Barony of Laval, raised to the status of a county (comté) in 1429, belongs to the Montmorencys, the Montforts and the Colignys.

Loches On May 11th 1429, Gilles and Joan of Arc travel to this château, situated on the Indre 40 kilometers west of Chinon, and where the future Charles VII likes to stay, to inform him officially of the liberation of Orleans.

Lodunois Tenancy of Gilles's, situated 80 kilometers south-west of Angers.

Loroux-Bottereau (le) Seignory of Gilles's, situated 20 kilometers east of

Nantes, comprising the village and a château. Catherine de Machecoul, Gilles's great-grandmother, founded a chaplaincy the profits of which are embezzled by Jean de Craon. Gilles rights this wrong on his grandfather's death. In 1422, Béatrice de Montjean and her younger sister, abducted on the orders of Jean de Craon, are imprisoned in the château before being transferred to Champtocé. On September 5th 1436, Jean V, fearing plots and surprise attacks, receives an oath of loyalty from Valentin de Mortemer, captain of the fortress of Le Loroux-Bottereau.

Loubert Seignory of Gilles's, situated 40 kilometers north-east of Angoulême.

Louviers When Joan is a prisoner of the English, an acknowledgment of debt to Rolland Mauvoisin, captain of Princé (26 December 1430), testifies to the presence of Gilles in Louviers, a village situated on the Eure, 30 kilometers south of Rouen. Some chroniclers speculate about an attempted raid there to free the Maid.

Lude (Le) In 1427, while he is captain of the fortress of Sablé, Gilles wins a spectacular victory at Le Lude, a village situated 20 kilometers south-east of La Flèche. Having stormed the fortress held by the English, he cleaves Captain Blackburn in two with a single blow of his sword.

Lyon see *Langres.*

Machecoul Situated in the Retz area 30 kilometers south of Nantes, the château becomes the residence of Gilles's parents upon the death of Jeanne La Sage (Joan the Wise) – who is buried there – in 1407. Despite the claims of some old chroniclers, it therefore seems unlikely that Gilles was born there in 1404 (see Champtocé), but it is in this stronghold established on the southern marches of Brittany that his brother René is born in 1407. Machecoul is identified as the location of the second wave of child-murders (1432-1433, after the first wave at Champtocé). According to testimonies, the first five children to disappear at Machecoul are Jeudon, Sorin, Roussin, Édelin and Chastelier. In 1435, Gilles founds his Chapel in Memory of *The Blessed-Innocents* here. In 1436, he transfers his old tutor Michel de Fontenay here from Champtocé, having abducted him in Angers. The château is again the scene of the conjuring of demons. On September 5th 1436, Jean V, fearing plots and surprise attacks, travels to Machecoul and here receives an oath of loyalty from the captains holding the fortresses belonging to Gilles in Brittany which have not yet been sold: Machecoul (commanded by Michel de Sillé and his lieutenant Jean de Dresneuc), Saint-Etienne-de-Mer-Morte, Pornic and Le Loroux-Bottereau. At the beginning of 1437, according to his confession, Henriet took a child (Catherine Thierry's brother) from Nantes to Machecoul to the "killing room". Poitou later informs him that the young boy has been killed. Gilles increases his trips between his residence at Tiffauges (a dependency of the crown) and his château and lands at Machecoul (a dependency of the duchy of Brittany, within which he believes himself to be under the protection of Jean V) where he burns the bones that are in danger of being discovered at Tiffauges after the raid by René de La Suze and André de Lohéac in October 1437. In November, the same brother and cousin seize Machecoul. According to the testimonies heard at the trial, Machecoul is the scene of the murders of those children who disappeared from Vannes, Nantes, La Roche-Bernard, Bourgneuf, Saint-Léger, Port-Saint-Père... At the end of 1439, Gilles and his companions leave Tiffauges, which is too vulnerable to the crown, and withdraw to Machecoul. Prelati and the Marquis de Ceva sleep in the high chamber of the château where they beat up Perrine Rondeau whose husband is dying. André Barbe, the village cobbler, insists that in February 1440, he heard a stranger lamenting the loss of a seven-year-old child in the Church of the Holy Trinity. On Easter Sunday 1440, Gilles spontaneously confesses his sins and then takes communion humbly among the crowd in this same church. Gilles, Prelati, Blanchet, Henriet and Poitou allow themselves to be arrested in the château on September 15th 1440.

Mans (Le) In 1427, while his grandfather becomes the lieutenant general of Yolande of Aragon, Gilles has his first taste of action against the English in the area around Le Mans – which is where Charles VI had started to go mad. But the French troups come to grief in front of the town. In Gilles's ecclesiastical trial, the bishop appointed to Le Mans, Guillaume de Malestroit, will be one of the assistants of the prosecutor, Guillaume Chapeillon. Around June 1439, Gilles sends Captain Jean de Siquenville to prepare an operation against Le Mans. He will never join up with him, and Le Mans will remain in English hands until 1448.

Maurière (La) Seignory of Gilles's situated 70 kilometers south-east of Nantes. It extends the seignory of La Mothe-Achard to the banks of the Auzance and also belongs to the marriage settlement in favour of Catherine de Thouars according to the agreement made with René de Rais in 1448.

Montaigu Château situated 15 kilometers west of Tiffauges, where the Dauphin, future King Louis XI, takes up residence on the occasion of his visit in 1439, the purpose of which is to put an end to the pillaging. Jean de Siquenville, whom he has arrested in Tiffauges, is clapped in irons here, but manages to escape.

Montluçon Returning from Orleans, Gilles stays at the Écu de France in

Montluçon in Autumn 1434, leaving behind a bill, half of which he is unable to pay.

Mortagne With the conjuring of demons and rumours of child-murders on the increase, Eustache Blanchet flees Tiffauges on All Saints Day in 1439 and takes refuge in Mortagne, 12 kilometers up-river on the Sèvre. Jean Petit, dispatched by Gilles, comes to his host's house to search for him in vain. The host, named Bouchard-Menard, spreads rumours of Gilles's crimes. Seven weeks after his flight, Gilles de Sillé, Poitou and Henriet capture Blanchet and take him via Rocheservière to Machecoul where he lives at liberty until the arrest of all parties.

Mothe-Achard (La) Vassal seignory of Talmond comprising a château belonging to Gilles, situated 65 kilometers south of Nantes. It is occupied by the Penthièvres in their struggle against the Montforts, its lands are laid waste in 1420 and the château is destroyed during the final violent clash between the Penthièvres and the Duke of Brittany. At the end of December 1437, Gilles promises to cede this stronghold to his brother in return for the restitution of Champtocé which he has occupied since October, but at the end of 1438, Gilles refuses to do so, and by force of arms, takes back from him the château of Saint-Etienne-de-Mer-Morte. On 15th January 1439, an agreement between the brothers allows Gilles to retain Saint-Etienne while René recovers La Mothe-Achard. The seignory becomes part of Catherine de Thouars's marriage settlement in 1448, in accordance with the agreement entered into with René de La Suze.

Nantes Capital of the duchy of Brittany (939-1532). In 1431, Yolande of Aragon marries François of Brittany, son of Jean, here. This union puts an end to the tension between Anjou and Brittany.

Biesse (meadow of) Place of execution of Gilles, Henriet and Poitou, situated to the south of the old centre of Nantes, on an island of the Loire (the present-day boulevard des Martyrs Nantais de la Résistance), where the condemned are led in procession, having passed through the Porte Poissonière. Shortly after the execution, a cross is erected anonymously near the place of execution, at the entrance to the bridge leading to the sandbanks of the Saulzaie, which will disappear in 1744.

Bouffay (Le) Fortress near the château where Gilles is taken on the day of his sentencing by the ecclesiastical tribunal, and where he repeats the confession of his crimes before the secular court.

Château of the Dukes of Brittany Gilles, arrested at Machecoul, is taken to a room high up in the New Tower (Tour-Neuve). His trial begins in the large upper chamber of the New Tower where the charges brought against him will be read out. In the lower chamber of the New Tower, the bishop and the inquisitor's assistant hear the accusations of the families against Gilles regarding the disappearance of their children.

Notre-Dame-de-Crée-Lait Shortly after the execution of Gilles, Henriet and Poitou, a sort of calvary is erected by the side of the Chaussée de la Madeleine. The calvary is formed from a recess containing a statue of the Virgin Mary, with St. Gilles and St. Laud on either side. Women come to pray here for plentiful milk for their children. In 1837 traces of this calvary could still be seen on a piece of wall opposite the Hotel de la Boule d'Or, between a house and the gates leading to the hospital courtyard. In 1867, the construction of a square necessitated the demolition of this strange little Gothic monument, which the people of Nantes called "Bluebeard's".

Notre-Dame-des-Carmes (or du-Carmel) Church that has disappeared now, but was situated in the medieval quarter, in the present-day rue des Carmes. It is here that, on the day of his execution, Gilles's body is taken in procession to be interred. The paving-stone beneath which lies the maréchal could still be seen at the entrance to the church next to the holy-water font until 1793 when the church was desecrated by revolutionaries.

Suze (de La) Mansion (Hôtel) no longer standing, belonging to Gilles, and situated in the rue Notre-Dame near the collegiate church. Gilles attempts to summon demons on several occasions here. Young Guillaume Delit, one of Gilles's kitchen-boys, disappears in February or March 1438. Jean Jenvret's nine-year-old son who frequents this house disappears around June 16th of the following year while Gilles is in Nantes. At the trial, Perrine Martin, otherwise known as La Meffraye, confesses to having taken the child to Machecoul, whilst Poitou states that he was killed in the Hôtel de La Suze. Around Midsummer's Day, another child from Nantes who also frequents the house, Jean Degrepie, disappears while Gilles is once again staying in Nantes. La Meffray is alleged to have taken him to Gilles in his chamber and the latter is alleged to have ordered that he be taken to Machecoul. According to other witnesses, little Jean Hubert was killed by Gilles in the mansion two days later. Around August 1439, there is another disappearance: Guillaume Avril's son. One of Gilles's men has promised to show him "the mansion of the Archdeacon des Merles" and to give him a cobloaf. Henriet admits that he delivered this nephew of Denis de Lemion's to his master, who "had relations" with him before he was "killed and burnt".

Orleans Occupied by the English, a key city on the Loire river, Orleans had become the de facto capital of France, but had aligned itself on the side of the Armagnacs behind the future King Charles VII. The city is recaptured by Joan of Arc, accompanied by Gilles and La Hire, who storm the fortress of Les Tourelles on May 8th 1429, after a siege lasting seven months. It is here on 26th March 1435, that Gilles, who has been staying regularly in Orleans since September, registers with two notaries the founding of his *Chapelle des Saints-Innocents* constructed in Machecoul. Moving here with his ecclesiastical household and his men-at-arms, he stages the ruinous performances of his *Mystery of the Siege of Orleans* which commemorates the deliverance of the city and the memory of Joan. In the mansion known as the Croix d'Or (or Golden Cross) placed at his disposal, Gilles attempts to summon demons on several different occasions. His brother is lodged at the Petit Saumon (or Little Salmon), his college at the Ecu de Saint-George (or St. George's Arms), his choristers at the Enseigne de l'Épée (or Sign of the Sword), his men at the Tête Noire (or Black Head), his captain and Gilles de Sillé at the Grand Saumon (or Great Salmon)... More than fifteen houses are thus reserved for his imposing retinue. On 28th December, he confers a power of attorney here on Roger de Briqueville, permitting his young Norman cousin to sell his master's property in Brittany and to marry off his daughter, Marie – who is four years old. In October 1439, the States General are held in Orleans.

Oudon Village situated 30 kilometers north-west of Nantes, on the right bank of the Loire, opposite Champtoceaux. It is here, in 1420, that Duke Jean V confirms the granting of salt rights to Gilles and Jean de Craon against their rivals by the Duchess of Brittany, together with income partly confiscated from one of the supporters of the Penthièvres, Ponthus de la Tour.

Paimpont See *Brocéliande* (*Cahiers Gilles de Rais* n^0 3).

Paris In 1417, the Parliament of Paris forbids Gilles's marriage to the rich orphan, Jeanne Pleynel who is still a minor. On 8th September 1429, twelve thousand Armagnacs, commanded by Joan of Arc and La Trémouille, to whom Gilles is subject, attack the gates of the city. Joan is wounded at the Gate of Saint-Honoré. On 13th September, the order to retreat from Paris is given by Charles VII, who leaves the uplands of Montmartre for Saint-Denis, then for the banks of the Loire. On 16th December 1431, Henry VI of England, aged ten, is crowned King of France at Notre-Dame. Paris will not be recaptured until 1436. Henriet, Griart and the alchemist Jean Petit are natives of Paris.

Parthenay Small seignory, property of Richemont, situated 50 kilometers west of Poitiers. In 1428, the High Constable retires here, having fallen into disfavour.

Patay Village situated 20 kilometers north-west of Orleans. It is taken back from the English by Joan of Arc and the High Constable of Richemont, accompanied by Gilles, La Hire and Xaintrailles, who take John Talbot prisoner on June 18th 1429.

Plessis-de-Reczac-lès-Redon It is in this village that Jean V announces the confiscation of Gilles's properties on September 9th 1440, just a few days before his arrest.

Poitiers On September 19th 1356, Jean de Craon's father is taken prisoner in the capital of Poitou and then heavily ransomed. The royal parliament of Charles VII which sits in this city fines Gilles and his grandfather for high treason in the affair of the attack by Président Adam de Cambray, who came to Pouzauges following the abduction of Béatrice de Montjean. Gilles accompanies Joan of Arc here the day following her visit to Chinon, in order that the Maid be examined by scholars and prelates as part of an ecclesiastical inquiry. Having abandoned his troups to his twenty-year-old brother while they were involved in the deliverance of Grancey in Burgundy and keeping his young favourites André Buchet and Jean Rossignol at his side, Gilles is appointed canon in the Church of Sainte-Hilaire in Poitiers – an honour hitherto reserved for the Dukes of Aquitaine alone.

Pornic Château and land of Gilles's (see *Rais*). On September 5th 1436, Jean V, fearing plots and surprise attacks, receives an oath of loyalty from Yvon de Kersaliou, captain of the fortress.

Port-Launay Village neighbouring Couëron, situated 15 kilometers from Nantes, on the right bank of the Loire estuary. The son of the late Jean Bernard leaves the village around September 1438 heading for Machecoul to ask for alms which are said to be given lavishly there, and disappears.

Port-Saint-Père Around May 15th 1440, a couple by the name of Aisé, who live in this village on de Rais territory, send one of their sons, aged about ten years, to beg in Machecoul, 15 kilometers to the north. A little girl tells her mother that alms were first of all given to the girls, and then she heard someone from the château say to little Aisé, who had not had any meat, that he would be given some. He was then let in to the château, and his parents did not hear from him again.

Pouzauges Vast seignory in the Lower-Poitou (Bas-Poitou) comprising a château with a huge square keep, situated 30 kilometers south-east of Tiffauges. The lands over which it has rights extend as far as the île de Bouin (Isle of Bouin) where the lord of Pouzauges possesses the Poitou rights and lord de Rais the Breton rights. From 1434, Catherine de Thouars is separated from Gilles and lives the life of a recluse here. Etienne Corrillaut, otherwise known as Poitou, who enters Gilles's service as a page at the age of ten years (around 1427), is a native of Pouzauges. Together with Tiffauges, this is the last great château to remain in Gilles's possession at the end of his life. Catherine will bring these two properties to her second husband in her dowry, the year following Gilles's death.

Précigné Lands of Gilles's, situated 45 kilometers north of Angers.

Prigny Château and lands belonging to Gilles, situated 5 kilometers north-west of Bourgneuf (see *Rais*).

Princé See *Rais*.

Puisaye Property of Georges de La Trémouille, situated on the right bank of the Loire, between Sully and Auxerre.

Rais This barony, inherited from Jeanne La Sage (Joan the Wise) by Guy II of Laval and Marie de Craon, relatives of Gilles's, is made up of around forty parishes stretching between the Loire and the Free Marchlands (Marches Franches) of Poitou and Brittany. It controls part of the Poitou frontier. The châteaux and lands of Machecoul, Le Coustumier (Machecoul and Bois-de-Cené), Bourgneuf, Princé, Vue, Pornic, Touvois, Saint-Michel-Chef-Chef, Saint-Etienne-de-Mer-Morte, Prigny and half of the île de Bouin are amalgamated by Gilles.

Reims Since Clovis, it has been the custom for French Kings to be anointed in this city, in the church of Saint-Remi. Thus, Charles VII is crowned here on 17th July 1429, with Joan of Arc standing on his right and Gilles on his left, bearing the holy chrism. On this same day, he will be appointed maréchal de France, the King granting him an additional coat-of-arms of a surround of fleurs de lis on a blue background.

Rivière (La) Small amount of land next to Machecoul which Gilles gave to one of his favourites, Jean Rossignol.

Roche-Bernard (La) Coming back from Vannes to Machecoul in September 1438, Gilles stops in this town, having travelled 40 kilometers. He stays with Jean Colin, and through Poitou, gets Peronne-Loessart to entrust his ten-year-old son to him. The latter travels to Machecoul where his throat is cut.

Rochelle (La) The only Atlantic port to which Charles VII has access. The allied Castilian navy lands reinforcements here from Scotland and harasses enemy convoys between England and the duchy of Guienne held by its vassals. In 1430, Richemont, supported by the Anjou faction, threatens this strategic location. La Trémouille responds by dispatching his men to Poitou and Gilles to Anjou where he pillages the countryside. Jean Rossignol, a choir-boy in the chapel at Tiffauges and a favourite of Gilles's, is a native of La Rochelle.

Rocheservière See *Mortagne*.

Rouen After being condemned as a heretic and witch by an ecclesiastical tribunal presided over by the Bishop of Beauvais, Pierre Cauchon, Joan of Arc is burnt at the stake in Rouen on 30th May 1431. A desperate Gilles is present at the execution.

Sablé In 1430, after Joan has been sidelined by La Trémouille and abandoned by Charles VII, Gilles is appointed captain of this fortress under Richemont's command. Sablé is situated 50 kilometers south-west of Le Mans at the junction of the Sarthe, the Erve and the Vaige rivers. He occupies Sablé in the conflict between La Trémouille and Yolande of Aragon and having taken Jean de Bueil prisoner at Château-l'Hermitage, locks him up in a large tower.

Saint-Cyr-en-Rais Village bordering Bourgneuf from which the young Bouer boy leaves to beg in Machecoul on Sunday 12th April 1439, never to return.

Saint-Etienne-de-Mer-Morte Village situated 10 kilometers south of Machecoul, where Gilles owns a château which he cedes to his brother in 1434. But on 15th January 1439, an agreement concluded between the two brothers allows Gilles to recover Saint-Etienne from René in exchange for La Mothe-Achard. Towards the end of 1439, Jean Petit is locked up in the dungeons of Saint-Etienne-de-Mer-Morte for failing to bring back Eustache Blanchet who had fled to Mortagne. Geoffroy Le Ferron, the Treasurer of Brittany, has acquired this château and its lands, but Gilles questions the transaction, and on Whit-Sunday 1440, leading a band of 60 armed men and brandishing a guisarme, the former owner bursts into the chapel of the château "in a furious and reckless manner" while the treasurer's brother, Jean Le Ferron, is celebrating mass. He insults him and threatens to kill him, abducts him and holds him prisoner, having forced him to open up the château which his brother Geoffroy had entrusted to his keeping. This violation of ecclesiastical privilege infringing the rights of the Duke of Brittany will prove fatal to Gilles. Jean de Malestroit, Bishop of Nantes, has ecclesiastical jurisdiction over the diocese to which this place of worship belongs.

Saint-Etienne-de-Montluc On 28th August 1439, Jean Toublanc, an inhabitant of this village situated 20 kilometers north-west of Nantes, and guardian of a 13-year-old boy, whom he has left in his house, cannot find him. At the end of June 1440, Jamet, a boy of about eight years, and son of the late Guillaume Brice, disappears from Saint-Etienne.

Saint-Florent-le-Vieil Seignory of Jean de Craon's, situated down-stream from Ingrandes but on the left bank of the Loire. On their way from

Florence, Eustache Blanchet and Prelati stop off here during the last days of April 1439 before joining up again with Gilles at Tiffauges. On 5th September 1436, fearing plots and surprise attacks, Jean V receives an oath of loyalty from Conan de Vieilchatel, captain of the fortress of Saint-Etienne-de-Mer-Morte.

Saint-Léger-les-Vignes About a fortnight before Christmas 1439, Jeannette Drouet, an inhabitant of this village situated 20 kilometers south-west of Nantes, sends two of her young sons to beg for alms in Machecoul. She will never discover what happened to them.

Saint-Michel-Chef-Chef Château and lands of Gilles's, situated 40 kilometers west of Nantes (see *Rais*).

Saint-Père-en-Retz Fief of Gilles's not belonging to the de Rais barony and situated 35 kilometers west of Nantes.

Savenay Seignory of Gilles's, situated 35 kilometers north-west of Nantes. The little fief of Roche-en-Savenay extends over five parishes.

Sigon Lands of Gilles's, situated 5 kilometers north-west of Poitiers.

Sillé-le-Guillaume In March 1434, accompanied by a sumptuous retinue, and appearing for the last time in the royal army commanded by Richemont after La Trémouille has fallen into disfavour, Gilles takes part in a show of force at Sillé – 33 kilometers north-west of Le Mans – fief of his mother-in-law's, of his grandfather's widow and of his cousin Gilles, where the French and the English eye each other without fighting. Having withdrawn into a neighbouring village, the English finally give way and return to Sablé whence they had come. Then they attack Sillé which capitulates three days later.

Souché Small seignory of Gilles's, situated in the parish of Saint-Aignan-de-Grandlieu, 15 kilometers north-east of Machecoul.

Sully-sur-Loire Château situated 50 kilometers south-east of Orleans, on the left bank of the river, and inherited by Georges de La Trémouille from his mother. This stronghold commands navigation on the river on the borders of French, English and Burgundian territories. Having accomplices in the English camp, La Trémouille ensures that his château is not attacked when Orleans is besieged. Joan of Arc accompanies Charles VII here in 1430, but since this hospitality is a pretext to keep a watch on her, she flees.

Suze (La) Important château and lands situated 20 kilometers south-west of Le Mans, comprising a fortress and extending over about fifteen parishes. Gilles is forced to cede it to his brother in 1434.

Terre Sainte (Holy Land) After the deaths of Joan of Arc and Jean de

Craon and and having started to commit his crimes, Gilles is wracked with disillusion and remorse, and expresses a desire on several occasions to go on a pilgrimage to the Holy Sepulchre in Jerusalem, a desire that he never fulfils.

Tiffauges One of the principal vassal seignories of the Viscounty of Thouars, comprising an imposing château (the boundary walls have 18 towers), situated 45 kilometers south-east of Nantes, where Poitou, Anjou and Brittany meet, and constituting one of the most important places in Gilles de Rais's possession, which had come to him through Catherine de Thouars's dowry. He retires here after the victory of Lagny in 1432, and later, after the performances of the *Mystery of the Siege of Orleans* in 1435, and spends the last months of his life here. At the beginning of May 1439, the Florentine, Prelati is brought to Tiffauges where Gilles, with the help of the Parisian goldsmith, Jean Petit, installs his alchemical ovens, dreaming of regaining wealth and power. Prelati, Blanchet, Petit and the old Perrote woman sleep in the same room. The large lower hall in the château and a neighbouring meadow become the locations for the summoning of demons, especially on the occasion of June 1439 during the course of which neither Barron nor Beelzebub nor any of the others appears to Gilles, unlike the events of August of the same year when, in a place which he does not recall, Prelati obtained "a large quantity of gold bullion" guarded by "a large green-coloured serpent as big as a dog" which, upon seeing the crucifix brandished by the fearful Gilles, reduced the precious metal to "a kind of tinsel" before disappearing... But in December, the young Dauphin, the future Louis XI, forces Gilles to destroy his equipment, following a visit of inspection, and Jean de Siquenville is arrested upon his return from Le Mans. Prelati reports that, at the end of 1439, he saw a child lying dead in the large hall where the conjuring of demons took place. Poitou tells of a further offering to the demon of the hand and heart of a child, carried in a glass by Gilles to Prelati. Right at the end of the year, Gilles leaves Tiffauges to return to Machecoul, and therefore Brittany, where he believes himself to be under the protection of the Duke. But having kept Jean Le Ferron prisoner in the Château de Saint-Etienne-de-Mer-Morte since Whit-Sunday 1440, Gilles transfers him to Tiffauges which is situated in Poitou and so is a dependency of the crown. On August 24th 1440, the High Constable de Richemont seizes the château and delivers the cleric at his brother's request, though ostensibly acting in the name of the King. Together with Pouzauges, this is the last great château to remain in Gilles's possession at the end of his life. Catherine de Thouars will bring these châteaux to her second husband in her dowry the year following Gilles's death. In the village of Tiffauges, La Meffray's house can still be seen standing and inhabited today.

Tourelles (Les) See *Orleans*.

Touvois In February 1440, Mathelin Thouars, an inhabitant of this village situated 6 kilometers south-east of Saint-Etienne-de-Mer-Morte, reports the disappearance of a child of 12 years.

Troyes The city where Queen Isabeau of Bavaria had sought refuge with Charles VI of Valois, moving the parliament here from Paris and signing the treaty (1420) that delivered France to the English, disinheriting the future Charles VII. Troyes is recaptured on July 10th 1429 by Joan of Arc, accompanied by Gilles. In 1427, Jean V, abandoning the French faction, had had the treaty of Troyes approved by the parliament of Brittany.

Vannes It is in this Breton town that in 1419, the contract is signed, promising Gilles to Béatrice de Rohan, although nothing will ever come of it. On November 2nd 1437, fearing that Anjou may go to war with Brittany, Jean V calls a meeting in Vannes of the vassals of the entire duchy. He exchanges letters of military alliance with Gilles and offers him the General Lieutenancy of Brittany, withdrawing it from André de Lohéac because he suspects the Lavals of plotting against him. At Christmas, Gilles comes to stay at Vannes, accompanied by his chapel. It is here that the Duke, whose protection he seeks, is holding court. His finances in ruins, he agrees to let Jean V have Champtocé, which is currently occupied by his brother, in exchange for one hundred thousand gold ecus. André Buchet, a choir-boy at the chapel of Tiffauges, and a native of Vannes, sends him a boy from this town dressed as a page, through the intermediary of a certain Raoulet. Coming back from Josselin in July 1440, Gilles lodges in Vannes outside the walls in a place called La Mothe, at the house of a certain Lemoine . Buchet brings him a boy of about ten years, Jean Lavary, whom they take to a house nearby belonging to a man named Boetden. The child's head is cut off and then burnt in the room where Gilles is staying, while the body is hidden by Poitou in the latrines. On August 24th in Vannes, the Duke confers with his brother, Arthur de Richemont, and launches the operation against Tiffauges.

Verneuil In 1424, Charles VII suffers a terrible defeat under the walls of this château situated on the Avre, 30 kilometers west of Dreux. Verneuil will not become French again until 1449.

Voûte (La) or *Voulte (La)* Seignory comprising a château belonging to Gilles, situated 20 kilometers east of Poitiers.